KIDS FOR CASH

KIDS FOR CASH

Two Judges, Thousands of Children, and a $2.8 Million Kickback Scheme

WILLIAM ECENBARGER

The New Press gratefully acknowledges the
John D. and Catherine T. MacArthur Foundation
for supporting publication of this book.

Published in the United States by The New Press, New York, 2012
Distributed by Perseus Distribution

LIBRARY OF CONGRESS CATALOGING-IN-PUBLICATION DATA
Ecenbarger, William.
Kids for cash : two judges, thousands of children, and a $2.8 million kickback scheme /
William Ecenbarger.
         p.   cm.
Includes index.
ISBN 978-1-59558-684-1 (hc.)
1. Juvenile detention—Pennsylvania—Case studies.   2. Juvenile courts—
Pennsylvania—Case studies.   3. Juvenile justice, Administration of—
Corrupt practices—Pennsylvania.   4. Bribery—Pennsylvania—Case
studies.   5. Corruption—Pennsylvania—Case studies.   I. Title.
HV9105.P22E34 2012
365'.4209748—dc23
2012021136

Now in its twentieth year, The New Press publishes books that promote
and enrich public discussion and understanding of the issues vital to our
democracy and to a more equitable world. These books are made possible
by the enthusiasm of our readers; the support of a committed group of
donors, large and small; the collaboration of our many partners in the
independent media and the not-for-profit sector; booksellers, who often
hand-sell New Press books; librarians; and above all by our authors.

www.thenewpress.com

Composition by dix!
This book was set in Fournier MT

Printed in the United States of America

2   4   6   8   10   9   7   5   3

For Angie and Bill

Listen! If everyone must suffer in order to buy eternal harmony with their suffering, pray tell me what have children got to do with it? It's quite incomprehensible why they should have to suffer, and why they should pay for the harmony with their suffering.

—Fyodor Dostoyevsky, The Brothers Karamazov

CONTENTS

ACKNOWLEDGMENTS

Most of all, I am grateful to the kids and parents who agreed to talk to me about their experiences in the Luzerne County Juvenile Court. Among this group, I am especially indebted to Laurene Transue, who showed Mark Ciavarella and his accomplices in injustice that one of the most dangerous places in the world is between a mother and her child.

This book could not not have been written without Juvenile Law Center and its two leaders, Bob Schwartz and Marsha Levick, who set out some four decades ago to change the world and did. They, along with their colleagues Marie Yeager and Laval Miller-Wilson, educated me in how a juvenile justice system ought to work. I thank them for their intelligent suggestions and patience.

As a journalist for a half century, I have covered many "blue ribbon" panels that were set up to study serious problems and then proceeded to ignore them. The Interbranch Commission on Juvenile Justice is a sterling exception. Chairman John Cleland is a judge who, unlike Conahan and Ciavarella, takes his oath of office seriously. He and several of his colleagues on the commission were steady, trusted presences in the process of writing this book.

Special thanks also to Thomas Baldino, Thomas Crofcheck,

Richard Gold, William Kashatus, Bart Lubow, Chester Muroski, Robert Wolensky, and Clay Yeager.

Susan Stranahan, my onetime colleague at the *Philadelphia Inquirer*, read early drafts and made her usual perceptive criticisms.

I am also grateful to those individuals who agreed to talk to me on condition that I not use their names. You know who you are, and so do I.

My thanks to two esteemed institutions for their generous support toward the writing of and production of this book: the Annie E. Casey Foundation and the MacArthur Foundation.

Anita Bartholomew, my agent, encouraged this project right from the beginning and connected me with The New Press and executive director Diane Wachtell, whose immediate enthusiasm for the project persuaded me to go with The New Press. Over the next year, she persevered through great personal tragedy to shape my manuscript into its final form. Marc Favreau, editorial director at The New Press, also made important suggestions that were heeded.

Finally, writing a book is a solitary, consuming experience and therefore hard on the people the writer lives with. No one knows this better than my wife Susan, who not only put up with me but served as my first-read editor, making constructive suggestions, aligning verb tenses, eliminating misspellings, blocking unwise metaphors, and knocking down pretentiousness.

AUTHOR'S NOTE

I was on a magazine assignment in the Peruvian Amazon in January 2009 when the kids-for-cash story broke, and I didn't catch up with it until early March when I read Ian Urbina's page one article in the *New York Times*. As I read and re-read the article, it called to mind Mark Twain's dictum: "The difference between truth and fiction is that fiction must be believable."

Over the spring and summer of 2009, I was distracted by other matters, and the story was only at the rim of my awareness, until one night in October 2009 when I got a call from Vernon Loeb, the deputy managing editor of the *Philadelphia Inquirer*. A staffer in the Harrisburg bureau had become ill, and he needed coverage of an important hearing the next morning. Could I fill in? I had spent most of my career covering state government at the *Inquirer* and had recently started writing freelance pieces for it. But these were feature articles, and this was hard news: the first hearing by a special committee created to look into the judicial debacle in Luzerne County. "Sure," I told Loeb. The story would occupy me for the next two and a half years. I interviewed more than two hundred people, including forty-three of the judges' child victims and their parents, juvenile justice experts, prosecutors, defense lawyers, state officials, federal agents, victims' advocates, and local attorneys, politicians, teachers, and judges (though not the two miscreants themselves). I covered hearings, trials, and sentencings, and I read thousands of pages of court documents.

Because it is the clear intent of the juvenile justice system that children be treated differently from adults, a euphemistic terminology has grown up that avoids some of the harsher words of the adult courts. In Pennsylvania, this gentler, softer language includes words like "delinquent" instead of "criminal," "disposition" rather than "sentencing," and "placement," not "imprisonment." I have tried to be sensitive to this issue, but I have not always followed these strictures. For example, "placement" is not always adequate to describe the process by which a child has his or her freedom taken away and is placed behind locked doors, and so I have from time to time in this book called it "incarceration." My defense is that, in an effort such as this, it is always more important to be understood than it is to be polite.

I have chosen to use only the first names of nearly all the juveniles who came before Judge Ciavarella. Many of them have had their full names published in news accounts, but their court records were sealed and now have been expunged, and there is no need to perpetuate their unfortunate encounters with the Luzerne County Juvenile Court between 2003 and 2008. Exceptions to my rule are Hillary Transue and Jessica Van Reeth, whose status as lead plaintiffs in Juvenile Law Center's landmark suit make them special cases. In addition, they have consented to having their full names appear in this book.

1

MATTHEW, ANGELIA, LISA, AND CHARLIE

At the age of thirteen, Matthew was a quiet boy whose benign, gentle features seemed to demand that a violin be placed in his hands. But inside, the seventh-grader was strung taut between his mother and his father, who had been in a protracted custody battle over him since he was ten. Four days after Thanksgiving 2004, Matthew got into a disagreement with his mother's boyfriend. There was some shoving and angry words, but it wasn't much of a contest. Matthew stood four foot three and weighed eighty-two pounds. His adversary was six foot two and weighed about 210 pounds.

No one was injured in the momentary scuffle. Nevertheless, his mother called the police, and an officer came to Matthew's bedroom, pushed him against the wall, and jabbed a finger at him: "You think you're tough, but you're not. I've dealt with people like you before, and it's no big deal." Then his mother told the officer that Matthew had thrown a piece of steak at her beau, and she wanted to file assault charges against her son.

A month later, three days after Christmas, Matthew was in the dark-paneled Courtroom Four of the Luzerne County Courthouse. He was accompanied by his father and the lawyer his father had retained. Matthew had been assured that even if he was found guilty, his punishment would be light because he had no prior record of offenses. The boy knew he had done nothing wrong, and he believed the justice system would work and treat him fairly. Even so, Matthew's senses were on full alert because he was standing before Judge Mark A. Ciavarella, who had already spoken at Matthew's school three times and warned students that he would be tough on any child who came to his courtroom.

The lawyer told Ciavarella that the incident was part of an ongoing dispute between Matthew's parents, and he asked that Matthew be placed in his father's custody. But his mother and her boyfriend testified that Matthew had thrown the steak. Matthew kept shifting his feet and pushing his glasses up the bridge of his nose. Ciavarella doodled absently on a scratch pad during the testimony and seemed to regard the entire proceeding as an intrusion. Finally, the judge turned to Matthew and asked if he threw the piece of meat. Matthew, his voice squeaky with adolescence, said he had not. Words of explanation formed in his throat, but Ciavarella cut him off and said, "Remanded!" The word hung in the air for a few seconds. Matthew, bewildered, didn't even know what it meant.

Suddenly, two officers, each grabbing an elbow, were escorting all eighty-two pounds of him to an adjacent holding room. He was saucer-eyed with disbelief as they patted him down for weapons. Then they were putting handcuffs on his wrists and shackles on his ankles. Both sets of restraints were attached to a belt around his waist. His mouth went cottony with fear, and he started crying. The restraints were too tight and little darts of pain shot at his wrists and ankles. He begged his captors to loosen the cuffs and the shackles, and they finally did. Then he shuffled out to a waiting van with another boy and two girls, and was driven away. He wondered if this was really happening to him.

He reached out and touched the wire mesh barrier in the van. It was real.

About twenty minutes later, the van drove into what appeared to be a garage. But then the door went down behind the vehicle and locked as another door opened in front and the van drove forward and stopped. Because his father was a prison guard and had told him about them, Matthew knew this was a sally port, an entry point to a secure facility that was once a feature of many medieval castles. In modern times, they are used for prisons. Matthew had been taken to PA Child Care, a privately owned, for-profit juvenile detention facility in Pittston, Pennsylvania, that had been opened just two years earlier. It was a state-of-the-art "juvie," but to Matthew it was an ugly jail.

Matthew, his face frozen into a fright mask, was hustled inside, where a woman at a desk took all of his personal items, including his wallet, keys, and a religious medal that said, "I Am a Catholic. Please Call a Priest." He was handed gray sweatpants, a gray sweatshirt, and black plastic flip-flops, and directed to a room to change his clothes. He was ordered to take a shower and wash his hair with an anti-lice shampoo. That night he lay on his bed and stared at the ceiling. Tears rolled down his temples and into his ears.

Ciavarella had sent Matthew to PA Child Care to await a psychological evaluation. In the interim, Matthew went to classes, which he found very easy. They used stapled photocopies of textbooks rather than the books themselves. Fridays they watched movies. Time creaked along, the days passing by like centuries. Finally, on the sixteenth day, Matthew met with the psychologist for about an hour, and the therapist's eventual conclusion was that Mattthew was depressed. "Who wouldn't be?" Matthew asked plaintively years later. Because he blamed her for his predicament, Matthew steadfastly refused to speak to his mother. County probation officers told Matthew he would not be released until he did.

But a week after Matthew's incarceration, his father launched an all-out, frantic effort to get his son out of PA Child Care. He tried to contact his local congressman, state legislators, county officials, the office of Governor Ed Rendell, the state Judicial Conduct Board—anyone who might help. He knocked on doors, wrote letters, made phone calls, and sent emails. He also got in touch with the Wilkes-Barre *Times-Leader*, which eventually ran a story outlining Matthew's plight. Five days after the article appeared, Matthew got another hearing before Ciavarella. He was brought to the courthouse in shackles, and as he got off the elevator a woman waiting to step on exclaimed in amazement, "Look at that little kid! What could he have done?" Matthew was released and placed on probation. He had been deprived of his freedom for forty-eight days.

During his seven weeks at PA Child Care, Matthew saw the movie *Napoleon Dynamite* three times. He came to hate it. When he was not in class, he was confined to his room. He was not allowed to lay on his bed during the day and instead had to sit on a backless stool at a metal desk. "Being in jail is a terrible thing," he said. "I was locked up like an animal."

Matthew returned to the seventh grade and worked hard to get his grades back up to the B level. Many of his former friends avoided him. "Their mothers didn't want their sons hanging around with a juvenile delinquent," he recalled bitterly. He graduated from high school, but seven years after his confinement he still jousted with depression regularly. He wants to be an airline pilot, but he is unable to take the first step toward higher education. "I picture myself in college," he says, closing his eyes with the imagining. "But I just can't do it." At the age of twenty, he is estranged from his mother and lives with his father. He works full-time in a restaurant, making pizzas and serving takeout pasta. There is a lost look about him, as though he has been permanently startled.

When Angelia was fourteen, she and a friend scrawled "Vote for Michael Jackson" on five stop signs with a black felt marker. There had been a spate of stop-sign graffiti all over her hometown, and police decided to charge the girls with all of the offenses—eighty-six counts of vandalism and defacing public property. When Angelia's mother protested that she was only responsible for a few stop signs, she said the officer told her that unless her daughter pled guilty to all of the charges, "he'd make sure she'd see Judge Ciavarella on a day Penn State lost the previous weekend because Judge Ciavarella sends all juveniles to jail if Penn State loses."

Penn State's football season was over by the time Angelia and her friend got into Ciavarella's courtroom, but most of the twenty-minute hearing was taken up by discussions among the judge, court officials, and local police about the National Football League playoffs. The previous weekend, the Pittsburgh Steelers and the Philadelphia Eagles had won divisional playoff games, and there was talk of an all-Pennsylvania Super Bowl.

Ciavarella seemed to resent being distracted from the gridiron speculations, and he ignored conflicting testimony from an alleged eyewitness who described Angelia as having short black hair. Angelia's long blonde hair reached down to her waist. Angelia and her co-defendant admitted vandalizing five of the signs, but said they had nothing to do with the other eighty-one. Nevertheless, the judge said that even though it had not been proven that the girls had defaced all eighty-six stops signs, he was going to use them as an example to deter others. He ordered them shackled and taken away by juvenile probation officers.

Angelia's mother protested that her daughter was epileptic and subject to seizures under stress, and she shouted to the probation officers leading her away, "She can't go without her medication!" But by this time Ciavarella was part of a rising tide of repartee over the Super Bowl, and he ignored the frantic mother. At PA Child Care, Angelia was placed in a locked room with a bunk and a stool. It felt like a prison. Her mother contacted officials at PA Child Care and warned them Angelia's seizures were brought on by stress. "Her stress level is too high, and I know she's going to have a seizure," she said.

On her second night at the detention center, Angelia's muscles suddenly contracted and she lost consciousness. Her body violently alternated between relaxation and rigidity. The savage muscle contractions lasted about two minutes. When she regained consciousness, she had a throbbing headache. Angelia had had a grand mal seizure. She had banged her head against the cement wall next to her bed so hard that she cracked her dental braces.

The next day she was before Ciavarella again, shackled, handcuffed, and weak from her trauma. As her mother held her upright, she remembered Ciavarella saying, "There's people with worse illnesses in jail. Don't think I won't throw you back." He then released Angelia from detention and placed her under house arrest. However, despite the fact that Angelia had been an A student, Ciavarella refused to allow her to return to her school for three months as part of her punishment. She managed to finish her freshman year with Bs and Cs. But throughout high school Angelia suffered from her brief encounter with Judge Ciavarella.

"She rarely left the house in her teen years," her mother said.

"I had to force her to go to her own prom just to have some kind of high school experiences. She never went to football games, never went to anything. And I feel it was from what happened that one time, the very first time she got into trouble. You know, she should maybe have gotten a little bit of punishment, but not an ax thrown at her. It's taken a lot of years for her to come out of that shell. And I blame him for that."

Angelia said she believed her youthful experience changed her outlook permanently: "I've learned that people we put in power just aren't always the ones we should trust. Judge Ciavarella, I thought maybe he could see I wasn't a bad kid. Yes, I did deserve a slap on the wrist. Yes, I did deserve to be punished. Did I deserve what I got? No. Was I punished too harshly? Yes. I just think I was punished too harshly, and I just don't think it was very fair."

Nevertheless, eight years after her encounter with Ciavarella, she was about to graduate from college and planned to pursue a doctorate in sociology so she could teach at the college level.

In November 2003, some members of the literary club at Crestwood High School decided to pull a prank designed to get one of them summoned to the principal's office. It was an asinine idea—the kind of thing adolescents sometimes do. Sixteen-year-old Lisa penned a note that said: "I like to shoot, shoot, shoooot young men. I will tell you now of my Evil Plans. On Nov. 26, I will bring my father's 5 PM semiautomatic handgun to school. I will shoot the kneecaps of innocent young men." Lisa signed the name of another club member. The note was left on a table for easy discovery. It was senseless and insensitive, foolish and foolhardy—especially for someone with a 3.8 grade point average who had never been in trouble before. Lisa was quickly identified as the true author, and by the time she got to the principal's office, she realized she had "done something really stupid." She was contrite, wept, and even offered to get on the school public address system to apologize. Her mother and her grandmother came in, and it was agreed that she should be suspended for three days.

Lisa was ashamed—it was the first time she was ever disciplined in school—but she thought that would be the end of it. Who would actually take her threat seriously? Her father lived in another state, no one else at her home owned a handgun, and there's no such thing as a 5 PM semiautomatic. Lisa was an unlikely terrorist. She often carried spiders and insects outside her house and released them, rather than killing them inside. She didn't believe she had the right to kill anything.

But the next morning she was seated at the dining room table studying her geometry textbook when the doorbell rang. Only her grandfather was home, and he was upstairs, so Lisa went to the door. She was surprised to see two uniformed police officers, who said they were taking her into custody. They stepped into the kitchen, handcuffed her, and as her grandfather stood by helplessly, began to escort her outside. It was cold, and she asked to wear her jacket. Because she was handcuffed, she had to wear it like a blanket. They perp walked her out to the cruiser and ducked her head as they guided her into the backseat. Her eyes brimmed with tears, and then spilled over when she passed her high school. Her friends were inside, sitting in class. She was in the back of a police car in handcuffs.

Lisa was taken to PA Child Care to await a hearing before Ciavarella. But it was the day before Thanksgiving, and the court had closed until the following Monday. She was locked in a room, behind a dead-bolted metal door, for the night. Lisa lay down on her cot and sank into her thoughts. She wasn't afraid. She wasn't angry. She was just lonely. She questioned her self-worth. What did everyone think of her? Would her friends be her friends when she returned to school next week? Did everyone hate her? Did they laugh when they heard what happened to her? The next day she had a cafeteria-style turkey dinner with canned carrots and peas. She sat next to a girl named Michelle who the previous night had tried to carve her name into her forearm with a nail file but had succeeded only as far as "MICH."

After five days in PA Child Care, Lisa, shackled and handcuffed, was taken to the courthouse for a hearing before Ciavarella on charges of making "terroristic threats." Did she write that note, Ciavarella asked. Lisa said she did. She started to explain that she never intended to harm anyone, but the judge silenced her with an admonitory finger. Her attorney told the judge Lisa's note was "a bad prank" and asked the she be placed on probation. Ciavarella interrupted him and sentenced Lisa to an indefinite term at a wilderness camp for girls. The entire proceeding took less than five minutes.

At the camp, some of the girls were tough, inner-city teenagers convicted of violent crimes. But others were there for stealing their father's credit card to buy clothes and for unintentionally bringing a pocketknife to school. At one point while among a group of girls cleaning portable toilets, she began singing the orphanage song from the Broadway musical *Annie*:

"It's a hard-knock life, for us! It's a hard-knock life, for us!"

Before long, most of the other girls had joined in.

"Steada treated, we get tricked. Steada kisses, we get kicked!"

Nine days after Lisa arrived in detention, Ciavarella ordered her released following appeals from school authorities and recommendations from camp counselors. She had missed two weeks of school, and she had a criminal record. She was ashamed and embarrassed in school. She withdrew from activities. She felt guilty. Some of her former friends and their parents said she deserved what she got and should have been kept in detention for months. She lost her driver's license for a year, and when she got it back the insurance company raised her rates because of her record. She didn't apply for a job if the applications asked for arrests and convictions.

But Lisa graduated from high school, went to college, got a teaching job after earning her BA degree, and got married. Then she and her new husband applied to the Peace Corps. Lisa's application was flagged and put on hold. Sixteen months and many questions later, the couple was finally approved, and in September 2011 they began their assignment in Mozambique. Lisa is still embarrassed about her ill-advised misstep at the age of sixteen.

Charlie had a passion for motors and vehicles, and when he spotted a used motorbike for sale in the summer of 2006, he wanted it. It was a bright red Greenline "beach cruiser." It was only $60. At fifteen, Charlie was a troubled, anxious boy. "We thought it might cheer him up," his mother recalled, "so we bought it for him. He was overjoyed." Like his father, Charlie had considerable mechanical aptitude, and he alternately rode and tinkered with his new possession.

But several weeks later, two police officers knocked on the door of his house. Charlie was home alone and thought he was in trouble for riding the Greenline without a helmet. Instead, the officer told him the bike was stolen. They said they'd be back later. When Charlie's parents came home that night, the police returned. The adults tried to explain that they thought they had legitimately purchased the bike, but all three of them were arrested. Later, the charges were dropped against the parents, but Charlie was ordered to appear before Ciavarella.

Charlie thought he would just explain what happened to the judge, and his problems would be over. Probation officers advised his parents that he did not need an attorney. But as he and his mother sat on folding chairs outside the courtroom awaiting his hearing, his mother noticed a disturbing pattern: Parents were going into Judge Ciavarella's courtroom with their children, but only the parents were coming out. A low-watt anxiety surged through her. Each time the door opened, his mother heard a jangling sound. She didn't realize it just then, but it was the sound of shackles. Concern turned to panic when they got before the judge and found out Charlie had been charged with receiving stolen merchandise—a felony.

Charlie, a shy, pudgy, bespectacled youth, stood there with his hands in his pockets and fear on his face for the entire three-minute hearing. Even though he had had no prior run-ins with law enforcement authorities, Ciavarella adjudicated him a juvenile delinquent. Charlie was neither advised of his right to a lawyer, told of the consequences of pleading guilty, nor given a chance to explain how he had innocently come to own the motorbike. If Charlie had been an adult, he would have received a sentence of either probation or a maximum of one month in prison under state sentencing guidelines. But as a juvenile, Charlie received an indeterminate sentence. As it turned out, he would be locked up for most of the next three years for a crime he did not commit.

Before he even understood what had happened to him, the boy was being shackled and handcuffed. His mother reached out to comfort him, but he was hustled away from her and out of the courtroom to a crowded holding cell with other children. Indeed, there were so many other youths in the room that all of the benches were filled and Charlie was obliged to stand against the wall. Later, a sheriff's van sliced through an angular, sleeting rain and took everyone to PA Child Care. A psychological evaluation there concluded that Charlie suffered from anxiety and depression. His parents were charged $250 for the evaluation. When they asked for a second opinion from a physician covered by their medical insurance, they were turned down by county authorities.

After six weeks in PA Child Care, Charlie was sent to a "boot camp" designed to teach wayward adolescents discipline. He was placed in a cabin with boys who had been convicted of drug dealing and gun-related offenses. Here his mental state worsened. He couldn't sleep, and he said he didn't speak to anyone for three months. The camp doctor placed him on the mood stabilizer Seroquel, and he showed some improvement. Three months later, he was released and returned to high school. But he had fallen behind his junior-year classmates, and his grades dropped. He was shunned as a troublemaker and delinquent by many of his former friends. When his infant niece was killed in a tragic apartment fire, his anxiety and depression returned. He began using drugs and missing appointments with his probation officer. Soon he was again before Ciavarella, who sent him to back to PA Child Care. He would be in and out of detention facilities for three years. When he was finally released, he sent a plaintive Twitter message to his friends: "i am about to go home from being in placement for 3 years for something i didn't do i can't wait."

Charlie got out of the juvenile justice system when he turned eighteen, but as an adult, he has had more trouble with the law, including receiving stolen goods and using fraudulent credit cards.

• • •

Matthew's, Angelia's, Lisa's, and Charlie's cases were not deviant, aberrant miscarriages of justice. They were part of a routine and systematic form of child abuse that took place in the juvenile court of Luzerne County, Pennsylvania, between 2003 and 2008. During that time, *several thousand* young defendants were needlessly handcuffed, shackled, and summarily dispatched to incarceration that typically lasted between one and three months. After the briefest of hearings, parents who had accompanied their children to court and expected to return home with them, left instead stunned and bewildered, alone.

Seldom was Ciavarella's tough-love justice tempered with mercy. No matter how young the defendants, no matter how clean their records, no matter how cringing their hesitancy, no matter how wobbly-voiced or jelly-kneed they appeared in his courtroom, most left shuffling in their shackles to vans that took them away.

While these proceedings were closed to the public, they were witnessed by assistant district attorneys, public defenders, other lawyers, probation officials, and court officers, including clerks and messengers. Often police officers, teachers, and school administrators were also present. The air was heavy with unspoken words and unacknowledged guilt, yet for six years, through thousands of hearings, no one spoke out effectively in opposition.

In failing to do so, public servants, educators, and others charged with protecting our children served as enablers for one of the worst judicial scandals in American history. For as he meted out these injustices, Judge Ciavarella and his behind-the-scenes co-conspirator, Judge Michael T. Conahan, were being paid millions of dollars by the owners of PA Child Care. In exchange, the judges provided the owners a steady stream of inmates. Children became commodities in a kids-for-cash scheme.

The scandal became public when federal prosecutors held a news conference on January 26, 2009, detailing the kickback scheme that had allowed two judges to wrongfully imprison thousands of children for the judge's own financial benefit. Initially, however, there was little negative reaction in northeastern Pennsylvania among community leaders—educators, prosecutors, public defenders, probation officers, or even the Luzerne County Bar Association. Indeed, two administrators at the Wilkes-Barre Area Vocational Technical School wrote a letter to the editor of the Wilkes-Barre *Times-Leader* praising Ciavarella. "His dedication to working with our students created a bond of trust and confidence among him, the students and the staff," the administrators wrote. "Students who had personal experiences with the judge have expressed gratitude for his involvement in their lives. His concern for their well-being after adjudication is what makes him so special. He has made a tremendous difference in the school's educational process."

But as the breadth and nature of the kids-for-cash wrongdoing spread beyond the immediate area, other voices rose. Robert Schwartz, executive director of the nonprofit Juvenile Law Center, which was instrumental in bringing the scheme to an end, said, "Children in Luzerne County were treated as commodities, with a for-profit provider as purchaser, and the juvenile court as supplier. The Luzerne County juvenile court was in the business of inventory control. This was done publicly and without comment from other professionals in the room. This is hard to believe."

Within weeks, the international press took notice. The *Sunday Times* of London ran a 750-word article headlined, "Judges Took

Bribes to Jail Teenagers," calling it "one of America's most sinister judicial scandals of recent times." *The Economist* magazine headlined its piece "The Lowest of the Low." In Sydney, *The Australian* proclaimed, "Judges Paid off to Keep Jails Full," and the *New Zealand Herald* announced, "U.S. Judges Jailed Kids for Cash."

In early March, the *New York Times* ran a front-page article by Ian Urbina, which began: "Things were different in the Luzerne County juvenile courtroom, and everyone knew it. Proceedings on average took less than two minutes. Detention center workers were told in advance how many juveniles to expect at the end of each day—even before hearings to determine their innocence or guilt. Lawyers told families not to bother hiring them. They would not be allowed to speak anyway."

How could two judges conspire over five years to deprive thousands of children of their most basic constitutional rights and send them off in shackles to detention centers in which these judges had personal financial interests?

There were many ingredients in the Luzerne County judicial scandal—official evil, greed, opportunity, public indifference, secrecy, and place: Luzerne County, Pennsylvania, has a history of corruption, nepotism, and mob-related violence dating back decades, so perhaps it should not be a surprise that the juvenile justice system there was corrupt as well.

Although the Luzerne County kids-for-cash scandal resulted from a unique confluence of factors, it was allowed to thrive in part because of a dangerous, nationwide opacity in America's juvenile justice system. Matthew, Angelia, Lisa, and Charlie were among the approximately one hundred thousand American children who, on any given day, are either confined to correctional facilities or held in detention centers awaiting trial or placement.

Fewer than one-third of these youths are being detained for serious, violent crimes. Many of the rest, like Matthew, Angelia, Lisa, and Charlie, are incarcerated for nonviolent infractions, including behaviors common among adolescents in our society.

Some of them, like Angelia and Lisa, rebound and begin productive lives. Others, like Matthew, suffer prolonged emotional stress, long-term psychological damage, truncated educations and careers, and develop deep disdain for a justice system that failed them. And many of them, like Charlie, become adult criminals. The lack of transparency at the court level as well as inside juvenile detention centers—particularly those run as private, for-profit companies—is a recipe for abuse and an environment in which scandals such as Luzerne County can be perpetrated out of public sight. Rather than affording extra protections to the most vulnerable among us, we have set up a system of justice for children in this country that too often criminalizes standard adolescent behavior, treats adolescents more harshly than if they were adults committing similar infractions, and is not open to public scrutiny.

The egregious miscarriage that took place in Judge Ciavarella's courtroom offers a chilling and telling caricature of a system prone to abuse, yet nonetheless entrusted with the care of millions of American children.

2

BARONS AND GODFATHERS

Forty years I worked with pick and drill
Down in the mines against my will
The Coal King's slave, but now it's passed
Thanks be to God I am free at last.
—Gravestone of Condy Brisbin (d. 1880), Saint Gabriel's
Catholic Cemetery, Hazleton, Pennsylvania

A freak of geology placed nearly all of the world's supply of high-grade anthracite coal—"hard coal"—inside an area of some 1,700 square miles at roughly forty-one degrees north latitude, seventy-five degrees west longitude in the crescent-shaped Wyoming Valley of northeastern Pennsylvania. Anthracite was formed some 300 million years ago and lay undiscovered until around 1800. Local folklore has it that a farmer named Necho Allen dug a hearth in the earth, and when he set a campfire, it burned untended for weeks. Some versions are that this miracle occurred on Christmas Eve 1795. By whatever means anthracite came to human attention, by 1830 it had become a popular source of heat among local residents. It burned cleaner and gave off more heat than conventional bituminous coal, which comprised 99 percent of the nation's supply. Already bankers and other financiers from Philadelphia and New York were buying up vast parcels of farmland and forest beneath which the miracle fuel lay. To find a wider market, anthracite needed transportation, and so these first "coal barons" built railroads. Thus they prospered doubly—first from mining anthracite, then from moving it.

To get cheap labor to extract the anthracite while maximizing profits, the coal barons recruited aggressively in Europe. The successive waves of immigrant miners—first Welsh and Irish, then Italians and Slovaks—moved into tiny towns called "patches" that were centered on the mining operations. The miners' relationship with the coal companies was close to slave-master. They lived in company-owned housing under leases that could be canceled at whim. The miners were required to buy all of life's necessities from the company store, which charged exorbitant prices. Itinerant peddlers with better prices were not allowed in the patches. These "coal-crackers" labored fourteen hours a day, often in near darkness standing in knee-deep water or lying flat on their stomachs. Death and injury were their constant companions. Their entire existence was permeated with threats—loss of home, loss of job, loss of life. Insecurity and submission to authority became part of the coal-cracker gene pool.

By the turn of the last century, some 100,000 miners worked in the anthracite region, but demand dropped sharply after World War I, and northeastern Pennsylvania slipped into the Depression well before the rest of the nation. World War II brought a brief revival of prosperity before a permanent malaise set in at midcentury. By 1960, fewer than 8,000 men worked in the mines.

From the beginning, the coal barons formed alliances with anyone who could be helpful, and one powerful group that became intimately associated with the mining business was organized crime. The first mob boss in northeastern Pennsylvania was Sicilian-born Santo Volpe, who ran bootlegging, gambling, and prostitution operations while heading up several coal companies. Volpe's political connections got him a seat on the Pennsylvania State Coal Commission, and from here he helped Mafia family members take over local coal companies. Joseph Barbara assumed mob leadership in 1940, and it was at his summerhouse in Apalachin, New York, that an infamous meeting of America's top Mafia leaders took place in 1956. Around 1960 Barbara was succeeded by Russell Bufalino, who would become one of the nation's leading organized crime figures with interests in loan-sharking, gambling, and legitimate businesses like coal companies. By this time the mobsters' influence permeated not only the ownership side, but the United Mine Workers union as well. Sweetheart labor contracts became common.

Moreover, the big coal companies had been selling or leasing the mines to small, Mafia-controlled operators who hobbled the UMWA and other unions and bribed state mining inspectors. This cleared the way for mine owners to engage in unsafe practices, especially "robbing the pillars"—the practice of mining from the columns of coal that had been left behind by earlier operations to support the roofs of the mines. In September 1958, a federal grand jury in Scranton began investigating organized crime's infiltration of the anthracite industry. Dozens of company and union officials testified under subpoena.

Then, on the unseasonably warm evening of January 22, 1959, the roof fell in—literally. The icy waters of the Susquehanna River broke through the roof of the pillar-robbed Knox Coal Company River Slope mine near Pittston. Twelve men were killed and the mine was flooded. It took nearly five hundred railroad cars and 25,000 cubic yards of dirt, rock, and boulders to seal the hole. Billions of tons of anthracite were made inaccessible. The grand jury indicted August J. Lippi, the local UMWA president, and several subordinates for accepting bribes from Knox Coal. Company officials and state mine inspectors were charged with conspiracy and involuntary manslaughter. Most of them eventually went to jail on lesser charges, but the trials exposed the widespread corruption of the anthracite industry by organized crime.

The Knox Disaster, as it came to be called, hastened the already inevitable decline of the anthracite industry. But according to Robert Wolensky, a sociologist who grew up in northeastern Pennsylvania and co-authored a 1999 history of the disaster, there was a far deeper legacy: "Owners, bosses, inspectors and mineworkers alike knew that illegalities had become epidemic. They realized that powerful corporations with Wall Street addresses used contractors and lessees to accomplish questionable or illegal goals. They knew that organized crime had become part of the cancer. Finally, they knew that the UMWA had turned away from the mineworkers to become an accomplice in the scandal. Many otherwise upstanding citizens participated in the crooked dealings. The culture of corruption that had engulfed the industry caused serious damage to the community's social and moral fabric, leaving wounds that remain to the present."

With the mines shutting down, people looked elsewhere for jobs, and the most likely sources were municipal governments, because there were so many of them. This was yet another legacy of the anthracite industry. These tiny municipalities were the descendants of the old mining patches, which had been originally established by the coal barons to give them iron-fisted control over taxes and laws. Luzerne County alone still has seventy-six municipalities—four cities, thirty-six boroughs, and thirty-six townships. Some examples: Sugar Notch Borough occupies one square mile and is home to 1,023 people; Bear Creek Village, two square miles, 284 residents; Nuangola, 1.3 square miles, 671 residents; and Pringle, one-half square mile, 991 residents. They have mayors, councilmen, and supervisors. In addition to these little fiefdoms, there are school boards and hundreds of commissions, agencies, and authorities. Each of them is headed by a public official with the power to hire and fire.

Dr. Thomas Baldino, a longtime political science professor at Wilkes University, said that at first local politicians merely handed out jobs to their relatives and friends, "but before long patronage moved into pocket-lining." Baldino was born and raised in South Philadelphia: "Therefore, I am no stranger of crooked politicians. But the difference is that in Philly we have at least had episodes of reform, like Joe Clark and Richardson Dilworth in the 1950s. Here, there's never been a reform movement. What we're seeing here today is the way it's always been." Wolensky, who now teaches sociology at the University of Wisconsin but returns regularly as an adjunct professor at King's College in Wilkes-Barre, concurs: "The level of corruption is unbelievable—it's epidemic. It wasn't until I moved to Wisconsin that I realized that corruption wasn't a normal part of government. Paying to get a job is viewed as the proper thing to do—a way of saying thank you."

Even some of the public schools are highly politicized. A generation ago graduate students in the University of Scranton's Department of Education were openly advised how much one had to pay to get a teaching job in parts of Luzerne County. It cost $2,500 in some corrupt districts, $3,000 in others. Payment was usually in cash placed in an envelope and usually slid across the table with the applicant's résumé. Baldino said the old ways continue today: "It still costs a couple of thousand dollars to get a job in certain school districts. I have bright students who graduate but can't get jobs here because they can't afford to pay for it." William C. Kashatus, a local historian who has written five books about the anthracite region and teaches at the Luzerne County Community College, said corruption has led directly to inferior schools: "We tell our best education students not to apply for jobs around here."

There is a very high tolerance for crooked politicians. Joseph Vadella was forced to resign as Carbondale mayor in 1997 after being sentenced to federal prison in a ballot-tampering scheme. Just two years later, Vadella was elected mayor again—even though his name wasn't on the ballot and had to be written in. In Moosic Borough, Mayor John Segilia and Councilman Joseph Mercatili were forced to resign in 1992 after pleading no contest to charges of fixing parking tickets and manipulating drunken driving cases. Both were elected to the same offices in 2009. Congressman Joseph M. McDade easily won reelection in 1992 and 1994 while he was under indictment on federal racketeering, conspiracy, and bribery charges. McDade was eventually acquitted.

But the best example is Daniel J. Flood, the flamboyant longtime congressman from Wilkes-Barre, who was elected to a sixteenth term in 1978 while under federal indictment for bribery and perjury. Even today, the Wilkes-Barre Area School District includes the Daniel J. Flood Elementary School. Flood finally resigned from Congress in 1980 after pleading guilty to accepting kickbacks for government contracts. He died in 1994. Kashatus has written a biography of Flood that recounts how Flood mastered the machinery of Congress to bring federal largesse to his district. He brought the area a veterans' hospital, a regional airport, and he got Interstate 81 routed through Hazleton and Wilkes-Barre. However, his shining moment came in 1972 when Hurricane Agnes flooded the entire region. Flood rushed back to

Wilkes-Barre in a Defense Department helicopter and declared, "This is going to be one Flood against another!" Flood led the recovery effort with enormous success. Even when he was up to his waxed mustache in corruption charges, Flood remained popular. Kashatus recalls: "When Flood was running for reelection in 1978, I would say to people, 'Don't you know that Daniel Flood is corrupt?' They would say to me, 'We don't care what anyone says about Daniel Flood. He's one of us.' "

Throughout his career, Flood maintained very cozy relations with the northeastern Pennsylvania Mafia. Indeed, Santo Volpe was a guest at Flood's wedding, and years later the congressman regularly obtained federal contracts for a close associate of Russell Bufalino. Nevertheless, Dan Flood is Luzerne County's most legendary politician and remains a local folk hero. In 2010, an official state historical marker honoring him was placed in Wilkes-Barre's public square. It reads: "Dan Flood, U.S. Congressman from Pennsylvania's 11th district, was a colorful and controversial figure in Washington, D.C., from 1944–1980. His seniority on the House Appropriations Committee and his genius for the legislative process resulted in the passage of such national Great Society programs as Medicare, Appalachian economic development, and urban redevelopment. Charged with improprieties in arranging federal contracts, Flood resigned from Congress in 1980. His Wilkes-Barre office was at the corner of W. Market and Franklin Streets."

In 2002, federal authorities launched a widespread investigation of public corruption and organized crime in northeastern Pennsylvania that is still going on. By 2012, it had resulted in indictments and convictions of more than three dozen public officials, including judges and school board members accused of taking bribes for teaching jobs. One of them was Greg

Skrepenak, a Luzerne County commissioner who pleaded guilty to taking multiple payoffs from a developer who obtained a government-subsidized loan through a county authority. Skrepenak, a former All-American football player at the University of Michigan and subsequently an offensive lineman in the National Football League, told reporters that he didn't know the kickback was illegal until his indictment. "Things have been like this for so long," Skrepenak explained, "that I don't think many people see a lot of wrong in what they've done."

Today there is a plaque at the Wilkes-Barre/Scranton International Airport listing the names of six county commissioners who were in office when the facility opened in 2006. Three of them have since been jailed on public corruption charges. Nevertheless, a motion to remove their names from the plaque was defeated by the airport's governing body in October 2011.

Kashatus sees a distinct contrast between the politicians like Dan Flood and the current crop of local miscreants: "The difference today is that the old pols were pouring money back into the system—to the party, giving jobs to people, getting funds for local projects. Today they're just putting the money into their own pockets. The anthracite culture may be dead, but the mentality it created is still here. Until the outsiders outnumber the descendants of the miners, it will be here."

The juvenile justice scandal of the first decade of the twenty-first century is the worst manifestation of a legacy of official wrongdoing in Pennsylvania's anthracite coal region, which includes the cities of Wilkes-Barre, Scranton, and Hazleton. Here, there is a "culture of corruption" that has snared judges, congressmen, legislators, councilmen, and school directors for decades.

Indeed, back in 1909, when the mines were booming, there

was a burst of civic pride as the new Luzerne County Courthouse, a magnificent structure of Ohio sandstone and concrete, opened on the banks of the Susquehanna River in Wilkes-Barre. But the early arriving courthouse workers were greeted by rats that were expelled only after two months of efforts involving traps, cats, and ferrets. Next, there were flooded offices brought on by a faulty cooling system. In the ensuing controversy, a grand jury charged that the project had been "riddled with fraud and gross negligence." The following month criminal warrants were brought against the commissioners, county controller, architect, and subcontractors. Among the allegations were overcharging, kickbacks, and the use of inferior building materials.

The allegations eventually were dropped and soon forgotten, and today the courthouse is a stately, if timeworn, Victorian structure with wide corridors, stained glass, Italian marble, bronze statuary, paintings, and mahogany paneling. The most impressive feature, visible for miles, is the rotunda dome.

3

SCOOCH AND THE BOSS

A finespun morning fog erased the landscape around the eighty-seven-year-old Luzerne County Courthouse and shrouded its neoclassical lines, sandstone walls, and terra-cotta roof. By noon, the stained-glass windows of the dome were being pecked at by snowflakes—the advance guard of the record-shattering blizzard of '96 that would bury the city in a few days. The interior base of the dome carried a circular inscription: "O Thou Who Art High above All the Earth, Cause Thy Face to Shine upon this Habitation of Justice, this Dwelling-place of Wisdom and Probity!"

Beneath that dome, in the arched rotunda, a short, wiry forty-six-year-old man stood on the marble floor poised with his right hand raised and his left hand on a Bible held by his wife, Cindy. With his three children—Lauren, fourteen, Nicole, twelve, and Marco, nine—watching proudly, he intoned, "I, Mark A. Ciavarella, do solemnly swear that I will support, obey and defend the Constitution of the United States and the Constitution of this Commonwealth, and that I will discharge the duties of my office with fidelity."

Then the new judge's face creased into a smile as his parents helped him slip into his black robe. Ciavarella had several reasons to be pleased on January 2, 1996. He was on the cusp of a ten-year term as judge that he had won the previous November after a bruising, expensive election campaign. Today was his parents' fiftieth wedding anniversary. And last night his beloved Penn State football team had trounced Auburn 43–14 in the Outback Bowl.

Among the honored guests was Judge Michael T. Conahan, who exactly two years earlier had stood in the same rotunda and sworn to uphold the same two Constitutions. Conahan, too, had become a judge after a costly, combative campaign in which he promised he would uphold the judicial ideals of integrity and independence.

Within a few years, Conahan and Ciavarella would become close personal friends and next-door neighbors on a pair of socially prestigious acres in the pricey suburb of Mountain Top. And they would become secret business partners in a scheme that would have devastating consequences for thousands of Luzerne County children and their families.

Mark Arthur Ciavarella Jr. was born on March 3, 1950, the second of three children of Mark and Mary Ciavarella. He grew up with his two sisters in a six-room house that sat halfway up a hill in Wilkes-Barre's East End section, which is a cluster of mom-and-pop stores and fifteen-hundred-square-foot wood-frame homes huddled neatly and sociably around the Holy Saviour Church at the very top of the hill. Its twin spires, visible for miles, loomed over the neighborhood like admonishing fingers. It was a place of confessing, communicating, baptisms, confirmations, marriages, funerals—life chasing its own tail. His father worked at the local Stegmaier Brewery and his mother was a Bell Telephone Company operator. Decades later, Ciavarella would recall that hardly anyone in his neighborhood locked their doors. And if they did, they left the key under the mat. People treated each other as though they would meet again very soon. The Ciavarellas worshiped regularly at Holy Saviour, and both parents were stern disciplinarians. Nevertheless, Mark was in and out of trouble as an adolescent, and several times he was suspended from school for getting into fights. When he was fifteen, he was arrested with some friends for stealing a car they wanted to take for a joyride. He was not charged. Instead he was sent home to face the wrath of his parents. "My poor mother was absolutely devastated," Ciavarella told a newspaper reporter nearly four decades later. "When I saw how much I hurt her, I woke up and saw I was not the only one with consequences. I wasn't the only one who would suffer for what I do. I vowed then, I would never do anything again to hurt her."

Young Ciavarella soon came to be known by his father's nickname—Scooch. It is a frequent Italian sobriquet, meaning "pest," that is often applied to unruly children. He was a good athlete who pitched a Little League no-hitter in 1962 and was a starting guard on the St. Mary's High School basketball team that won the Catholic League championship in 1968. Scooch Ciavarella received a prelaw bachelor's degree from King's College in Wilkes-Barre in 1972; three years later he received a law degree from Duquesne University in Pittsburgh. He was admitted to the Luzerne County bar in October 1975, and quickly developed a reputation for brashness. "He was loud, he was sure of himself, but he always came up just short of being obnoxious," recalled James A. Gibbons, an attorney from nearby Scranton who is now a district magisterial judge. Ciavarella took on difficult cases— and sometimes got burned. In 1993 he sued Wilkes University on behalf of a woman who claimed her husband died from exposure to a toxic chemical in a school lab. Four years later the woman pleaded guilty to murdering her husband with slow doses of rat poison placed in his tea. In the 1990s, he coached the Wyoming Valley Catholic Youth Center girls' swim team, which won nearly one hundred consecutive meets. Despite his emphasis on discipline and hard work, he was well liked by both the young athletes and their parents. Then, in 1994, Ciavarella decided that "the next logical step" in his career was to run for a county judgeship.

Pennsylvania is one of thirty-nine states where judges have to run for election; the other states choose members of the judiciary through some sort of merit selection process similar to the federal system. There is no perfect way to choose the men and women who preside over courts, but election is one of the worst. In an arena where integrity and independence are paramount, candidates are subjected to the corrupting influence of cash campaign contributions.

In politics, money not only talks—it keeps up a running conversation. And so, not surprisingly, among the most regular contributors to judges' campaigns are the lawyers who will practice before them—a stark state of affairs that has led former U.S. Supreme Court Justice Sandra Day O'Connor to warn, "This crisis of confidence in the impartiality of the judiciary is real and growing. Left unaddressed, the perception that justice is for sale will undermine the rule of law that courts are supposed to uphold."

Nor is it surprising that the judiciaries in these thirty-nine states are regularly rocked by scandals. In Pennsylvania in the 1980s, more than a dozen Philadelphia judges were found to have accepted cash from the leaders of the local roofers' union. Two of them went to jail and thirteen others resigned or were removed from office. And in 1994 a state Supreme Court justice was impeached by the state House of Representatives, convicted in the Senate, and ousted from office. Those are just the ones that got caught. But these black marks on the judiciary were mere prefaces to what Judges Ciavarella and Conahan would bring to Pennsylvania's checkered judicial history.

The other problem with electing judges is that our system of justice needs stewards who are steeped in the law and not afraid to make unpopular decisions. But in partisan elections, candidates do well when they tell voters what they want to hear. Thus it was that when Mark Ciavarella announced he was a candidate for a vacancy on the Luzerne County Court, he stood in front of a banner reading, "A Re 'Mark' Able Choice for Judge," and told a gathering of some three hundred supporters in a downtown Wilkes-Barre hotel ballroom, "It's time for people who break the law to realize they'll be punished." He said he would be a "citizens' judge" and pledged to "return to a time when values had importance."

In the May 1995 primary election, Ciavarella won the Democratic nomination by a scant 378 votes and prepared to face Joseph Yeager, the Republican nominee. During the long campaign, Ciavarella several times danced very close to the line between ethical and unethical behavior for judicial candidates. "He said he would not accept plea agreements," recalled Judge Gibbons. "This was outlandish and the product of a mind that had never been in criminal court, at least not very often." Candidate Ciavarella denigrated courts' attempts to prescribe alternatives to jail time, saying, "I believe our system is no longer a punishment system in many instances. The greatest rehabilitative tool we have is punishment." In his campaign appearances, he challenged voters to keep score on the tough-on-crime pledge, and he drew standing, protracted ovations with this line about sex offenders and drug dealers: "Those individuals will get the harshest punishment I'm allowed to impose under the Pennsylvania sentencing guidelines. If you violate our rights, you're going to pay, you're going to pay dearly." Armed with $450,000 in campaign contributions, Ciavarella carried this message in television, radio, and print advertising. A lot of this money came from local attorneys, but when Ciavarella was asked if this would present any conflict-of-interest problems when he got on the bench, he snapped, "Anybody who has donated money to my campaign and thinks they're going to get anything other than a level playing field wasted their money." Yeager, with a budget of only $70,000, was defeated by nearly six thousand votes.

Among the new judge's staunchest supporters were Lori Umphred, a friend; Donald Rogers, Ciavarella's law partner; Joseph O'Hara, the basketball coach at St. Mary's High School; and an up-and-coming commercial real estate developer named Robert K. Mericle. Soon after taking his oath in the Luzerne County Courthouse, Ciavarella handed out three jobs—Umphred as his secretary, Rogers as his law clerk, and O'Hara as his tipstaff. Far bigger things were in store for Rob Mericle.

Just a few months after graduating from Temple University Law School with mediocre grades in 1977, Mike Conahan managed to become a district magistrate in his hometown of Hazleton, Pennsylvania, in southern Luzerne County, some twenty-five miles down Interstate 81 from Wilkes-Barre—a minor miracle considering that Conahan was only twenty-five years old. Nevertheless, he was appointed to the post by Gov. Milton J. Shapp to temporarily fill a vacancy that opened when the incumbent magistrate resigned while under investigation by the Pennsylvania Crime Commission for ties to organized crime. No one was stunned that the local magistrate would have such ties. Hazleton is that kind of place.

Magistrates are the lowest rung on the judicial ladder in Pennsylvania—there are more than five hundred of them—and are charged with handling minor criminal matters, traffic cases, and small claims. Nevertheless, Conahan's leap from law student to magistrate was remarkable and due in no small part to his father, Joe Conahan, the local funeral director and three-time mayor who had connections reaching all the way to Harrisburg.

Conahan had grown up in Hazleton in the 1960s as one of nine children of Joseph and Elizabeth Conahan. He attended St. Gabriel's Catholic elementary school, Hazleton High School, and Villanova University, before going to Temple in 1974. He met his wife, Barbara, in the ninth grade.

Two years after his interim appointment, Conahan was elected to a full six-year term as magistrate in 1979, and he won reelection in 1985 and 1991. During his sixteen years as magistrate, Conahan developed many outside business and professional interests. As a private attorney, he handled real estate deals for the Scalleat family, which has been repeatedly identified by state investigators as part of the Bufalino organized crime family of northeastern Pennsylvania. Joseph Scalleat was well known for his 1951 appearance before the U.S. Senate Special Committee to Investigate Organized Crime in Interstate Commerce in which he repeatedly refused to answer questions by invoking his Fifth Amendment rights. Conahan also was a business partner with the Scalleats in a so-called gentlemen's club called the Golden Slipper Lounge.

On February 27, 1993, Conahan stood at a podium at the Ramada Hotel in downtown Wilkes-Barre and announced he was running for county common pleas judge. He pledged to turn down any campaign contributions from local lawyers or their spouses so he could preside from the bench impartially. "This will guarantee that there will not even be the remote possibility that when I am hearing a case my mind could in any way be clouded between the arguments of a lawyer who contributed to my campaign and perhaps one who didn't," he claimed. In his campaign, Conahan portrayed himself as having more integrity than his opponent—and in the world of Luzerne County politics, he may have been right.

After a nasty campaign, Conahan won both the Republican and Democratic nominations in the spring primary, guaranteeing his landslide election in November. Conahan told voters they should elect him because of his proven abilities as a crime fighter. But, as it turned out, Conahan already was part of the local crime problem rather than an agent of its solution.

Indeed, in August 1994, just eight months after Conahan put on his judge's robes, a transcript surfaced from the 1991 trial of Ronald Belletiere, who was convicted of operating a large-scale cocaine ring in Hazleton during the 1980s when Conahan was magistrate there. A witness at that trial, Neal DeAngelo of Hazleton, testified that Conahan had called him in 1986 to warn him against buying drugs from a man who was under investigation and offered instead to put him in contact with Belletiere to buy cocaine. DeAngelo said Belletiere later called him "at the direction of Mike Conahan to see if we can do some business." The trial transcript also showed that the federal prosecutor referred to Conahan as an "unindicted co-conspirator."

But Conahan was never charged in this matter, and he survived an inquiry by the state Judicial Conduct Board, which is supposed to investigate alleged misdeeds by judges. Conahan called the charges "outrageous and unfounded" and said they came from "common criminals trying to help themselves at my expense." However, he did admit knowing Belletiere and DeAngelo and performing legal work for them. Indeed, he said he was the godfather of Belletiere's daughter.

Belletiere served four years in prison as a drug trafficker, but that did not deter Conahan from maintaining business and personal relationships with him. Barbara Conahan, the judge's wife, and Belletiere opened a Mercedes-Benz dealership in 2004. And Belletiere was registered as a permanent guest at the Conahans' condominium in Jupiter, Florida.

Judge Conahan soon struck up a close relationship with William D'Elia, who became the organized crime leader in northeast Pennsylvania in the waning years of the twentieth century. As he consolidated his power around the Luzerne County Courthouse, giving jobs to friends, taking them away from enemies, Mike Conahan became "the Boss." He also eased into a friendship with another newcomer to the Luzerne County bench—Mark Ciavarella. In the beginning, common pleas judges were paid $90,000 a year, plus generous benefits. Within ten years, they would each be getting $158,000 in salary. It wouldn't be nearly enough.

Eight months after he joined the court, Mark Ciavarella was named juvenile court judge. Growing up in Luzerne County was about to get a lot more difficult for some kids. True to his campaign promises, Ciavarella began imposing maximum sentences on child defendants. He was especially tough on school violence, and in October 1998 he imposed a policy that students found guilty of violent acts on school grounds would automatically spend one month in an out-of-home detention facility—and their parents would be required to pay up to $400 a month to help defray the cost. Ciavarella was able to do this because, as the only juvenile court judge, he effectively was empowered to set policy for juvenile proceedings. The get-tough stance won quick support from District Attorney Peter Paul Olszewski Jr., who said it would be a deterrent. "I think it's going to have an effect, because word is spreading," he said. School administrators were even more enthusiastic. Jeffrey T. Namey, superintendent of the Wilkes-Barre Area School District, praised the new policy because he said students who once argued verbally were now turning directly to physical force. "Judge Ciavarella is very responsible and holds young people accountable for their actions," Namey added.

There were only a few objectors. Ferris Webby, a local defense attorney, pointed out that taking a child out of the home for a month might be too severe a step for first-time offenders who might do something as minor as push another student. But mostly the approximately seven hundred members of the Luzerne County Bar Association kept quiet. After all, Ciavarella heard juvenile cases only two days a week, and on the other three days he handled adult criminal issues and civil cases. The lawyers who appeared before him in juvenile court were the same lawyers who had to argue before him the rest of the week. And Ciavarella, like all judges, had the power to impose extreme penalties on them. He could send lawyers to jail for up to six months if he found them in contempt. Any judge who was willing to abuse this power, as Mark Ciavarella was, could influence the outcome of cases and intimidate the attorneys who came before him.

The only serious opposition to Ciavarella's courtroom conduct came from Juvenile Law Center, a Philadelphia-based advocacy group, which accused him of incarcerating a thirteen-year-old boy, Anthony, in 1999 without advising the boy of his right to a lawyer. The Pennsylvania Superior Court agreed with the Law Center and overturned Anthony's adjudication. The court's decision was inescapably clear: "When a respondent appears without counsel at any stage of a delinquency proceeding, the court has both a constitutional and a statutory duty to inform the child of his right to counsel, and his right to have court appointed counsel if he cannot afford representation." Publicly, Ciavarella was contrite and told the *Times-Leader* it would never happen again in his courtroom: "They obviously have a right to a lawyer and even if they come in and tell me that they don't want a lawyer, they're going to have one." Privately, he summoned the entire juvenile court staff to his chambers and said in mocking tones, "Everyone's going to have an attorney now because the Superior Court says that's how it's going to be."

But Ciavarella's pronouncement was a monstrous lie.

The American idea that children ought to be treated different than adults in courts of law had halting origins in the early days of the nation. The first institutions designed specifically for juveniles were called houses of refuge and they appeared in the first quarter of the nineteenth century. The houses were intended to get wayward youth off the streets, set them on the moral path, and then return them to society. Next came reform schools that added the dimension of education. But a nine-year-old girl named Mary Ellen Wilson brought the nation's attention to the need for society to protect children in 1874. A missionary found Mary Ellen in a New York City tenement, where, abused and starving, she was imprisoned by her mother, who had adopted her as an orphan. The girl had been repeatedly struck with a whip and slashed with scissors. When the social worker tried to rescue her, she found there was no appropriate agency to take her in. In desperation, she turned to the American Society for the Prevention of Cruelty to Animals, which persuaded a court that the child was a member of the animal kingdom and therefore deserving of protection like a stray dog or cat. There was a storm of protest about Mary Ellen's vulnerability and then an energetic reform movement to protect children in general.

The first juvenile court was established in 1899 in Chicago by reformers who were appalled at seeing children, some as young as eight years old, housed with adult criminals in the Cook County Jail. Other states soon followed, and before long there was a national movement of creating separate systems of courts, law, and facilities for children. By 1925, forty-six states and the District of Columbia had separate courts for juveniles, part of a larger social movement centered on the idea that the state had an obligation to protect its young people. Child labor laws were passed, restrictions were placed on the sale of tobacco and alcohol, and safety regulations were enacted for toys.

One of the central points of the juvenile reforms was that children are developmentally different from adults and therefore less responsible for their misdeeds, as well as more likely to be rehabilitated. Children should not be viewed as "little adults," but rather as individuals distinct from their elders and requiring the guidance of responsible adults. Because of these differences, the society in general had a moral responsibility to serve as a kind of super parent to endangered children. For the juvenile court system, this meant focus on rehabilitation rather than punishment.

At the same time, however, there was always widespread public fear about juvenile delinquency. Few generations escaped the perception that they were experiencing a juvenile crime wave. In the early days of nationhood, there were worries about wayward youth in Boston, Philadelphia, and New York. Successive generations were convinced that the "youth of today" engaged in much more dangerous and antisocial behavior than their own generation did. In the early years of the twentieth century, there was great concern about "bad literature," including newspaper stories that gave "details of such criminals as Jack the Ripper" and "bad theaters" showing movies like *Buffalo Bill* that led to "uncontrolled excitement and a craving induced in the poorer children which leads them to steal in order to get the entrance fee." By 1920, the automobile and "un-chaperoned rides" had been added to movies and jazz as sources of youth corruption. After World War II, FBI Director J. Edgar Hoover warned of a "flood tide" of youth violence, and the U.S. Senate held public hearings on the rising problem of juvenile delinquency. The chairman, Senator Estes Kefauver, a Tennessee Democrat, opened the hearing by proclaiming that no town in America was safe from the epidemic. There were efforts to censor movies and books, especially comic books, from spreading the wrong values.

Near the end of the twentieth century, an increase in violent acts by juveniles led state legislatures to blur the line between childhood and adulthood. Contemporary adolescents were believed to be more mature than those of past generations and therefore needed to be treated more as adults. Perhaps the most extreme manifestation of this attitude was displayed by a Texas legislator who advocated executing eleven-year-old miscreants because "some of the kids that are growing up today just aren't the Leave It to Beaver kids that I grew up with."

Zero tolerance—a policy of mandatory punishment for given offenses without regard to the special circumstances of the individual—started with the Gun Free School Act of 1994, which required expulsion or suspension for any student bringing a firearm to school. Soon, zero tolerance was expanded to include any weapon, then drug and alcohol use, fighting, disrupting class, foul language, skipping school, and many other forms of misbehavior. Disciplinary matters once dealt with by school authorities now became matters for the police.

Then, on Tuesday, April 20, 1999, two seniors at Columbine High School in Colorado shot to death twelve students and a teacher. The response in schools across the nation was to impose additional security measures such as metal detectors, computerized student identification cards, locker searches by drug-sniffing dogs, and see-through backpacks. In Luzerne County, Pennsylvania, Mark Ciavarella rode this tsunami of public opinion and not only embraced zero tolerance, but bracketed it and gave it a coefficient.

Zero tolerance is a kind of push-button justice. It is justice without thought, or nuance. Any thoughtful person knows that, both in and out of the courtroom, the truth is not simple; it has many nooks and crannies. But zero tolerance is a one-size-fits-all prescription that quickly brought about absurdities everywhere it was adopted. Two elementary school boys in New Jersey were charged with terrorism for playing cops and robbers with paper guns. An eight-year-old in Georgia was suspended for bringing to school a pair of cuticle scissors she used to unwrap her breakfast. A Florida boy was arrested for passing gas on a school bus.

Nevertheless, there was a widespread belief, fueled by the media, that the nation was threatened by a new kind of adolescent—a "super predator" needing to be brought under control with punitive measures. Legislators and school directors expanded zero tolerance to include other student misbehavior—class disruption, truancy, profanity, and dozens of other vague offenses such as "insubordination." But rather than end school violence, zero tolerance merely pushed children out of school and into the juvenile justice system. And this went against a mountain of research showing that once juveniles get enmeshed in the criminal justice system, they tend to stay in the system and become adult offenders and expensive burdens to taxpayers. In fact, one recipe for a career criminal is take a troubled adolescent and toss him into jail with real criminals. The American Bar Association went on record in 2001 in opposition to zero tolerance on the grounds that it violates the civil liberties of children while failing to be an effective force against juvenile crime. Judges, defense lawyers, and even many prosecutors came to agree that zero tolerance was counterproductive. Pennsylvania avoided many of the excesses of zero tolerance with a system of "balanced and restorative justice" that sought to hold juveniles accountable for their misdeeds while simultaneously providing treatment and rehabilitation designed to make them productive citizens rather than social encumbrances. But in Luzerne County, Ciavarella was going his own way, and no one was stopping him. Indeed, when Ciavarella received a video presentation on balanced and restorative justice that had been prepared for juvenile judges, he tossed it in the trash can after reading the title.

At the invitation of admiring school administrators, he started making regular appearances in school assemblies, where he got attention not with judicial temperance but with a set of bared teeth. Teachers and students remember that his standard talk included these words: "Do you know who I am? You never want to come in front of me. You should be frightened of me. But I'm fair. If it's your first time and it's nothing major, I'll give you a break. If you come in front of me a second time, I'll throw the book at you." Although his appearances were unfitting behavior for a judge, Ciavarella stoutly defended them. Indeed, he seemed to believe that had he just been allowed to give his talk before the students of Columbine High School, the massacre could have been avoided. Students' response ranged from lukewarm to hostile, but the adults at school—administrators, teachers' unions, and many teachers—were delighted. Many infractions that were normally dealt with reluctantly by principals and superintendents were now being handled quickly by Ciavarella. "Everybody loved him," said Judge Chester B. Muroski, Luzerne County's longtime family court judge. "He was putting bad kids away. That's how it was perceived."

At some point in his early years on the juvenile bench, Ciavarella decided it was time to replace the county-owned juvenile detention center, which was known as the River Street Center. The facility was mainly used as a holding facility to temporarily house juveniles who were either awaiting court hearings or awaiting placement in long-term detention accommodations. It was an ugly, red-brick, rust-scabbed structure built as a women's prison in the 1930s, and it was far from an ideal resource. Ciavarella enlisted Conahan's support, and the pair worked behind the scenes to try to force the county to build a new center. When that didn't work, Ciavarella went public in April 2000, casting himself as an advocate for better conditions for the troubled youth of Luzerne County. "The place is old," he said. "It suffers from leaky pipes that we can't get to because they're buried behind two-foot-thick concrete walls and the interior is infested with cockroaches and rodents." When county commissioners—the three elected officials charged with overall responsibility for running the county—resisted the idea, Ciavarella turned in May 2000 to the biggest private developer in northeastern Pennsylvania—his lifelong friend, Rob Mericle.

• • •

While still a twenty-year-old undergraduate at the University of Pennsylvania's prestigious Wharton School in 1983, Robert K. Mericle felt the spur of the moment dig into his flank when Cabbage Patch Kids dolls became a national obsession. Mericle contacted Coleco, the manufacturer, and ordered ten thousand of them, which he then resold to eager retailers. It was risky, but it paid off. He estimates he made a fast $75,000 on the deal; but this would be pocket change compared to the deals he would work over the next twenty-five years to become northeastern Pennsylvania's number 1 commercial real estate developer.

He was already out of the toy business when he graduated from Penn in 1985 with a degree in economics and returned to his native Wilkes-Barre, where his parents operated an old-fashioned hardware store. He founded Mericle Properties, passed the exam for a general contractor's license, and studied local building codes and zoning ordinances. He had an extraordinary knack for paying the right price for the right building at the right time. His first big project was the purchase of fifteen rundown homes in Wilkes-Barre, which he rebuilt and sold at a profit. With these proceeds he bought an old shoe factory, which became a Sallie Mae Bank that handled student loans. He built shopping centers, business parks, and industrial parks. Typically, Mericle built a facility and then got tenants to sign long-term leases. His name—appearing in huge letters on signs all over northeastern Pennsylvania—became synonymous with quality construction, job creation, and economic development. Within fifteen years, his website would claim that Mericle Properties was responsible for ninety-one buildings in which some ten thousand people were employed.

Mericle was brilliant and willing to take risks, but he also was helped immensely by state grants and loans and local tax incentives. In pursuit of this largesse, it is not surprising that he became a major contributor to political campaigns. Between 1998 and 2008, his donations to politicians totaled nearly $445,000. Most of the money went to Democrats, including Governor Edward Rendell (2003–2011), who received $110,000, and Bob Mellow, a powerful state senator, who got $117,000. This money was not wasted. For example, Mericle received $25 million in state grants and loans to develop a warehouse complex during Rendell's tenure.

Mericle also made contributions to his friend and attorney, Mark Ciavarella, when Ciavarella ran for judge in 1995 ($1,000) and for retention as judge in 2005 ($2,500). Mericle had known Ciavarella since he was sixteen and considered Ciavarella to be a "big brother." While he was in private practice, Ciavarella represented Rob Mericle and Mericle Properties in a number of legal matters. While he was still in college, Mericle began giving Christmas presents to Ciavarella. Indeed, the first gift was fifteen Cabbage Patch dolls. By the time Ciavarella became a judge in 1995, Mericle was a rich man. He began giving his friend the judge travel certificates worth $5,000. But this became cumbersome and so Mericle decided to let Ciavarella decide where he wanted to travel, simply placing $5,000 cash in an envelope, which he tucked into a travel magazine. This went on year after year until 2009.

Thus when Ciavarella summoned Mericle to his chambers on May 3, 2000, to discuss building a new juvenile detention center for Luzerne County, there was an overlay of familiarity and cordiality to the talks. When Mericle expressed an interest in the project, Ciavarella put him in touch with another rags-to-riches local boy—forty-one-year-old Robert J. Powell, the son of a West Hazleton brick plant worker. Powell had gotten into St. Francis College in Loretto, Pennsylvania, on a basketball scholarship and then worked his way though the New England Law School at night. He returned to northeastern Pennsylvania in 1987 and within a few years established himself by winning product liability and personal injury cases. His six-foot-three frame and booming foghorn voice made him a formidable courtroom figure. In the mid-1990s, he parlayed political connections and generous campaign donations into lucrative municipal finance work. As he won seven-figure verdicts, his reputation and wealth grew. Powell became a perennial all-star on Super Lawyers, a national rating service.

Given the county's continued refusal to provide money for a new facility, the two judges, Powell, and Mericle decided secretly in early 2001 that Powell would build a private detention center and then sell or lease it back to the county. For the project Powell took on a partner, Gregory Zappala, a Pittsburgh attorney-businessman and the son of former Pennsylvania Supreme Court Justice Stephen A. Zappala. Mericle was assigned the task of looking for a site. The Powell-Zappala entity was named PA Child Care, and in July 2001 the firm sent the Luzerne County commissioners an unsolicited proposal: We'll build a new juvenile detention center and lease it to you for $37 million over thirty years.

But the commissioners balked at the PA Child Care proposal, still preferring to use the existing River Street facility. Meanwhile, Powell brought Mike Conahan into the negotiations to help with financing. The judge had a close relationship with the Minersville Safe Deposit Bank and Trust Company in nearby Schuylkill

County, and a deal was struck. Using money lent by the bank, Powell bought a tract of land in September 2001, in an industrial park in Pittston, a few miles northeast of Wilkes-Barre. Mericle Construction submitted the low bid for the project, and the contract was awarded.

Mericle was pleased, and in July 2001 he went to the Luzerne County Courthouse to see his friend Ciavarella. There was good news in his eyes. The construction budget for the juvenile detention project included a "finder's fee" of $997,600, which was roughly 10 percent of the overall cost. "If anyone should get this fee, it should be you, Mark," Mericle said. He assured the judge that this was a standard industry practice. Ciavarella claimed he took this advice to heart and did not scruple over whether the proposed payment could be construed as a bribe or a kickback. Instead, Ciavarella thanked his friend and former legal client for what he would later describe as "manna from heaven." He decided that Conahan should share in this largesse, and he ran to his chambers. Conahan, he said, threw a pencil in the air in joy. "I can't believe that," Conahan rejoiced. "That's one hell of a friend." For Ciavarella, the coming money was especially timely, for he had fallen deeply into six-figure debt, apparently in the effort to keep pace with his wealthier friends, the Powells, the Mericles, and the Conahans.

One obstacle remained. Ground could not be broken for the project without a green light from the elected county commissioners. But the land had been purchased and the contract to build the center had been signed—and Conahan had no intention of giving up on the project. On Christmas Eve 2001, Powell and Conahan drove to the undeveloped site of the new center for an inspection. According to Powell, the judge said, "When we get this thing done, we're going to have to do something to take care of Mark." Powell said he was surprised by the remark because from his vantage point the project was still very much in doubt; but he claimed it was his first indication that the judges were expecting to be compensated for their efforts on behalf of the center. He says he was unaware of Mericle's finder's fee.

Powell was having trouble lining up further financing for the project. And how were they going to get around the commissioners' opposition? Conahan had the answers. For one thing, he had just been elected president judge by his fellow jurists, giving him broad supervisory authority over the entire Luzerne County Common Pleas Court. Less than a month after he became president judge on January 3, 2002, Conahan signed a secret "Placement Guarantee Agreement" with PA Child Care assuring that the court would pay annual rental installments of $1,314,000 to house juvenile offenders. This guarantee—that the center would have a steady stream of juveniles whose stays would be financed by state and county taxpayers—paved the way for the financing of the construction.

Mericle began building the center immediately, and in October 2002 President Judge Conahan dropped the other shoe: He ordered the Juvenile Probation Department to stop sending young people to the county-owned River Street facility, effective December 31. Conahan and Ciaverella said the building was unfit for further use, even though the state Public Welfare Department had just inspected and renewed its license, and two other agencies—the state Labor and Industry Department and the Wilkes-Barre Health Department—had found it acceptable.

To push the new center, which they were now acutely aware would bring them each at least $500,000, the two judges began a media campaign emphasizing the grievous conditions at River Street. In November, Conahan arranged a media tour of the facility that revealed cockroaches, leaky pipes, rusty sinks, and peeling paint. In an interview, Conahan said the building had no handicapped facilities and improper schooling, counseling, and treatment facilities. "The courts put the commissioners on notice well over a year ago," he intoned. "The conditions are deplorable." Then he allowed that he didn't care what the county commissioners did so long as they replaced River Street. But he warned that he wouldn't wait too much longer for the commissioners to act: "They have a job to run the county and protect taxpayers. We have a job to do, too—focusing on the safety and welfare of the juveniles up there. Sometimes the two jobs conflict."

Conahan waited less than a month before choking off funding for the county-operated juvenile center, effectively closing it and paving the way for PA Child Care to begin receiving juveniles when it opened in February. Despite their stated preference for sticking with the county-owned facility, the county commissioners went along with Conahan's edict.

In January, Conahan and Ciaverella began receiving their initial $997,000 finder's fee, but the payments were concealed through a money-laundering scheme. Disguised as a broker's fee, the cash went from Mericle to Powell and then disappeared into a befogged quagmire before reemerging into bank accounts controlled by Conahan and Ciavarella. Ciavarella received his first finder's fee installment of $330,000 on January 28, 2003. When he paid off his debts, there was little left. But more money was on its way.

PA Child Care's forty-eight-bed juvenile detention center opened on Sathers Drive in Pittston Township on February 4, 2003. Hundreds of people attended the ceremonies, including Bob Powell, who was in a defensive mode because of murmurings of discontent about his involvement in the project and his vast political connections through various positions, including county planning commission solicitor. He said the new center had nothing to do with politics or undue influence or even making money. Rather, he said, he was inspired to build the center after talking to a man who was extremely fearful that his son was about to be placed in the River Street facility. "This was about the children," Powell said.

Neighbors were in a not-in-my-backyard state of mind. They complained that there were no public hearings for them to air opposition. Indeed, they said they didn't even know the nature of the building that was going up in late 2002. Even the local zoning officer was bewildered, explaining that he signed PA Child Care's application thinking it was for a recreational facility. "When I think 'youth center,' I think basketball and other activities like that," he said.

For many years, the Luzerne County Juvenile Probation Office had been a forgotten agency, housed in cramped offices in the old River Street Detention Center. They operated without files, secretarial help, or a voice mail system. Now all that was changing under Ciavarella. When River Street closed, the probation offices would be moved to a county offices building in downtown Wilkes-Barre. So there were no objections when Ciavarella summoned all probation officers to his chambers late in 2002 and told them, "I want PA Child Care filled at all times, and I don't care if we have to bankrupt the county to do it. Is that clear?"

Three days after PA Child Care opened, Ciavarella expanded zero tolerance to require the automatic detention of any child who skipped school or violated probation. This provided an even larger pool of potential inmates for the new institution. The license for the now-closed River Street facility was returned to the state Public Welfare Department, which was puzzled by the receipt since it had just renewed its license and said that with some improvements it could become a safe and effective juvenile facility. But before it would reimburse the county for detentions at PA Child Care, the state required a ramping-up process to prepare it to receive juveniles. When Conahan learned that children were not immediately being sent to PA Child Care, he was furious and believed that the delay was the fault of Sandra Brulo, the Luzerne County juvenile probation director, who was summoned to Ciavarella's office in late February.

Ciavarella handed her his telephone and said "the Boss" was on the other end. "Judge Conahan began screaming at me and accused me of being responsible for the ramping-up limits," she recalled later under oath. "He said Robert Powell had bills to pay and that the ramping limits were limiting the admissions." Brulo told Conahan that she was not responsible for the delay in admissions. Conahan ordered her to file weekly reports with Ciavarella indicating the number of beds in use at PA Child Care. In turn, Brulo told probation officer Tom Lavan, who was responsible for placements, that PA Child Care was to be kept full at all times.

The judges' single-minded pursuit of using PA Child Care raised eyebrows around the courthouse, and it was whispered in the corridors that Conahan and Ciavarella must have some vested interest in the new facility. But Conahan kept a full-nelson grip on the court staff by populating it with his political cronies and relatives. Together, Scooch and the Boss imposed a reign of terror on the century-old courthouse, where questionable practices went unquestioned—and became accepted practices. Justice and the Luzerne County Juvenile Court had parted company.

4

MINDING THEIR
OWN BUSINESS

Within a few months Ciavarella was filling up beds at the new
PA Child Care Center with assembly-line efficiency, and zero tolerance picked up a tailwind. A fifteen-year-old boy was held there
five days without a hearing on charges growing out of a family
argument. He was eventually charged with a misdemeanor for
showing disrespect to his grandfather and placed on probation.
A seventeen-year-old boy was charged with violating his probation by staying out past his curfew. Without a lawyer present
and without allowing the youth to speak at his hearing, Ciavarella sentenced him to six months in PA Child Care. A fourteen-
year-old girl who drove her mother's car around the block spent
thirty-three days at the facility—even though her mother did not
press charges and the probation officer recommended probation
rather than incarceration. A seventeen-year-old boy arrested for
shoplifting spent three days there before he got a hearing. Another seventeen-year-old boy got into a fight and was charged
with simple assault in 2003; Ciavarella sent him to PA Child Care
for three months.

One of the first children detained at PA Child Care was
sixteen-year-old Rachelle, who appeared before Ciavarella in
December 2002 on aggravated assault charges involving an

incident at school. She was accompanied by her mother and an attorney—even though she had been warned by the court's probation officers that having counsel would "make matters worse" before the judge. She was initially sent to a boot camp, but then Ciavarella sentenced her to the just-opened PA Child Care center for ninety days. Rachelle immediately began suffering from acute separation anxiety, and within a few days she attempted to kill herself. She had nightmares about her experience for years after her release.

Another early detainee was sixteen-year-old Jeffrey, who was sent away by Ciavarella for operating a motorized trail bike on a highway shoulder while intoxicated. His father explained that Jeffrey had borrowed the vehicle from the family garage and ridden it to a friend's house, where a group of boys drank alcohol for several hours. As he was returning home after dark, Jeffrey was stopped by a policeman because the bike did not have any lights, and subsequently he was charged with driving under the influence. His father said Jeffrey had been acting strangely, hearing voices and experiencing paranoia, for several months. "When I looked into his eyes, I knew something was wrong and I wanted to get him some help," his father recalled. Two months later Jeffrey stood before Ciavarella, rocking slowly back and forth. When the judge asked him if he was pleading guilty, he just nodded affirmatively and kept swaying. His father tried to intervene and tell Ciavarella that his son needed mental health counseling, but the judge would not let him speak. The boy did not have a lawyer, and Ciavarella did not explain—as required by law—the consequences of being unrepresented or of pleading guilty.

Jeffrey spent eight and a half months in detention, including two and a half months at PA Child Care. Here he was evaluated by Dr. Frank Vita, who would conduct hundreds of such appraisals during Ciavarella's tenure as juvenile judge. Vita was Conahan's brother-in-law and designated court psychologist under a noncompetitive contract with the court. Vita did about eleven evaluations per month. Often the youths were detained in PA Child Care for a week or more before seeing the psychologist. Vita's recommendations were nearly always the same— "placement," meaning incarceration.

Jeffrey first went to PA Child Care and then to a private school for troubled boys in nearby Wyoming County, Pennsylvania. Here he was diagnosed with a bipolar disorder and returned to his home. At the age of twenty-three, Jeffrey was still living at home without a job or a high school diploma. "I would drive him to school, drop him off at the door, but he'd just walk out and come home," his father said. "He has few friends. He still goes out and gets into trouble drinking. He refuses to take medication for his mental problems, and he refuses to go to therapy. He doesn't trust anyone because he's afraid if he agrees to treatment they will lock him up. He's terrified of that."

Jeffrey's parents were assessed $5,925 for their son's ordeal—$4,500 for the detention expenses, $1,200 in court costs, and $225 in probation fees. The money was deducted from his father's disability check and garnished from his mother's paycheck. Similar charges were assessed against the parents and guardians for hundreds of other juvenile defendants.

Indeed, between 1999 and 2004, Ciavarella ran a kind of special "fines court" that would send children to detention centers until their parents could pay outstanding fines imposed by magisterial district judges. One of the victims was eleven-year-old Ryan, whose troubles began in May 2004 when he got into an argument with his mother after he left home without permission to play basketball. When his mother locked him out of the house to teach him a lesson, the boy called the police. When she explained to the responding officer that she was having behavior problems with young Ryan, he suggested that she allow him to cite the boy for harassment. She agreed after being assured there would be no fine, and so when she got a letter several weeks later asking her to pay a fine, she refused. This got her and her son before Ciavarella.

"Ryan, how old are you?" asked Ciavarella.

"Eleven."

"Do you have $488.50?"

Ryan shook his head in the negative.

"Very good," Ciavarella said. "He's remanded. He can stay there until he pays the fine."

Ryan's mother then informed the judge that there was an additional fine outstanding on a separate charge.

"We'll get that," Ciavarella said. "By the time he gets out he'll be able to go back for the next one. You're having a great day. Put the cuffs on him and get him out of here."

Ryan was handcuffed and placed in leg shackles. He stood four foot two and weighed sixty-three pounds. His shocked mother tried to speak, but Ciavarella silenced her with a dismissive wave. She never got to tell the judge that Ryan had not committed any crime and that it was he who called the police in the first place.

Ryan spent the next two months in Camp Adams, the wilderness camp for delinquents in Jim Thorpe, Pennsylvania. Within a few days, he was twisted into an emotional pretzel. He told counselors he was going to have a mental breakdown. He became so incensed while he was there that he tried to stab another resident with a plastic fork. Four years later, he had stayed out of further legal troubles, but he was still angry, bitter, and did not trust the legal system.

Ciavarella ignored the fact that the goal of the juvenile court is markedly different from that of adult court. The juvenile justice system is supposed to be the shallow end of the pool, a place where bad habits can be corrected before they become ingrained behavior. Being mature, after all, is like hitting a baseball or driving a car. It takes practice. While adult court is about punishment, juvenile court is about rehabilitation, tied inextricably to accountability and community protection. Its twin pillars are treatment and rehabilitation that will redirect children toward responsible adulthood. Juvenile courts even have their own terminology. There are no trials, only hearings; instead of convictions, there are adjudications; sentences in juvenile court are called dispositions; adjudicated children are called delinquents rather than criminals, and their punishments are called placements rather than imprisonments.

There has always been a disparity, sometimes a cleft, sometimes a chasm, between this ideal and the reality. From the very beginning of the juvenile court system in 1899, society has wavered in its approach to youth crime. The pendulum has swung between the goals of child welfare and community safety, emphasizing one, then the other. But another source of disparity is that juvenile justice is local. There are fifty-one juvenile justice systems in the United States, and each one has its own rules, procedures, structures, and philosophies. Within many states, including Pennsylvania, there are significant differences from one county to another. Moreover, juvenile judges are accorded enormous power and wide latitude in dealing with the children who come before them.

Unlike adult court, the juvenile systems of all states except Washington have no guidelines for dispositions. This is intended to afford young defendants the benefit of a doubt, but it also leads to significant variances in penalties from one court to another for the same offense. Juvenile judges are given extraordinary leeway in Pennsylvania, as they are in most states, and there are fewer checks and balances on their official behavior than there are on adult court judges. This makes them ripe for abusive practices. Ciavarella carried this discretion to the extreme, virtually setting his own rules. He took full advantage of his broad discretionary powers, and kids guilty of nothing more than adolescent mischief, who should have been been sent home under supervision instead ended up in detention facilities like PA Child Care. He also extended his influence to the probation officers, giving him even more power to impose injustice on so many children. He was supposed to take into account a variety of factors, including the youth's family situation, schooling, and the presence of drug abuse. But as long as he could claim that he was doing what was in the best interests of a child before him, he was free to punish unfairly—so long as no one spoke up. In Ciavarella's court, juveniles got the worst of both worlds because they were denied both proven rehabilitative treatments and legal due process.

It is an irony that Pennsylvania became the site of the worst juvenile justice scandal in American history, for the state has a national reputation among professionals for progressive policies in dealing with young offenders. The state actually has a relatively low rate of incarcerating young people, and its system of balanced and restorative justice aims to protect society and compensate victims while helping errant children transition into successful adulthood. When many states responded to popular demands for more punitive juvenile laws, Pennsylvania resisted the trend and kept its eye on the wiser goals of treatment and rehabilitation. Much of Pennsylvania's separation from the pack was the result of the relentless efforts of Juvenile Law Center.

In 2004—just one year after the first million-dollar kickback was paid in Luzerne County—Juvenile Law Center was designated by the MacArthur Foundation to lead a juvenile justice reform effort in Pennsylvania called "Models for Change," designed to make juvenile justice fairer and more effective. Among the project's primary goals were diverting children from formal juvenile court processing, establishing community-based alternatives to incarceration, and improving legal representation. Pennsylvania was one of only four states initially chosen by MacArthur, and the Luzerne County ignominy, though an aberration, was acutely embarrassing to the state's juvenile justice professionals.

Despite Ciavarella's frequent claims that he believed he was acting in the best interests of the children he was sending into placement, a mountain of evidence proves that he was acting contrary to the best interests not only of the juveniles, but also of the community and the taxpayers.

George D. Mosee Jr., a deputy district attorney in Philadelphia who heads the juvenile division, says his office makes a sharp differentiation between violent and nonviolent offenders: "If a child hurts someone, or if they even use a gun or a knife, the response is to protect the community. But these are a minority of the cases. With most kids, we look for the least restrictive means that we can to deal with them. What can we do to keep them out of the system and increase the odds that they will not become a problem as an adult? We are always looking for opportunities to keep them out of the system." Research over the past thirty years shows that detaining young offenders far from their homes and families is almost a guarantee that they will repeat their bad behaviors and become criminals as adults. Incarceration has lasting and detrimental affects on teenagers, disrupting their educations, socialization, job prospects, and passage into adulthood. "If you send a kid away, you take him out of his normal development trajectory," says Juvenile Law Center's Robert Schwartz. "Send kids away who scare you, not kids who annoy you."

Yet studies across the nation show that the majority of adolescents in detention are sent there for substance abuse, property crimes, and so-called status offenses like running away from home. Ciavarella carried this misguided policy to an extreme in Luzerne County. Sixteen-year-old Daniella spent fourteen months in detention centers, including nine at PA Child Care, for simply failing to pay a $286 fine imposed after she got into a fight with another girl in school. When he was twelve, Eric took his mother's car for a joyride and crashed it. His mother only pressed charges because her insurance carrier refused to pay a claim without a police report. Ciavarella—even though he himself had gotten off free after he took a stolen car for a joyride when he was fifteen—sent Eric away for *two years*. Alissa got into an argument with her grandmother when she was thirteen. Although her grandmother did not file charges, Ciavarella sent Alissa to PA Child Care for three weeks, the start of a downhill spiral that ended with the girl being incarcerated for nearly four years for substance abuse and probation violations.

The removal of children from their homes, families, schools, and friends often is accompanied by shame, guilt, and anxiety. Desirae was a Girl Scout and a cheerleader when she was arrested at the age of fourteen for possession of a controlled substance. As her mother stood by numb with disbelief, Ciavarella had her shackled and taken to PA Child Care. She left the courtroom screaming, "I'm sorry, Mommy." Desirae spent thirty-one days in the Pittston detention center. It was the first time she had ever been separated from her mother, who says her daughter never recovered from the experience. She dropped out of high school. Five years after her time in PA Child Care, she suffered from depression and feelings of worthlessness and was unable to keep jobs or maintain relationships.

The MacArthur Foundation Research Network on Adolescent Development and Juvenile Justice released a study in 2009 showing that expensive institutional placement, regardless of how long, produced few beneficial results for the community at large and that less costly rehabilitative services were just as effective in reducing recidivism. "Longer stays in juvenile facilities do not appear to reduce offending," the foundation said. "However, continued probation supervision and community-based services provided after a youth is released do make a difference."

In 1992 the Annie E. Casey Foundation launched a Juvenile Detention Alternatives Initiative that has shown that there are safe alternatives to incarceration of kids in most cases. "Youth are often unnecessarily or inappropriately detained at great expense, with long-lasting negative consequences for both public safety and youth development," according to the Casey Foundation.

Unnecessarily locking up young miscreants is not only bad social policy, it's bad business. Under Ciavarella, for example, Luzerne County was paying out about $16 million a year to juvenile detention facilities. One day at PA Child Care could cost as much as $300. After he left the bench and fewer kids were sent away, these costs plummeted to about $4 million with no rise in juvenile offences.

Nationally, the average daily cost of juvenile detention is around $250. The Justice Policy Institute, a Washington-based think tank, estimated in 2009 that some $5.7 billion in public funds was being spent to imprison children, most of whom committed nonviolent offenses. The institute estimates that cheaper home- and community-based alternatives to incarceration would save billions of dollars and result in substantially fewer juveniles going on to become adult criminals.

It often took many years for the full consequences of Ciavarella's zero tolerance policy to be realized. Shane first appeared before the judge when he was thirteen years old. It was February 11, 2002, and Ciavarella was in the process of working out details with Rob Mericle to launder the $997,000 finder's fee by first sending it to Robert Powell, who would get it to the two judges in a roundabout fashion. When Shane stood before Ciavarella, construction of PA Child Care had just begun, and it would not open for a year. A few months earlier, Shane and two of his friends had explored a long-abandoned elementary school building that was not far from their homes. They pried a plywood cover from a window opening, climbed in, and turned on a flashlight. State police officers arrived on the scene and arrested the boys. They were charged with criminal trespassing and Ciavarella sent them to Camp Adams for two weekends. When informed that Shane was a seventh-grade honor student, Ciavarella told his mother that he "could be 'smart' at camp." Shane and his fellow trespassers spent two winter weekends at the wilderness camp, joining other delinquents from all over eastern Pennsylvania who were there for dealing drugs, burglary, and other similar offenses. That spring Shane got into trouble again when he and his friends found a backpack containing paintball equipment. The owner of the backpack did not press charges, but since Shane was still on probation from the trespassing charge, he was sent back to Camp Adams for another weekend.

His mother recalled his departure: "Shane cried. He was dropped off at the juvenile detention center on River Street on Friday at 3:00 p.m. A bus would come and take him to camp in Jim Thorpe. They slept outside, the temperature was in the teens. No showers for youths that were there for just the weekend. My son came home on Sunday afternoon dirty, smelly, and starving. He is not a picky eater. He was spit on by the youths who were staying there for months. They did have a pavilion they slept under in army surplus sleeping bags."

Once Shane's weekends at the detention center became common knowledge, some parents of his friends forbade their children to associate with him. "It tightened up who I could hang out with," Shane said. "There weren't too many good people around me after a while." He failed to pass the ninth grade, and then in 2005 he and other boys broke into a bar and were arrested. Ciavarella sent Shane to Camp Adams for three more months and then placed him on probation. By this time, he was a sixteen-year-old alcoholic and drug addict. He was in and out of juvenile detention centers until he was eighteen, when he began ending up in adult prisons.

His mother concedes that Shane is responsible for the behavior that got him into such difficulty, but she believes things might had been different had Ciavarella shown more compassion for a thirteen-year-old honor student whose only real crime was adolescent curiosity.

Meanwhile, the Conahans and Ciavarellas were enjoying their new wealth. Conahan bought a house next to Ciavarella on Deer Run Drive in Mountain Top, a leafy suburb of substantial homes moated by lawn and landscaping south of Wilkes-Barre. Another Mountain Top resident was Robert Powell, whose family often joined the judges for weekend pool parties and cookouts. The view from society's box seats was good. The Ciavarellas and Conahans, enriched and unscathed, bought a recreational vehicle together, which they used for vacations and for tailgate weekends at Penn State football games. Then they raised their sights on leisure time and bought a three-thousand-square foot condominium in Palm Beach County, Florida, for $785,000. Unit 303 in the Mariner building at the Jupiter Yacht Club had a balcony view of the marina on the Intracoastal Waterway. To facilitate the purchase, the judges created an entity they called Pinnacle Group of Jupiter LLC, a Florida-based company that was set up in the names of their wives, Barbara Conahan and Cindy Ciavarella.

Ciavarella was not nearly as wealthy as Conahan or Powell, and in anticipation of Mericle's finder's fee for PA Child Care, he borrowed $150,000 from Barbara Conahan. He also signed up for dozens of credit cards and took thousands of dollars in cash advances on each. When he finally received the first $330,000 in laundered money from Mericle in January 2003, he spent $310,000 of it just to pay off his debts. Ciavarella received an additional $75,000 in Mericle money in April and another $75,000 in July. Despite the total of $480,000 from Mericle, plus his judicial salary of $158,000, by the end of 2003, Ciavarella's main bank account had only $4,333.

Late that year Ciavarella met in his chambers with Powell and Conahan—when Powell says he learned for the first time that he, too, was also expected to pay the judges. "You mean you blew through one million dollars already?" Powell asked incredulously. "They both kind of laughed and said, 'yeah.' " Powell said Ciavarella produced a sheet of statistics giving his estimates of the profits from the operations of PA Child Care. "You guys are doing very, very well," Powell said the judge told him. "I know what's going on up there." And, of course he did—because he was sending the kids there. When Powell protested that Ciavarella's estimates did not take into account one-time startup expenses, he said: "Judge Ciavarella started to get animated. He said, 'I don't care. I know what you got up there, and I want to be paid.'"

And so Powell agreed to a scheme in which he would funnel cash to the Pinnacle Group, owned by Barbara Conahan and Cindy Ciavarella. The payments would be disguised as monthly rentals on the judges' condominium and as various fees for docking Powell's fifty-six-foot sport fishing boat, the *Reel Justice*, at the adjacent marina. All through 2004, Powell wrote checks for such items as "slip rental fees" ($78,000), "leases expenses April May June" ($75,000), and "rent prepay" ($52,000). The Pinnacle Group also received two wire transfers totaling $220,000 from Vision Holdings, a Cayman Islands entity owned by Powell. Powell later told federal investigators that he paid $585,000 just to rent the condominium—even though it was only available in the hot summer months and even though the judges had paid only $785,000 to own it. Even while it was still a useless, unfinished, unfurnished shell, Powell agreed to a $15,000-a-month lease over ten years—or a total of $1.8 million—for the condominium. But in fact he paid thirty-nine months' rent—or $585,000—in just the first nine months of 2004.

Ciavarella's draconian demeanor soon became a courthouse rubric, and the word spread among police, attorneys, and probation officers that juveniles often were better off without a lawyer—and if they had one, they would fare better if they pled guilty. Not only was this bad advice, it was inaccurate. Among the juveniles who appeared before Ciavarella between 2000 and 2008,

60 percent of those without lawyers were sent to detention while only 22 percent of those with representation were placed. When twelve-year-old David was arrested in 2004 in connection with a rock-throwing incident by a group of boys who broke several windshields near a busy highway, his parents consulted a lawyer. They were advised that David should plead guilty—even though the boy said he had not been one of the rock throwers. Somewhat reluctantly, the parents went along with the advice, but they brought with them a file of commendations David had received and presented it to Ciavarella. After accepting the plea, Ciavarella dug into the file, pulled out a Boy Scout citation David had received from former Governor Tom Ridge, and regarded young David with head-cocked amusement.

"Well, Mr. Big Shot Boy Scout, Governor Ridge is now the secretary of Homeland Security. Perhaps I should tell him that we have a terrorist loose on the streets of Luzerne County." David was handcuffed, shackled, and taken away from his parents and placed in a wilderness camp for thirty-five days.

By this time Ciavarella's courtroom was a busy, sometimes chaotic place on Tuesdays and Thursdays when he held juvenile court. There were twenty or more hearings per day, and cases were moved quickly. Ciavarella often announced near the end of a morning that he was in a hurry because "I have a one o'clock tee time." David described how it looked the day of his hearing: "There were lots of people in the courtroom at the time. I know there were other people being charged that were sitting around the corners of the courtroom already in handcuffs and shackles. There were lots of people behind us too. I don't know who they were." David's father added, "The courtroom was filled, and I mean filled. It was packed. It looked like a marketplace. There were children, young people, not adults, in orange jumpsuits with the belts and the hands and the shackles on the feet standing kind of like off to the side."

Juveniles often spent days and weeks at PA Child Care even before getting in to see Ciavarella. Fifteen-year-old William spent five days at the Pittston facility before getting a hearing at which Ciavarella asked him if he had disrespected his grandfather. When William said he had, he was placed in Camp Adams for sixty days. William did not have a lawyer and he did not plead guilty to any charge. In 2003, thirteen-year-old Fred was held at PA Child Care from November 3 until he finally got a hearing on November 26. Seventeen-year-old Ruth was in PA Child Care for seven months on a simple assault charge.

In 2003, the mother of thirteen-year-old Fred called police "to scare him" because he was misbehaving at home. But when the officer came to the home, rather than lecture Fred, he arrested him on disorderly conduct charges, even though his mother protested. He was held at PA Child Care for nineteen days before he got a hearing. When Fred finally went before Ciavarella, his mother assumed he would be ordered into counseling and so she didn't retain an attorney. But after a two-minute hearing, Fred was taken away in shackles to Camp Adams for three months. His mother was assessed several court costs plus $480 a month that was garnished from her wages. She was forced to take money from her retirement plan, incurring taxes and penalties for early withdrawal.

Within five months of the opening of PA Child Care, there were not enough beds to accommodate the targets of Ciavarella's zero-tolerance policy. Powell and Zappala decided to open another facility—Western PA Child Care, a ninety-nine-bed facility in Butler County, Pennsylvania—about 230 miles from Wilkes-Barre. The company was created just four months after PA Child

Care opened, and Mericle was designated as the contractor. Once again Mericle paid a finder's fee to Conahan and Ciavarella. This time it was an even $1 million, disguised as a "registration and commission" agreement. Mericle paid the money to Powell, who in turn got it to the two judges in a series a money-laundering maneuvers. The money landed in the Pinnacle Group owned by Barbara Conahan and Cindy Ciavarella. Powell later told federal investigators that he allowed Mericle to run the money through him because if Powell didn't he feared the judges would bankrupt him—Powell and Zappala had a $12 million mortgage on PA Child Care—by refusing to send more children to the two private detention facilities.

Ciavarella found an opportunity to help his old friend and new benefactor Rob Mericle in September 2004 when Mericle Properties sued three tenants over a lease dispute in an office building in Scranton. Scranton is not in Luzerne County, but in neighboring Lackawanna County. Nevertheless, Mericle filed the suit in Luzerne County, and Conahan assigned the case to Ciavarella. Lawrence Durkin, the attorney for the tenants, filed a motion asking that the case be shifted to its proper venue, Lackawanna County, but Ciavarella ignored the request and proceeded with the case. Ciavarella granted Mericle an unusual request for a preliminary injunction blocking the tenants from removing anything from the offices. The case was even eventually settled out of court. However, at no time during the proceeding did Ciavarella disclose that he already had received $505,000 from Mericle as a finder's fee for PA Child Care and was in line for another $500,000 that would be paid in a few months for his role in setting up Western PA Child Care.

When a fourteen-year-old boy tried to hang himself with a

bedsheet in December 2004, Ciavarella was quick to praise the PA Child Care staff for prompt action to prevent the suicide. He said he had been generally pleased with the treatment at the facility: "I've sent kids to other locations and at other locations they've tried to harm themselves. That does not mean people are not doing their job."

Ciavarella's tough anti-crime stance didn't always extend to adults—especially if they were well connected politically. On August 6, 2002, Trooper Jerry Sachney of the Pennsylvania State Police arrested a man who had carjacked a Dodge minivan along Interstate 81 and driven off to Wilkes-Barre International Airport with two terrified children—aged eleven and twelve—in the backseat. Their mother told police that she had witnessed the crash of an SUV, and when she stopped to see if she could help, the driver jumped into her vehicle and took off with her kids. They were found an hour later unharmed.

Police traced the SUV to its owner and arrested Louis Pagnotti III, whose wealthy family had founded one of the largest anthracite firms—the Pagnotti Coal Company. Pagnotti was charged with seven offenses, including motor vehicle theft, interference with the custody of children, and unlawful restraint. As the arresting trooper, Sachney waited to be called to testify, but months dragged by without any action. Conahan initially handled the case, and preliminary hearings were canceled twice. Ciavarella took over the case in May, and on June 23, 2003, he dismissed three of the most serious charges. Five months later, the only remaining felony, theft by unlawful taking, was dismissed by Conahan, who then accepted Pagnotti's guilty pleas to three misdemeanors, fined him, and placed him on probation. Sachney was amazed: "I couldn't believe it. This guy had endangered the lives of two kids and he got off."

As word of Pagnotti's wrist-slapping spread, courthouse rumors held that the case had been fixed. But no one wanted to challenge Ciavarella—let alone the Boss. Besides, law enforcement officials said that Pagnotti was involved in various enterprises with William W. "Big Billy" D'Elia, the former bodyguard and personal driver for Russell Bufalino, who was now the head of organized crime in northeastern Pennsylvania. Federal authorities said D'Elia had been like a son to Bufalino and was now a powerful crime boss with ties to mob families in Philadelphia and New York. Conahan and D'Elia had been personal friends for most of their adult lives, and their association was widely known throughout the Luzerne County Courthouse and beyond. "It was no big deal," says William Kashatus, the local historian. "Politicians and the mob have been married up here for a long time. Conahan's association with D'Elia was well known—and it only added to the mystique that made people afraid of him."

Nor was it any secret that the judge and the mobster were regulars for breakfast, sometimes as often as three times a week, at the Perkins Family Restaurant just outside Wilkes-Barre on State Route 309, just four miles from the judge's chambers at the courthouse. They always sat beneath a big-bladed ceiling fan at a special booth in a section that was usually off-limits to other patrons. They would talk over coffee and ham and cheese omelets and then, hunched on the edge of red vinyl seats, they would spread file folders and papers on the Formica top and engage in earnest discussions. Sometimes pending cases at the courthouse were discussed. On other occasions, D'Elia stopped off at the courthouse, summoned a security guard, and handed her a sealed envelope with instructions to give it directly to Conahan.

Ciavarella thought the openness of the relationship was unwise, but his objections were dismissed by Conahan, who said D'Elia and he had been breaking bread together for thirty years. "He's been a friend," Ciavarella would recall Conahan as saying. "I see no reason why I should stop." But Ciavarella's misgivings were on target. The U.S. Attorney's Office, the Federal Bureau of Investigation, and the Internal Revenue Service already were looking into that very relationship.

However, these investigations were in incubation in 2003, and that November Luzerne County's electorate voted overwhelmingly to retain Conahan on the bench for another ten-year term. Under the Pennsylvania Constitution, judges are first chosen in partisan elections, as Conahan had been in 1993, but then can continue in office after ten years by running unopposed in retention elections. It is exceedingly rare for sitting judges to lose a retention election—fewer than one in every 200 have since the system took effect in 1970. And although there was no visible opposition to keeping Conahan on the court, the judge accepted donations totaling about $283,000, including about $120,000 from local lawyers. Taking this money represented a complete about-face from Conahan's pledge in his first campaign in 1993, when he said he believed taking campaign money from lawyers was improper. This time he not only took $283,000 in contributions, he spent only $61,000 of it on the campaign. The rest of the money, about $222,000, he paid to his wife and himself—supposedly for a loan they made to the 1993 campaign.

About the same time Louis Pagnotti III walked out of Ciavarella's courtroom a free man, seventeen-year-old Edward was coming in. Unlike Pagnotti, the boy had no connections with the power elite at the courthouse. His story would become a painful reminder that confining juvenile offenders makes it far more likely that they will become adult offenders.

Edward was about to begin his senior year at Coughlin High School, where he was a star wrestler who barely missed the state championships in his junior year. This year he hoped to make it to the finals and then get a college athletic scholarship. But that summer he had been keeping late hours, drinking and associating with what his parents thought was "the wrong crowd." Fearing that he was jeopardizing a life filled with promise in general, and a college scholarship in particular, they decided to put a scare into him. His father planted drug paraphernalia on the boy's truck and then tipped off police. His parents were delighted by the prospect of Edward going before a tough-but-fair judge like Mark Ciavarella, who would intimidate him and give him probation. His parents didn't think their son needed an attorney.

Although he was not advised of the impacts of a guilty plea or of appearing without a lawyer, Edward pled guilty to a misdemeanor in connection with the drug paraphernalia charge and his mother and father awaited a stern lecture and probation sentence. But Ciavarella had something else up the black sleeve of his judicial robe. He found Edward delinquent and, as his parents watched in stunned grief, Edward was taken away immediately to PA Child Care. He was there for a month. His coaches and teachers wrote letters to the court urging leniency, but instead Ciavarella sentenced him to four months at a military-style boot camp. Here he joined violent juveniles and gang members. According to his mother, Sandy Fonzo, "My son was never the same. Ciavarella ripped him out of his home." Edward missed his senior year and the 2003–2004 high school wrestling season.

After his release, Edward was placed on probation, and one week before the probation expired he got into a fight. Facing simple assault charges, the boy was certain Ciavarella would send him away again so he fled to Florida. He came back with his parents in about a month. The system didn't catch up with him for two years, but in October 2005 he was involved in a minor traffic accident, and he was before Ciavarella again—this time for violating his original probation. Edward was nineteen years old, had a construction job, and was working toward his high school degree, but Pennsylvania law allows juvenile courts to retain jurisdiction over individuals until they reach twenty-one. Ciavarella sent Edward to Western PA Child Care for 120 days. Upon his release in early 2006, he was ordered by pay some $5,000 in fines to cover the costs of his two incarcerations. Ironically, he was tried and acquitted in adult court of the assault charge that had prompted him to flee to Florida.

Edward was now a six-foot-one, 230-pound angry young man, and in 2006 he got into a fistfight at a party and beat his opponent so brutally that the other young man needed two operations. Edward was convicted of aggravated assault and sentenced to a three-to-six-year term in state prison. He was paroled in May 2010. He was depressed and drinking. On June 1 he shot himself in the heart. He was twenty-three years old.

Sandy Fonzo said later her son's suicide was the result of a downward spiral that began when Ciavarella sent him to PA Child Care at the age of seventeen. She says there were many other factors involved in his demise, and she does not absolve herself or his father of responsibility. But she believes he would be alive if he had not been sent away in 2004. Her personal conclusion coincides with the positions of nearly every expert on juvenile justice, including Juvenile Law Center's Schwartz: "While it would be an exaggeration to portray adolescence as a proverbial 'last chance,' it is not an overstatement to say that it is much easier to alter an individual's life course in adolescence than during adulthood. Events that occur in adolescence often cascade into adulthood, particularly in the realms of education and work, but also in the domains of mental and physical health, family formation, and interpersonal relationships. As a consequence, many adolescent experiences have a tremendous cumulative impact. Bad decisions or poorly formulated policies pertaining to juvenile offenders may have long-term consequences that are very hard to reverse."

In February 2004, reporter Mark Guydish, reporter for the Wilkes-Barre *Times-Leader*, was covering a routine meeting of the Crestwood School Board, when an outraged mother complained vociferously about the treatment of her daughter by school authorities and the Juvenile Court. This girl was Lisa, the girl who had written a prank note about bringing a gun to school and shooting young men in the kneecaps. The mother's anguish seemed real and her story plausible, so Guydish talked it over with a colleague, Terrie Morgan-Besecker, who covered the courts and knew Ciavarella. They decided to look further. They discovered that a report committing Lisa to the camp found that for the girl to remain in her home "would be contrary to the welfare of the child" and that placement in the camp "is necessary because reasonable efforts were made prior to the placement to prevent or eliminate the need for removal of this child from his/her home." But the journalists discovered that no one had visited Lisa's suburban home nor interviewed her mother or grandfather, who also lived in the home. The journalists also learned that no one had talked to her teachers and that Lisa had not met with a guidance counselor or been evaluated during her five days at PA Child Care. These events seemed implausible, but when they went to Ciavarella and asked him about it, the judge not only confirmed it, but was unapologetic. Instead, he asked, "Was it my fault, or the system's fault, that she passed the note?"

A story appeared in the *Times-Leader* on May 16, 2004, under Guydish's byline. It began:

> Cops knocked on the door while mom was at work. Handcuffs clicked around the slim 15-year-old wrists as a baffled grandfather watched.
>
> Police questioned her alone as they fingerprinted her. She waited five days in jail before a judge heard her case. When he did, he took only a few minutes to send her to a camp for delinquent kids.
>
> Until that moment, Lisa had been a model student, a participant in choir, plays, and the Science Olympiad. Suddenly she was a problem child, convicted of making "terroristic threats," yanked from her family and shipped away to correct her wayward life.
>
> Five months later, Lisa's mother, Laurie—she asked that last names be withheld—still talks about her daughter's ordeal like a shell-shocked victim of friendly fire.
>
> What rattles Laurie, as she sits in her middle-class living room in a quintessential suburban development, is how kids charged with crimes get treated. It's a world shrouded with secrecy in the name of confidentiality, and it is not what most adults think.
>
> Ask what she saw once caught behind the veil, and Laurie paints this picture:
>
> A school system that cuffs first and asks questions later, that bypasses guidance counselors in favor of police.

A legal system that questions kids before parents know about the arrest and that jails youngsters for days before they get a hearing.

A review system that deems a home unfit without visiting the home and that holds hearings at which no one from the family is heard.

And a sentencing system that unnecessarily rips families apart by sending kids across state and even across country, setting students behind in school work by weeks.

Lisa's story became the opening salvo of a *Times-Leader* series in 2004 that ran over three days, examining the county's juvenile justice policies and pointing out that Ciavarella's tough stance had quadrupled the cost of placement and treatment in just five years. Contrary to most expert opinion on the topic, Ciavarella said that probation usually doesn't work and only detention is an effective deterrent. "If a child believes the consequence will be anything other than placement (detention), they don't care," he told the *Times-Leader*. He said keeping juvenile offenders in the home environment often was counterproductive: "You just don't understand how little these children have in terms of supervision at home, in terms of guidance, in terms of people that are helping them make the right decisions. By sending them back to that environment, it will be a waste of my time and their time."

Given the seriousness of the problem of school violence, Ciavarella said his placement of Lisa was justified, though he did concede he may have been mistaken in some cases: "Are there probably times that kids get placed, that maybe it was not necessary? Yeah, I'm sure there are. But I also believe there are a whole host of times we make the right decisions." He said even though parents initially oppose his placement of their children, they change their mind: "I get letters all the time from parents who thank me. 'You turned my daughter's life around.' 'We finally have the son we knew we could have.' "

But no such letter ever came from Lisa's mother.

The series cited other questionable placements by Ciavarella, including three high school girls who got into a fight and were sent away to detention centers at a cost of nearly $50,000 to the taxpayers. "Years ago a case like this would likely have ended with a several-day suspension," the article pointed out. "But for juveniles who get in legal trouble in Luzerne County today, the days of a 'slap on the wrist' are long over."

Ciavarella had dismissed concerns over the rising juvenile detention costs in Luzerne County. "I'm not in the business to determine whether placement rates are up or down. I'm in the business of trying to help these kids," he said. "If it takes sending a child to an institution to help that child deal with his or her problems, that's what I'm going to do." But of course he was very much in the business of keeping placement rates up at PA Child Care. In fact, the two judges had received another $490,000 from Powell.

The *Times-Leader* series was solid journalism, and it outlined the reality of the injustices in Ciavarella's court. Only the kickback angle was missing. Morgan-Besecker and her colleagues were proud of their work on the series: "We thought, surely someone's going to see this story and someone's going to do something. But nothing happened."

There were many reasons for the lack of public outrage, not the least of which was that public knowledge of the kickbacks was some five years in the future. But some of the muted response had to do with flawed public perceptions about juvenile justice in general and juvenile offenders in particular, with stories about youth street gangs and "young predators" dominating the news out of juvenile court. In fact, however, only about 5 percent of juvenile arrests are for murder, rape, and other serious violent crimes. The overwhelming majority of young people's offenses are property crimes, including vandalism, and drug and alcohol abuse, and these were the sorts of offenses drawing disproportionate sentences from Ciavarella.

Indeed, Ciavarella's harsh policies with young defendants caused attorney Ferris Webby to seek to transfer some of his juvenile clients to adult court, where in Luzerne County they stood a good chance of getting a lighter sentence. For one thing, Ciavarella could set indefinite periods of incarceration while adult court judges were required to sentence within specified guidelines. Webby told Morgan-Besecker that he sometimes counseled parents that if their child went to adult court, he could assure them the child would not go to jail—but if they went before Ciavarella, he could make no such guarantee. Webby added that in most cases the trade-off was worth it.

Not only did Ciavarella routinely ignore the rules of juvenile court procedure, his courtroom manner was indecorous and unprofessional. He would interrupt defense attorneys without reason, waving his hand in dismissal as though swatting a fly. As witnesses testified, he bantered with conspiratorial hilarity with police officers and school officials, cracking wise about football games. He was an avid Penn State fan, and it was courthouse lore that appearing before Mark Ciavarella after Penn State lost a football game the previous weekend would land you in deep trouble. He showed up for court one day wearing a NASCAR cap. Another day he stalked out of his chambers into the courtroom complaining that he had spent the weekend in New York going to baseball games and that the Yankees had lost both games.

He once collected money from a probation officer on a sports bet just before sending a child to detention. Many of the juveniles who came before him found him terrifying, peering down at them through transition lenses with a kind of full-body sneer. Questioning his judgment only made matters worse. It was like trying to put out a fire with kerosene. Extenuating circumstances were dismissed with a mocking snort.

At the beginning of the twenty-first century, the Justice Policy Institute and the Northwestern University School of Law profiled twenty-five American adults who, as juvenile offenders, had been successfully rehabilitated: "They are prosecutors, politicians, poets, and probation officers; academics, attorneys, athletes, and authors; students, stockbrokers, and salespeople; football players and firefighters. They have worked at the highest levels of governments, as advisors to Presidents, and in the U.S. Senate. They have prosecuted, defended, and judged their fellow men and women. They have achieved unprecedented feats on the field of athletic competition. They have served their country honorably in the military. Yet when they were kids, every one of them was in trouble with the law. But for the protections and rehabilitative focus of the juvenile court—a uniquely American invention that was the brainchild of a group of Chicago women activists a century ago—many of them would simply not be where they are today. And most of them would be the first to admit it."

In their seminal 2000 book, *Youth on Trial*, Thomas Grisso and Robert G. Schwartz likened the juvenile justice system to a pipeline: "Along the pipeline are diversion valves, which are the decision points at which children are either diverted from the pipeline or continue through its various gates and locks—these are the points of arrest, detention, adjudication, disposition, and disposition review. One of the signal characteristics of the juvenile justice system is its many diversion options: at every point of the system 'valves' are available to send some children home, some to other systems, and others to noninstitutional care. Another characteristic that distinguishes the juvenile justice system from the adult system is the theoretical importance that the juvenile system places on a swift flow through the pipeline."

Juvenile court was supposed to be distinctly different from adult court, where persons convicted of crimes were fined or imprisoned (or both) under sentencing guidelines. Ciavarella's responsibility as a judge was to resolve each case that came before him as a special one—taking into account community safety and the crime victims while redirecting the child toward stable adulthood. To help him carry out this responsibility, juvenile law gave Ciavarella wide discretion in placement.

Ciavarella's approach was anchored firmly in airtight rectitude, antithetical to the whole concept of juvenile justice. Police arrested seventeen-year-old Kurt and charged him with being a lookout for a girlfriend who was shoplifting DVDs from Walmart. He was released, and a few weeks later a letter was sent to him at his father's house ordering him to appear in court. But Kurt was estranged from his father, and he never learned of the letter. Months later he was summoned to the school probation office, where a policeman was waiting with handcuffs. He was taken in a squad car to PA Child Care, where he spent the weekend. The following Monday he had a ninety-second hearing before Ciavarella, who sent him to Camp Adams for a minimum of ninety days. Ciavarella did not advise him that he had a right to a lawyer. Kurt actually spent four months there. He had not stolen anything, and was guilty only of playing a minor role in a minor offense.

The school-to-prison pipeline is a relatively recent phenomenon of students being arrested for what used to be considered normal adolescent misbehavior and being dealt with by school authorities without police involvement. The approach has led to absurdities nationwide. A five-year-old Florida girl was arrested by police for having a temper tantrum in her elementary school classroom. A fourteen-year-old Texas boy with Asperger's syndrome was cited by police for uttering an expletive in school. An eleven-year-old Colorado middle schooler was charged with theft after he took a lollipop from a jar on his teacher's desk. A Virginia eighth grader was suspended and ordered into a drug rehabilitation program after he borrowed a few ibuprofen tablets to deal with a headache.

In a 2010 Report, "Test, Punish and Push Out," a study group called the Advancement Project lashed out at the school-to-prison pipeline: "The absurdity of it is that most adults can recall multiple instances in which they committed these same sorts of acts when they were in school. Most of them subsequently learned their lesson without suffering serious consequences. Yet examples abound of districts that either mandate or endorse extraordinarily harsh punishments for behavior that—while it may need to be addressed—is actually quite typical and age-appropriate. As a result, the vast majority of punitive disciplinary consequences tend to result from relatively minor misbehavior or trivial student actions. The problem in most cases is not the student but rather the adults who react inappropriately to youthful behavior. Indeed, in a great many schools, it is seemingly no longer acceptable for young people to act their age."

• • •

During Ciavarella's reign, a good kid with a clean record could end up in detention for a single, thoughtless act. Sixteen-year-old Ashley was on her high school's honor roll, a Girl Scout, attended weekly Bible school, and worked on the school newspaper and yearbook staffs. She had no history of discipline problems in school, let alone a criminal record. During a family dispute involving her sister, police were summoned by her sister. Ashley tried to explain the situation to the officer, but he refused to listen and so she left and started walking to her mother's house. On the way, the policeman drove by and in anger and frustration she gave him the finger. She was taken to the police station, where she was charged with resisting arrest and disorderly conduct—even though her gesture is not a crime and is covered by First Amendment rights. She was kept at police headquarters for several hours until her father came to pick her up.

Two weeks later she and her father met with a juvenile probation officer, who told them Ashley would have to go to court, but since it was a minor matter, she didn't need to retain a lawyer and could use a public defender. She estimated that her hearing before Ciavarella lasted two minutes. According to Ashley, the public defender said, "Good morning" to Ciavarella, who returned the greeting and then flipped through a stack of papers about three inches thick. He said that it was her record even though she had no record. Before another word was said, Ciavarella told her to sit down, her hands and feet were shackled, and she was taken to PA Child Care in a van.

Once she settled in, her first concern was her schoolwork. She asked how she would be graded in her studies at PA Child Care and was told that there were no grades. She said the classes reminded her of her days in the second grade, including working in coloring books. After two months, she had a court-ordered evaluation by Dr. Vita, who concluded she was narcissistic and had anger problems. "They said I needed more structure in my life," she recalled, and so she was sent to Adelphoi Village, a residential facility for young people with emotional and behavioral problem near Pittsburgh—about 250 miles from her home. She spent the next six months there. Again she found the education inadequate. She finally persuaded her teacher to get her some high school texts, and she studied on her own, even giving herself tests to measure her progress. She did not fit in with the other girls, who had committed actual crimes, some of them violent. During this time, at least one family member managed to make the five-hour trip every weekend to visit her. Ashley was released in early summer 2005, and managed to catch up on her schooling, making it back onto the high school honor roll. She went on to Bloomsburg University, where she majored in criminal justice and made plans to go to law school and become a lawyer specializing in juvenile justice.

During her incarceration, her father sought legal advice on appealing Ashley's case, but she said he was counseled not to: "They said it would take too long, and it would cost some crazy amount of money to do it. And my time would run out before I would get anything done with the appeals." That was probably sound advice. Appeals from convictions and sentences, which are such a routine part of the adult criminal justice system, are rare in juvenile proceedings, even though Ashley's offense, a harmless display of disrespect toward a police officer, coupled with her lack of prior legal difficulties, made Ciavarella's adjudication and disposition vulnerable to challenge. Few reasonable people, lawyers or non-lawyers, would have agreed with it. Moreover, removing any child from her school and her home is a traumatic event and should be the last resort, not the first. But the appeals process in Pennsylvania and most other states is so cumbersome that Ashley likely would have completed her eight months of out-of-home detention before any relief was obtained. Had Ashley been an adult, she would have had the right to bail while her appeal was heard, and she would have had a very good chance of seeing her conviction overturned. But she was a child—and so she was shackled, denied her freedom, and taken away.

Ashley was plainly different from a seventeen-year-old gang member who was part of a drug-trafficking operation, but under zero tolerance both were delinquents. Research by the John D. and Catherine T. MacArthur Foundation finds it is impossible to place young people who end up in court under a single classification: "Adolescents who become involved in serious crimes are not a particular 'type' but a heterogeneous group, much like their non-offending peers. They differ substantially from one another on a number of relevant dimensions: parenting styles, social development, the timing of psychological development, mental health, attitudes toward the law, and the level of substance abuse. Seldom are these differences among them considered by courts, nor are they usually translated by service providers into different types of intervention."

Thomas P. Crofcheck's business card identifies him as Director of the Division of Audit and Review of the Bureau of Financial Operations of the Pennsylvania Department of Public Welfare. He joined the department thirty-three years ago right out of college with an accounting degree. Today, there's no CPA after his name. Instead, it's CFE—Certified Fraud Examiner. He is the head whistle-blower for the state agency that spends more than any other. One of the Public Welfare Department's many responsibilities is the child welfare system, including juvenile detention facilities like PA Child Care, which it inspects and licenses. Before 2006, most of the money for these facilities came from the department, which used a combination of state and federal funds to reimburse the counties. Crofcheck's role is to ensure that this money is being used wisely and appropriately.

Crofcheck lives in the Luzerne County community of Freeland, and one day he happened to come across a three-inch story in the local Hazleton *Standard-Speaker* stating that county commissioners were planning to "save money" on juvenile detention costs by replacing the current method of paying a fixed rate for each day a child is held with a long-term lease of the PA Child Care facility. Crofcheck was flabbergasted by the terms of the proposed lease—twenty years for $58 million. Then he remembered that back in May he had received a note from an alert department licensing monitor in Scranton saying that during its first ten months of operation, PA Child Care had realized profits of $1.2 million on income of just $4.3 million. Crofcheck knew that this level of profit—28 percent—was extraordinary for a start-up company—and it probably meant that the state was paying too much for these services.

On October 19, 2004, Crofcheck sent an email to senior management in the department's Child Welfare Services Bureau with the subject line "Bad Deal" and said he planned to audit PA Child Care. He said daily rates were too high and then added, "In the conversation with the county we were informed that the proprietors of the facility are anticipating building three more of these facilities across the state. We were also informed that the partners of PA Child Care include a number of influential people, including the son of a Supreme Court Justice." The department's Scranton field office normally would have done this audit, but it was too busy on another investigation. Crofcheck thought the PA Child Care situation was so grave that he would do the audit himself with the help of three other staff auditors. At this point, he believed that the Luzerne County commissioners were unaware that they were overpaying for juvenile detention services, and so on October 21 he informed the county of his plans to audit PA Child Care and suggested that the commissioners delay action on the proposed $58 million lease until the inquiry was complete. But just one day earlier the commissioners had given tentative approval to the lease.

Crofcheck had planned to begin the audit in January 2005, but now he moved in immediately. Within a few weeks his auditors concluded that the rates that the county was paying were 42 percent higher than any other county in northeast Pennsylvania, and it had been overcharged by at least $280,000. There were hundreds of instances of double billings, and generally poor financial oversight by the county. The auditors also criticized the proposed $58 million lease as "excessively slanted in favor of the landlord." The auditors determined that the county could build three juvenile detention centers for the cost of the lease. But when the auditors tried to delve further, PA Child Care officials denied them access to the facility's depreciation records on grounds that they were proprietary. Without these records, the audit was stymied. Crofcheck faxed an urgent letter to the commissioners on November 16, notifying them that the audit would be held up and urging them to delay action on the lease until the audit could be completed. Crofcheck said he wanted to help the commissioners "make an informed decision" about the lease. Crofcheck offered to meet with the commissioners and share his findings in greater detail. But two of the three commissioners—Greg Skrepenak and Todd Vonderheid—claimed they never received the fax, though the third one—Stephen Urban—did. The next day Skrepenak and Vonderheid voted to approve the lease over Urban's objections.

The decision drew the attention of Steve Flood, who as county controller was a kind of fiscal watchdog responsible for the money affairs of the county. Crofcheck telephoned Flood seeking further information. Flood asked for the working papers of the audit.

"I can't do that," Crofcheck said.

"What if I subpoena them?"

"That will do it."

"I'll fax you the subpoena."

Crofcheck received the faxed subpoena, scanned it into his office computer, and emailed it to the DPW legal department, which said it was valid. On the required date, Crofcheck traveled to Wilkes-Barre to deliver the audit information personally. Flood promptly leaked select documents to the *Times-Leader*, which quickly published a lengthy story on the critical findings. He also held public hearings on the lease and began questioning Skrepenak and Vonderheid at commissioner meetings. Flood came near to being ejected from one of the meetings because of the stridency of his opposition to the lease. Finally, in December, attorneys for PA Child Care filed a lawsuit against Flood, Crofcheck, and Leonard Pocius, another state official, in Luzerne County Court claiming they had released unspecified "trade secrets" by leaking the audit information to the *Times-Leader*. PA Child Care asked the court to seal all records in the case—and the motions were granted swiftly and conveniently by Judge Michael Conahan. The result would be a two-year delay in completing the audit.

Steve Flood was a flamboyant character who sometimes

over-stepped himself and propriety in his efforts to expose waste in county government. Although many officials privately agreed with him on the lease, they feared retribution from the Boss if they went public. And so Flood was widely portrayed around the courthouse as a kook who was way off base on the PA Child Care issue. When Flood failed to appear at a court hearing because of a mixup in communications in January 2004, Ciavarella threatened to put him in jail. Flood was running for county commissioner when he suffered a stroke in March 2007, leaving him unable to walk. He died in 2011.

Tom Crofcheck's troubles were just beginning. He had been sued personally by PA Child Care, deposed by PA Child Care's attorneys, and had his home telephone records subpoenaed. Eventually, he would be called on the carpet by his superiors in Harrisburg, labeled incompetent, and threatened with removal from his job. But not before he turned over the audit records to the FBI.

5

THE ELEPHANT IN
THE COURTROOM

In October 2005, sixteen-year-old John appeared in Luzerne County Juvenile Court to answer charges that he had shot out several windows in a Wilkes-Barre home with a BB gun. The boy had never been in trouble with police before, and even the homeowner asked the judge to be lenient. Nevertheless, Ciavarella, after repeatedly silencing the boy's court-appointed defense attorney, ignored the homeowner's request and in a matter of minutes banged his gavel, saying, "Adjudicated delinquent!" John was handcuffed, shackled, and taken in a van some fifty miles to Camp Adams, where he spent the next three months in the company of real delinquents serving time for stealing cars, drug dealing, and armed assault. The brief hearing in courtroom 4 was closed to the public, but it was witnessed by an assistant district attorney, the public defender, lawyers, probation officials, bailiffs, clerks, and other court staff. No one present spoke up against the inappropriateness of the sentence. Also silent outside the courtroom were the police, his teachers, and school administrators.

Silence is an extremely effective form of lying, but most silences are pauses, interludes, breaks in the action. The silence in Ciavarella's courtroom was deep and abiding, six years long, and it was never broken from within by the people who were closest to it. It was a conspiracy of silence. A large group of people agreed to ignore an unpleasant truth of which they were all aware. It is not an unusual phenomenon. Conspiracies of silence have existed at all times and at all levels of society. They happened in the antebellum South, where sexual relations between masters and slaves were common. For many years the Roman Catholic hierarchy kept mum about sexual abuse of children by priests. Baseball officials celebrated the shattering of long-standing home run records in the face of clear evidence that it was accomplished with the aid of steroids. During the civil rights battles of the 1960s, Martin Luther King warned us, "We will have to repent in this generation not merely for the hateful words and actions of the bad people, but for the appalling silence of the good people." A generation earlier, Mahatma Gandhi said, "Non-cooperation with evil is as much a duty as is cooperation with good."

In 2006 Eviatar Zerubavel, a Rutgers University sociologist, published *The Elephant in the Room*, a study of "silence and denial in everyday life." He said one of the underpinnings of group censorship was "knowing what not to know."

Thus, despite the fact that the Nazi deportations of German Jews to Eastern Europe were often carried out in public (not to mention the widespread rumors about what awaited them there), many Germans knew enough to know that it was better not to know more. By the same token, although people who lived near the death camps could clearly identify the unmistakable source of the smoke and the stench coming out of the crematoria, they nevertheless avoided asking "unnecessary" questions and, feigning ignorance, by and large tried to look innocent by not noticing. (Unlike

tactful, "civil" inattention, however, this was clearly motivated by fear and designed to protect oneself rather than
save someone else's face.) In other words, they pretended
to ignore what they otherwise could not help but notice.
[They] learned that if awareness of what was happening in
and around the camp was unavoidable, one might still look
away. Although cognizant of the terror in the camp, they
learned to walk a narrow line between unavoidable awareness and prudent disregard. In so doing, they thus came to
embody the type of citizen who makes the authoritarian re-
gime possible: not speaking, not looking, not even asking
afterward, not once curious.

Although juvenile court proceedings are not open to the public or media, there were always a dozen or more adults in the
courtroom when Ciavarella was violating the most basic constitutional rights of children. Stenographers, tipstaffs and other
court officers, prosecutors, public defenders, probation officers,
police, and attorneys with other cases all were witnesses. Many
of the onlookers were lawyers who had taken an oath to uphold
the Constitution. Under the Rules of Professional Conduct adopted in 1988 by the Pennsylvania Supreme Court, lawyers in
Ciavarella's courtroom were obligated to report the judge's
rights violations. Under rule 8.3, the lawyers aware of his actions
should have reported him to the Judicial Conduct Board or the
Supreme Court's Disciplinary Board. In addition, the prosecutors were required under rule 3.8 to report the huge number of
children appearing before Ciavarella without counsel.

Yet no one objected when the judge sent away eighty-two-
pound Matthew the steak-thrower, fourteen-year-old Angelia

the epileptic, and eleven-year-old Ryan, the boy who couldn't pay a $488 fine. Something very unusual and sinister was going on in the courtroom, and the truth was dancing before the spectators' eyes. A fifteen-year-old boy was sent away for three months for pushing a classmate into a locker. A fifteen-year-old girl was jailed for shoplifting a $4 jar of nutmeg. A thirteen-year-old girl was brought before Ciavarella for fighting on a school bus. The judge asked why she did it. Rather than answer, the girl started crying. Ciavarella sent her way for three months for not answering his questions.

At the center of this web woven by silence were three individuals: David W. Lupas, the district attorney; Sandra Brulo, the chief probation officer, and Basil G. Russin, the chief public defender. The common denominator among them and their subordinates was an acceptance of zero tolerance. There is no indication that any public defender ever interrupted one of Ciavarella's tirades against a cowering juvenile. No assistant district attorney ever appealed a case he had "won" because he knew Ciavarella's decision was wrong. No probation officer ever stood up to the judge when Ciavarella dispatched a child away from home for the flimsiest offense.

Together, they embodied the proverbial three monkeys—"see no evil, hear no evil, speak no evil." In Italy, the phrase refers to *omerta*, the Mafia code of silence, but in the rest of the Western world the three monkeys embody the acceptance of what is wrong by looking the other way, refusing to acknowledge, or feigning ignorance. They embody the official blink, moral laryngitis, systemic acquiescence.

During his tenure as district attorney between 2000 and 2007, Lupas never set foot in the juvenile court. Not even for a minute. He said he never received a complaint from his subordinates about the judge's treatment of juveniles. It was Ciavarella's courtroom, and no one dared to challenge him. The assistant district attorneys who practiced in juvenile court were young, naive, and unseasoned. Many of them were recent law school graduates seeking trial experience. They figured a judge like Ciavarella knew what he was doing, and they had no practical knowledge to counter that impression, and no guidance or supervision from Lupas.

There was a widespread feeling, common throughout the nation, that juvenile court was "kiddie court," a place where newcomers—prosecutors, defenders, and probation officers—got some trial experience and labored until they were ready for "the big time." In other counties and other states, the kiddie court mind-set even extended to judges, whose first assignment often was the juvenile court, with the understanding that they would "move up" if they did an acceptable job in this judicial apprenticeship.

Because of these newcomers' lack of experience and curiosity, no one questioned the fact that an exceptionally large number of kids were showing up in court without lawyers. Pennsylvania's 1972 Juvenile Act gives children the right to a lawyer from the time their cases begin until the end. Under the Supreme Court's Rules of Professional Conduct for lawyers, prosecutors are obligated to be certain that juvenile offenders understand the implications of waiving their right to counsel. Yet in Luzerne County more than half of all children did not have a lawyer. How unusual is this? During the same period, George D. Mosee was head of the juvenile division of the Philadelphia district attorney's office, overseeing the prosecutions of some 10,000 juveniles a year. He never prosecuted a single child who didn't have an attorney. Most juvenile judges in Pennsylvania believe that children charged as delinquents should be provided with continuous legal representation throughout the delinquency process. Judge Dwayne Woodruff, who has been a juvenile court judge in Allegheny County (Pittsburgh) since 2006, said the question of a waiver is never raised in his court. "Every juvenile has an attorney. Period." As a juvenile judge for twenty-one years in York County, John C. Uhler had some 20,000 young people charged with delinquency appear before him: "Every one of them had an attorney."

The restrictions on waiving counsel in Pennsylvania got even tighter on October 1, 2005, when the Supreme Court's new Rules of Juvenile Court Procedure took effect. The biggest change was Rule 152, which required that judges conduct a question-and-answer session—called a colloquy—with juveniles in open court to be sure that the young person is "knowingly, intelligently, and voluntarily" waiving the assistance of an attorney. Even when a waiver is permitted, the colloquy procedure must be repeated in every succeeding court appearance. Another major change was that only the child, not his parent or guardian, could relinquish legal representation. In sixty-six of Pennsylvania's sixty-seven counties, the change had a dramatic effect, cutting the number of waivers in half, from 8 percent to 4 percent of all juvenile cases. But in Luzerne County, little changed because Ciavarella—as well as the prosecutors and probation officers—ignored the rules. Over 50 percent of the children who came before Ciavarella had no legal representation.

Probation officers, who are employees of the court, advised juveniles either that they would not need an attorney or that they would fare better under Ciavarella without one. Ciavarella also manipulated the system by ordering the Juvenile Probation Department to set up tables outside the courtroom. Here youths or their parents arriving for hearings would routinely be asked to sign waiver forms. Often they were told they had to sign it, and many times they had no idea what they were signing. Ciavarella also pressured probation officers to recommend detention when the sentence was plainly incorrect. Ciavarella orchestrated a kind of festival of injustice, and everyone went along with it, murmuring Nuremberg-type rationalizations.

In affirming Ciavarella's demands that they ask juveniles to waive their right to counsel, and in doing this outside the courtroom, the probation officers violated basic legal requirements and rules of procedure. The result was that an extraordinary number of children, perhaps 2,500, were forced to navigate through the legal system by themselves, often with drastic results. Social scientists say that most teenagers are not able to make intelligent decisions about legal matters. For many years the American Bar Association has recommended a flat prohibition on allowing young people to waive their right to a lawyer. The MacArthur Foundation Research Network on Adolescent Development and Juvenile Justice concluded that adolescents are far less likely to make a decision that takes into account its risks and long-range consequences. It is clear that in most cases, neither the juveniles nor their parents knew what they were signing when they stepped off the elevator before entering Ciavarella's courtroom.

When a child came before Ciavarella, the judge usually had in front of him a folder containing not only the detailed recommendations of the Probation Department, but information on the juvenile's school record, parents, siblings, and other personal information, including any problems with drugs or alcohol. This information usually came from a so-called "intake report" based on an initial interview conducted by a juvenile probation officer early in the case. Typically, the file was given to Ciavarella by Brulo, even though it was against the law and a violation of court procedure for Ciavarella to have it, because information from the file could prejudice his final ruling. A juvenile judge is expected to hear a case with a clean slate and decide on the basis of the facts of the case whether the child committed the offense he or she is accused of. But by the time a child came before Ciavarella, the judge had already read his or her file and made up his mind about what to do. That's one reason most of the hearings were so brief.

Public defenders witnessed hundreds of instances of children's constitutional rights being violated, but they failed to speak up either on behalf of their clients or under their ethical responsibilities as lawyers. They failed to contact the state Judicial Conduct Board, they failed to contact the Luzerne County Bar Association and, with one exception, they failed to contact Russin, the chief public defender, who was in charge of twenty-two assistant public defenders—six full-time and sixteen part-time. Russin was the county's chief public defender for the entire time Ciavarella was the juvenile judge. In fact, Russin had held that post since 1980 and had served as an assistant public defender for four years before that. He worked at his public job about twenty hours a week, reserving the rest of his time for his private practice. As a part-time official, Russin did no in-the-courtroom supervision of his assistants, even though he knew they were inexperienced. There were no performance reviews or training in juvenile procedures.

During the Ciavarella years (1996–2008), Russin assigned only one of his twenty-two defenders to juvenile court, and that was on a part-time basis averaging four hours a week. As a result, public defenders handled extraordinarily few juvenile cases in Luzerne County. Russin estimated this number to be somewhere between 10 and 20 percent of all cases in which the offender had an attorney, meaning that between 2003 and 2008 no more than 250 juveniles had representation from Russin's office. Russin claimed he did not know the extent of Ciavarella's denial of legal representation to children, but said that the low number of defenders assigned to juveniles was due to his meager budget. Pennsylvania is one of only two states that do not provide funds for public defenders to represent juveniles. The entire burden falls on the counties, and therefore there are significant differences within the state in the quality of legal representation for child offenders. This disparity is sometimes known pejoratively as "justice by geography."

Russin felt so constrained by a lack of funds that even when one of his assistants came to him with a serious complaint, he did not address it. Jonathan Ursiak told Russin that huge numbers of juveniles were going before Ciavarella without lawyers, often after signing improper waivers. But rather than look into the possibility of constitutional violations, he told his young subordinate, "First of all, we're not going to seek clients. I'm not going to put up a sign and say, 'Please come in here, and we'll represent you.' We have to assume there's a proper waiver going on. We have to assume the judge has a waiver. We have to assume the district attorney knows the rules and the waiver and the juvenile probation office is doing the waiver. And we don't have the time or the manpower to intervene."

But, of course, all those assumptions were wrong.

One of the most egregious abuses Ursiak brought to Russin was Ciavarella's practice of placing children in PA Child Care to await evaluation by Dr. Vita, the court-appointed psychiatrist who was married to Conahan's sister. Matthew, the thirteen-year-old accused of tossing a piece of steak at his mother's boyfriend, was detained for sixteen days before getting to see Dr. Vita. Edward, the wrestler who eventually committed suicide, languished at the Pittston center for a month before getting his evaluation. Russin was troubled by the injustice of depriving children of their liberty in order to be evaluated under a court order, but he did not protest because he said he respected Ciavarella's judgment. Moreover, Russin was well aware that Ciavarella's zero-tolerance philosophy had strong support from the probation officers, who were taking their cues from the judge; the assistant district attorneys, who were getting convictions; and the police, who knew that when they charged a kid it would stick and youths would be sent away. But Ciavarella's adherents went well beyond the courtroom—and nowhere was zero tolerance embraced more warmly than in Luzerne County's eleven public school districts, where 50,000 children showed up for class every day.

By almost any standard, the public schools of Luzerne County were remarkably corrupt. Dr. Thomas Baldino, the Wilkes University political science professor and longtime critic of local public education, likens some districts to "job-selling cesspools." He adds: "For most respectable school boards, the biggest political issue is taxes, but in northeastern Pennsylvania, it's jobs. If you want a job teaching, you have to know somebody or pay somebody." Undeniably, the fourth R in Luzerne County schools was Relatives. Nepotism has been a way of life in northeastern Pennsylvania for so long that it is accepted and expected. School districts are loaded with the families and friends of school directors and top administrators. Not only do school directors see virtue in "hiring locally," the argument has even been advanced that it is a way to counter "brain drain," the migration of talented young people away from home. In 2009, Jeffrey T. Namey, superintendent of the Wilkes-Barre Area School District, claimed that a school board member's wife, a principal's son, and a teacher's son were all the best possible selections for elementary teaching positions among all the applicants. In 2002 a Wilkes-Barre Area school director had her son, daughter-in-law, and four cousins on the payroll earning a combined $270,000 in salary and benefits. The director defended her actions by saying everyone was doing it: "I have nothing against anybody else, as long as they're qualified. Every board member is pushing somebody for a job—friends' kids, neighbors' kids. I have helped many, many teachers in the district get jobs." Just before the 2002 election, the *Times-Leader* did a survey and found that fully one-third of the incumbent school directors who were seeking re-election in Luzerne County had relatives working in the school districts they oversaw.

By 2005, school officials were well aware that the one certain way to rid themselves of a troublemaker was to call the police, because this would get the child before Ciavarella. These kids were not only disciplinary headaches, they often were low achievers academically and dragged down test scores, making it doubly desirable to get rid of them. Behaviors that once were matters for in-school discipline—shoving matches, foul language, disrespect to teachers—were elevated to law enforcement issues. They were no longer handled by a visit to the principal's office or an after-school detention. In short, Luzerne County educators used Ciavarella as their chief disciplinarian. This despite the fact that under Pennsylvania law the only offense schools were required to report to police was the discovery of firearms and other prohibited weapons on school grounds. Around administrative offices and teachers' lounges, Ciavarella was praised to the point of eulogy. "The schools just loved him," said former Judge Chester B. Muroski, who served as juvenile judge in Luzerne County from 1982 to 1996. "It was so easy for them. When a kid got sent to the principal's office, even for something relatively minor, just call the cops." Muroski was removed as juvenile judge in 1996 partly because of complaints from school officials that he was too lenient in sentencing young people. Under Ciavarella, they pressed for disruptive students to be "placed"—and therefore out of their hair.

In feeding their problems to Ciavarella, Luzerne County educators ignored alternative steps that would be fairer to the children and less expensive to society. These include community service, after-school detention, loss of privileges such as extracurricular activities, and in-school suspensions that allow students to receive extra academic help.

Every autumn, early in the school year, principals, teachers' organizations, and parents' groups invited Ciavarella to speak at high schools, middle schools, and elementary schools. One parent remembers an elementary school principal introducing the judge to some 250 pupils this way: "And if all of that didn't scare you enough, here's Judge Ciavarella." Parents bathed him in a warm blanket of applause. Punctuating his sentences with his eyes and brows, he promised institutional placement for any school-related rules infractions or behavioral lapses. "I'm your friend," he said, "but there's one thing you must remember. If you don't behave, you're going to end up in my courtroom. You don't want that to happen." Then he mixed in with his audience, patting children on the head. Parents thanked him for taking time out from his busy schedule. The judge received similarly warm receptions all over the county, though in high schools there would be a scattering of catcalls and boos from students sitting in darkened auditoriums. "Ciavarella played on fear," Baldino said. "Parents were afraid their kids would be bullied in school. Old people were afraid they would be attacked by violent juveniles."

"Ciavarella took something good to a whole new level that was wrong," said James A. Gibbons, a district magistrate judge in nearby Scranton. "I go into schools and give talks, but mine are thematic and educational. I'll go in and talk about how the courts work and why to be wary of Internet predators. This guy went overboard and was threatening kids."

In 2005 Ciavarella went to faculty meetings and warned the teachers of the growing danger of gang members disrupting classes. "There are problems down there that don't get resolved," he said after meeting with the Hazleton Area School District faculty. "There is an element now beginning to participate in gangs. People don't want to say gangs are there and want to have a 'kids-will-be-kids' attitude. You can't do that and maintain a safe environment for our kids to go to school." To be sure, there was gang activity in northeastern Pennsylvania, partly because of easy access to drugs from New York City. In addition, two major national drug trafficking routes—Interstates 80 and 81—intersected in Luzerne County.

But no sinister gang inspired fifteen-year-old Paige to throw her sandal at her mother during an argument in the summer of 2005. Her mother filed charges to teach her a lesson. At a brief hearing, Ciavarella told the young girl, "Kiss your parents goodbye." Then he sent her to PA Child Care for six months. It was a difficult experience for her. She yearned to be home, and she didn't understand why she was interned with burglars, drug traffickers, and prostitutes. Nor was thirteen-year-old Sheree a threat to public safety when she took a joyride on a bicycle her mother said had been abandoned on the street. Ciavarella sent her away for a month, and thus began a long series of out-of-home confinements in several areas of Pennsylvania. The child became lonely, unstable, and began cutting herself. Fifteen-year-old Alyson was not a gang member when she got in a dispute over a candy bar with her mother and, at the height of the argument, hit her three times on the backside with a pillow. To teach her a lesson, her mother called the police, and suddenly she was before Ciavarella on assault charges. When the judge asked her how she was pleading, she said guilty. She got fifty-six days at Wind Gap, the wilderness camp in Carbon County operated by the Youth Services Agency.

The familiar scenario of parents bringing their children before Ciavarella to "teach them a lesson" has a long history. The very first juvenile courts of more than a century ago were used by working-class Americans to discipline their own unruly children. Sometimes parents were annoyed that their children refused to take factory jobs. "Working-class and immigrant parents used the courts as a club over rebellious children," writes Lawrence M. Friedman in his 1993 book *Crime and Punishment in American History*. "It was a weapon in a culture clash—a clash of generations, especially between old world parents, at sea in America, confused about values, horrified at the mobility, the laxity, the narcissism, the 'fatal liberty' that swallowed up their children and destroyed a nexus between parent and child that they had thought to be as sacred as a worshiped sun."

Fourteen-year-old Jamie came before Ciavarella on assault charges. She had gotten into a fight with another girl. They slapped each other once in a dispute over a boy at a bowling alley. Police and probation officers told her she did not need a lawyer. Ciavarella adjudicated her delinquent and sent her first to PA Child Care. She also spent time in two other detention facilities for a total time away from home of eleven months. During her confinement, other girls taught her about self-mutilation. She still bears the scars. Four years later, she told an interviewer, "It affected me dramatically. I've lost friends over this. People looked at me different when I came out, thought I was a bad person, because I was gone for so long. I'm still struggling in school, because the schooling system in facilities like these places is just horrible. Everybody gets put in the same level, and it's just horrible. I'm still struggling. I'm graduating this year. I was like an A-B student before I went, and now I'm just struggling with Bs and Cs."

Meanwhile, Conahan was a glowering, unsmiling presence in the century-old courthouse and dominated the courthouse staff by populating it with his political cronies and relatives. Even to Ciavarella, Conahan was the Boss. The courthouse teemed with ambition for raises and promotion, and fear of demotion and firing. When it came to questioning the violation of children's rights and the loss of their freedom, the courthouse became a hotbed of cold feet. Conahan and Ciavarella packed the courthouse with their friends and relatives. Dr. Vita, the court-appointed psychologist and Conahan's brother-in-law, was far from the only one of the judge's relatives to benefit. Indeed, it was joked that one probation office contained so many Conahan kin that "you didn't have to go far for a kidney if you needed a transplant." Conahan's cousin was the court administrator and another brother-in-law was jury management supervisor. Conahan's sister and nephew had jobs. Ciavarella's daughter was an assistant district attorney. Also holding county jobs were a former Ciavarella neighbor,

Ciavarella's daughter's boyfriend and former boyfriend, Ciavarella's wife's nephew, his wife's nephew's wife, the daughter of Ciavarella family friends, and Ciavarella's cousin.

The judges' intimidation powers extended well beyond the courthouse. In the American political system, there are few figures more powerful than judges, who are empowered to rule on the most basic aspects of everyday life and deprive any citizen of freedom and property. William Kashatus, the local historian, said this influence was magnified in Luzerne County: "The longtime residents are products of a regional culture that emphasizes deference to public officials and retribution for those who challenge authority. Much of the area's population is descended from poorly educated immigrants from eastern and southern Europe who worked in a once-prosperous anthracite coal industry. Congressmen, state representatives, and judges were among the most important authority figures in the lives of those immigrants, wielding significant influence and helping them navigate the challenges and uncertainties of their new home. At the same time, the immigrants feared retribution if they challenged authority of any kind, whether legal or illegal. Aspects of this mentality still prevail in Luzerne County. Ciavarella and Conahan realized that and preyed on it."

According to Robert Wolensky, the Wisconsin sociologist who grew up in Luzerne County: "There's always been a mentality here that if you don't do as you're told, you're going to lose your livelihood. But if you do as you're told, and don't make trouble, you'll be taken care of and you'll have a job. The pillars of this pattern were the coal companies, the aristocratic families, the church, and organized crime. Now it's the elected officials. Who's more powerful than a judge in his courtroom?"

Former Judge Muroski, who handled juvenile matters in

Luzerne County for twenty-three years, believes there is a strong "anti-kid" current that lent Ciavarella's stern policies popular support. Luzerne County has one of the oldest populations in the nation—about 18.1 percent of its people are over sixty-five, which is higher than even the state of Florida at 17.2 percent. "The city of Wilkes-Barre owns two golf courses, but there is no municipal swimming pool," says Muroski. "I rest my case." The judge remembers that when he was growing up in the 1940s and 1950s, there was a notorious juvenile facility called Kis-Lyn: "The kids were treated unbelievably brutally. They were beaten with razor straps. Parents, teachers, and principals told kids, 'If you screw up, you'll go to Kis-Lyn.' It was the worst thing that could happen to you. A teacher threatened me with it once. It scared the crap out of me." Kis-Lyn was closed in 1965 and the site is now a federal job training center. "Ciavarella became the new Kis-Lyn," Muroski said. "Parents and teachers tried to scare kids by threatening to send them to Ciavarella." Indeed, right after he became juvenile judge in 1997, Ciavarella tried to persuade the county to reopen Kis-Lyn for first-time offenders, whom he said would benefit from a boot camp atmosphere that featured strenuous physical activity, schooling, and counseling. "It would be a place where we could reinforce the fact that they don't ever want to break the law again," he said. The plan was dropped because the county did not provide funding. Anthony T. P. Brooks, executive director of the Luzerne County Historical Society, said the relative inattention to the welfare of children goes back to the mining days when preadolescent boys and girls were employed as breakers, sorting chunks of coal as they rolled down chutes, or as "spraggers," jabbing long pieces of wood under the wheels of mine cars to slow them down.

For many of the kids who were run through Luzerne County Juvenile Court and sent away, the worst part of the experience happened immediately—the shackling of their hands and feet. Many of them report feeling degraded and humiliated by the restraints. At the beginning of the day, a dozen or more sets of shackles would be brought in by court bailiffs. If the youths were placed by Ciavarella, sometimes they would be shackled by probation officers and escorted from the courtroom. On other occasions, they would be taken to a separate room to have the restraints attached. Several individuals recalled days when there were a dozen or more children standing in the courtroom shackled and wearing orange prison jumpsuits.

The hand and foot restraints were attached to a belt, forcing the juvenile to shuffle. Some of the handcuffs and leg cuffs used in Luzerne County were manufactured by the Hiatt-Thompson Corp. of Oak Park, Illinois, which has roots going back to a British firm, Hiatt & Company. This company started making handcuffs, manacles, leg irons, and other devices to shackle humans in 1780. Among their earliest customers were slave traders.

George D. Mosee said that in Philadelphia, juvenile offenders are not restrained unless they are a serious safety risk, and that in nearly all cases only handcuffs are used. And he said that the sheriff, not the judge, determined the issue of restraints on a case-by-case basis.

After sentencing seventeen-year-old Kevin to three months at Camp Adams for getting into a fight after a concert, he ordered the boy shackled. His mother said later, "Kevin has since told me that the most traumatic thing for him was the experience of being handcuffed and shackled in the courtroom, escorted out a side door, and shoved in a van. He was so ashamed to be treated like a serious criminal in front of people he knew in the courtroom. He was also worried about the emotional distress his grandfather experienced watching it all happen."

6

THE CASH FLOWS

The kind of silence that enabled Conahan and Ciavarella to milk their kids-for-cash scheme over six years often needs to be enforced.

Chester Muroski is a gentleman and a gentle man whose kindly, avuncular manner and pleasant voice made him a valued and admired courtroom figure very soon after he was assigned to the Luzerne County Orphans Court (a.k.a. "kiddie court") as a new judge in 1982. Most newcomers to the bench can't wait to be reassigned to other duties, but Muroski made a career of Orphans Court, which is better described as family court, handling both delinquency and dependency cases. He came to the court after spending fourteen years as a prosecutor, including a four-year term as district attorney. In that job, he earned a reputation as a maverick who was not afraid to tangle with the establishment. One notable prosecution was Francis Hannon, who was convicted of killing an elderly woman and burying her body in the basement of a Wilkes-Barre home. Hannon had strong political contacts—his mother worked for the mayor—and community prominence—he was photographed with the local bishop the Sunday before his arrest. Muroski not only pressed the prosecution of Hannon, but after Hannon's conviction Muroski publicly criticized the city police department for mishandling of the original investigation. After a department inquiry, the chief of police resigned.

As a juvenile judge, Muroski emphasized rehabilitation over punishment. He once told a symposium that institutional placement often resulted in making young people worse rather than better and ought to be avoided at all costs. This attitude ran afoul of the rising tide of zero tolerance, and pressures for tougher sentencing led to his removal from delinquency court in 1996. However Muroski remained as dependency court judge and oversaw abused and neglected children, handling cases involving divorce, custody, child support, and parental rights. As dependency judge, Muroski shared a budget with his new colleague, Mark Ciavarella.

There was harmony for about seven years, but as Ciavarella drastically increased the placement of juveniles in out-of-home facilities, the spending grew correspondingly. In fact, the court kept coming back to the county commissioners for additional money as the bills rolled in from PA Child Care, Camp Adams, Wind Gap, and other centers. (Only PA Child Care was paying kickbacks to the judges.) While $8 million was budgeted in 2003, spending totaled $10.5 million. The following year the county allocated $12.75 million, but actual spending was $15.8 million. This profligacy had a direct impact on Muroski, who often wanted to offer treatment programs to parents whose children were in foster care because the parents had abused or neglected them. Muroski's goal in most cases was to reunite the young people with their families after providing corrective services to parents. But because so many resources were being spent on the placements of kids Ciavarella had adjudicated delinquent, no money was available for these other programs. To his dismay, Muroski realized in 2005 that kids were being forced to stay in foster care for extended periods because their parents weren't getting treated.

"Once PA Child Care opened, slowly but surely the social services to these dependent children and their families became difficult to obtain," Muroski said. "There were waiting lists for parenting classes, family assessments, drug and alcohol evaluations and treatment, as well as other specialized services. Parents had to wait sometimes months to be given these services. This resulted in a child being in placement longer than necessary when the child hadn't done anything wrong, while the parents waited to complete services and the County had to pay to keep the children in placement."

Exasperated, Muroski finally wrote a remarkable letter to the county commissioners on June 15, 2005. It quickly got to Conahan, who must have felt the first tendrils of fear that the conspiracy was unraveling. Muroski noted in the letter that "a tremendous amount of money" was being spent on juvenile placements. He said he was frustrated because children were stuck in placements because their parents couldn't get treatment: "I really do not know why I cannot have the services I order made available. I just know it is not happening. Something has to be done." Then he threw in a zinger: "A reasonable mind might conclude this county places a higher priority on youth who are delinquent because of criminal conduct while the welfare and needs of dependent children who have been neglected, mistreated or abused are less important."

Next he challenged Ciavarella's claim that Ciavarella's strict policies had reduced recidivism. "Many argue the low rate of recidivism is misleading because a large number of juveniles remain in placement until they reach majority and sometimes longer.

Unfortunately there are not statistics on how many enter the adult criminal system, after their release, as adults." And finally Muroski threatened to ignore the budget restrictions and order treatment services—and hold the commissioners in contempt if they refused to pay for them: "I believe a contempt finding would be affirmed on appeal especially considering the enormous over budget expenses of delinquency court."

Muroski requested a meeting with the three commissioners on Monday, June 20. But on Friday, three days after his letter, Conahan, acting as president judge, transferred him out of the dependency court and reassigned him to preside over criminal cases. Not since his days as district attorney some twenty-five years earlier had Muroski been involved in a criminal jury trial. The notification came in the form of a written order sent through the mail. There was no personal communication from Conahan. It was a demotion, and it was demeaning to a widely respected judge. Muroski believes Conahan thought he'd quit rather than go back to criminal work. "He must have forgotten that I was DA here, and I knew my way around any courtroom. I had handled major murder cases."

Conahan characterized the change as part of a routine court organizational revision. In fact it was a slap in the face to Muroski and a message to the entire courthouse: do not challenge my authority or you will lose your job. If he can do this to an esteemed sitting judge like Chester Muroski, he can do it to anyone. If there were any lingering doubts about it, everyone who worked in the Luzerne County Court knew that they did so at the pleasure of Michael Conahan. The keys to staying on the payroll were blind eyes and deaf ears.

There was only one tiny voice of protest. Mary Pat Melvin, a veteran social worker who had appeared before Muroski dozens of times in custody, adoption, and addiction cases, said what everyone else was thinking: "Because he tries to do something to help the kids, he was slapped," she told Jennifer Learn-Andes of the *Times-Leader*. "I'm furious, absolutely furious. I don't care about what's going on in politics. What's right is right, and one thing I know for sure is that Judge Muroski should stay in family court." She said she knew that, as an independent contractor who depended on court-related assignments for much of her livelihood, she was taking a chance by criticizing Conahan. "Everybody's afraid of retribution. Everybody's afraid of losing their jobs. Everybody's so afraid. I think it's time someone in Luzerne County spoke up about this. Everybody can play ostrich and stick their heads in the sand, but I couldn't rest with myself if I didn't say something, because this is a very, very wrong move. The man is a very astute judge, and he genuinely cares about the kids in Luzerne County." But no other voices rose in protest, and Melvin stopped getting cases.

Muroski quietly took over his new duties, but he also began sifting through rumors and whispers that were circulating throughout the courthouse. He knew that large numbers of juveniles were being sent to institutions for relatively insignificant offenses. Alissa, thirteen years old, ended up in PA Child Care for getting into a fight with her grandmother. Thirteen-year-old David was picked up at school by police and taken to PA Child Care because police said he failed to appear as a witness to a school fight. David spent the weekend in custody before being released without being charged. Muroski knew that many kids were appearing without lawyers, but his big concern was the high rate of incarcerations. He knew that the courthouse was populated by the relatives and friends of Conahan and Ciavarella. He knew that Conahan's brother-in-law, Dr. Frank Vita, was being paid huge amounts of money for evaluations. He knew something was not right. He knew that Robert Powell had a private jet and a fifty-six-foot yacht named the *Reel Justice*.

Not long afterward Muroski went on a vacation trip to Florida with several friends, including two retired Pennsylvania State Police troopers and a lawyer he had served with in the district attorney's office. Just out of curiosity, they drove over to Jupiter to see the Conahan-Ciavarella condominium. They were staggered by the opulence of the place. Uniformed sentries waved Mercedes and BMWs past security checkpoints. Spacious landscaped grounds sported majestic palm trees and gurgling fountains. The condos overlooked the Intracoastal Waterway and a marina prickling with masts. The sweet smell of excess was everywhere. Properties similar to the judges' Unit 303 were for sale with asking prices of $1 million. Muroski knew he could not come close to affording such luxury on his judicial salary. He knew that Conahan had a variety of outside business interests and that his wife was from a very wealthy Hazleton family. But just as surely he knew that Ciavarella's means were far more modest. He returned to Wilkes-Barre convinced that Conahan and Ciavarella had access to huge amounts of money, and it probably had something to do with PA Child Care.

During most of Muroski's years on the dependency court, he heard cases in an annex across the street from the main courthouse. This, coupled with the fact that as president judge Conahan did not encourage meetings among the eight county judges, isolated Muroski from his colleagues. As a result, when he returned to the main courthouse in September 2005 to begin his new assignment, Muroski did not know many of the other judges very well. Nevertheless, he went to several of them individually, including Judge Ann H. Lokuta, and confided that he thought

Conahan and Ciavarella were taking kickbacks in exchange for sending children to PA Child Care. They thought that such a scenario was beyond belief. "They told me to keep my mouth shut. One said, 'You're going to get a reputation as a nut.' "

Next Muroski went to the FBI and learned that the agency was already investigating Conahan—not for bribery involving the juvenile court, but for his ties to organized crime. "When I suggested that Conahan and Ciavarella were taking bribes from PA Child Care, they were astounded and couldn't believe it. One of the agents said to me, 'Are you trying to tell me that these guys are making money by sending kids away? That's preposterous.' " At this point, the bureau was focused on Conahan's organized crime ties.

Muroski did not take his conclusions to the state Judicial Conduct Board, which is charged under the state constitution with investigating charges of unethical activities by judges. Surely, this was the place Muroski should take his concerns. But he didn't trust the JCB. Besides, the board was already investigating a Luzerne County judge. However, it wasn't Michael Conahan or Mark Ciavarella.

One of Pennsylvania state government's most secretive agencies is housed near the end of a hallway on the third floor of the Pennsylvania Judicial Center just across Commonwealth Avenue from the Capitol in Harrisburg. A piece of ordinary white bond paper, tucked into a protective plastic sleeve and taped to a window at the entrance says "Judicial Conduct Board" in half-inch letters. There is a small waiting room in suite 3500, but the door leading to the inner offices is marked with two signs: "Confidential Area. Do Not Enter Beyond this Point" and "The Procedures of the JCB Are Confidential. The Use of Cameras and All Recording

Devices Is Prohibited." The Judicial Conduct Board was created in 1993 to oversee Pennsylvania's 1,200 judges and protect its citizens from judges who abuse their power, either ethically or criminally. The twelve members of the board—three judges, three lawyers and six non-lawyers—are unpaid, part-time appointees. They consider about four hundred complaints a year—though much of the actual work is handled by its staff.

On September 28, 2006, the board received an anonymous eight-page, single-spaced complaint about Judge Michael Conahan that alleged links to organized crime, case-fixing, and an unusually high rate of placements in PA Child Care. In considerable detail, the complaint said Conahan met regularly with Billy D'Elia, the local mob leader; placed relatives and friends in jobs throughout the courthouse; decided cases involving personal friends and manipulated the assignment of other similar cases; and that there was a personal relationship among Conahan, Ciavarella, and Robert J. Powell. This was heavy material, well beyond the usual complaints about judges being too rough on lawyers or having poor courtroom manners. The complaint was organized under three headings:

- "Judge Conahan has used his judicial authority and power of appointment to benefit his family and friends and to contain and destroy his detractors."
- "Judge Conahan also falsely creates new titles for Courthouse employees in order to appear to comply with Supreme Court Directives, even though the Employee's functions remain the same. He also engages in political activities."
- "He routinely hears matters presented by Attorneys with whom he has close personal and long-standing business and friendships and refuses to recuse himself. In fact, it is his

practice to direct William Sharkey [then the Luzerne County court administrator, and Conahan's cousin] to switch cases, which are assigned to other Judges when the litigants or the Attorneys are his friends."

Each of these headings was followed by examples listing names, dates, the caption and docket numbers of cases, the names of the litigants and attorneys, and other identifying information. Lawyers who worked as law clerks for Conahan and Ciavarella also practiced before them—a violation of Supreme Court rules. Conahan ruled on appeals from decisions made by his sister, who was a court master—an appointed officer who made recommendations in civil cases. The complaint listed seven cases involving Powell that Conahan assigned to Ciavarella. In all, there were thirty-three specific examples of illegal and unethical conduct by Conahan. Ciavarella was mentioned several times.

It was an extraordinary document, a detailed road map for investigators. Nevertheless, the board did nothing with it for eight months. Then, acting on the recommendation of Joseph A. Massa Jr., its chief counsel, the board voted to table the complaint. The board was supposed to look at the complaint again at its October 2007 meeting, but the complaint never got on the agenda. Indeed, the board never took any action on the complaint.

Instead, the board staff spent much of its time and resources investigating a complaint against Luzerne County Judge Ann H. Lokuta, which alleged numerous violations of the Code of Judicial Conduct in her courtroom demeanor and performance. She was charged with being rude and intemperate to lawyers, witnesses, and the courthouse staff. It was also charged that she used court personnel to perform personal services, and that she often arrived late for court. These were serious charges, but when weighed against the criminal allegations against Conahan, they were reduced to trifles. As a result of the complaint, Lokuta eventually was removed from the bench. The campaign for her ouster was orchestrated in part by Conahan. It is widely believed that the complaint against Conahan came from Lokuta or someone close to her.

Throughout much of the board's long period of inaction, its chairman was Patrick Judge Sr., a Luzerne County businessman and political operative who had previously been involved with Conahan in several business ventures. At the time of the vote to table the complaint against Conahan, Judge informed the board members of his relationship with Conahan and did not vote on the question.

The board's refusal to investigate the complaints against Conahan was noteworthy, but it becomes phenomenal in light of the fact that in 1994 the same board already had received and dismissed serious charges against the same judge when he was a district magistrate. In that allegation, which the board never acted upon, Conahan allegedly leaked information about a criminal case and helped two would-be drug dealers hook up for a deal. In addition, the *Citizens' Voice* learned later, the board had received an unusual number of complaints against the two judges—twenty-four against Conahan during his sixteen years on the bench, and sixteen against Ciavarella during his thirteen-year career. These numbers were well above the average for all Pennsylvania judges. Despite later claiming that its resources were too limited to look into the allegations against Conahan, the board spent nearly $50,000 pursuing Lokuta.

Few Pennsylvanians outside the legal profession have heard of the Judicial Conduct Board. Only one Luzerne County parent claimed to have contacted the agency. The father of Matthew, the boy accused of throwing a piece of steak at his mother's boy-friend, said he called the board in Harrisburg to complain about the way his son had been treated in court. According to Matt's father, the conversation went like this: "You're calling from Luzerne County, aren't you? You're talking about Judge Ciavarella, right? We've had several calls about Judge Ciavarella, but you've got to understand, you've got to have a lot of ammunition against a judge. This will just be more fuel for the fire."

There was nothing further from the Judicial Conduct Board.

While the board was transfixed by Judge Lokuta's rude court-room manners, Ciavarella and Conahan were banking another $1 million in kickbacks. Western PA Child Care, the second detention facility in Butler County, was completed in July 2005, clearing the way for what would be a second $1 million "finder's fee." To begin the laundering process, Mericle paid the $1 million to Vision Holdings, the Cayman Islands company controlled by Powell. From here the money went into the Pinnacle Group, controlled by Cindy Ciavarella and Barbara Conahan, and then checks in smaller amounts were issued to the individual bank accounts of Conahan and Ciavarella. When Chester Muroski's misgivings about the wealth of Conahan and Ciavarella were being derided by his colleagues, the two had already accepted some $2.5 million in illegal payments.

In like manner, when the $1.5 million addition to the Pittston center was completed in February 2006, Mericle executed another broker's fee of $150,000 that went from the contractor to Powell's Cayman Island operation to Cindy and Barbara's Pinnacle Group and then to the two judges' checking accounts. By this time the judges had collected $2,150,000 from Mericle for finder's fees and another $590,000 from Powell in rentals and other fees connected to the condominium in Florida. None of this was reported to the Internal Revenue Service, state tax officials, or in the annual financial disclosures to the Judicial Conduct Board required of all judges.

But all this money, nearly $2.75 million from both sources, was not enough. According to Powell, the judges would summon him to their chambers and demand more money. Ciavarella said he knew how much money Powell was making from his half-ownership of the PA Child Care operation, and that he and Conahan wanted part of it. As Powell recalled, Ciavarella told him in June 2006: "It's time for you to step up. I know how much money you have going in there. You can't bullshit me. I know you have a lease, I don't have to send kids there anymore." That was a reference to the $58 million, twenty-year lease that took effect in 2005.

Powell felt squeezed. He believed Ciavarella and Conahan had the power to bankrupt him by urging judges in other counties not to refer delinquents to PA Child Care and Western PA Child Care. Moreover, Powell regularly tried big cases before both judges, and he knew they were not above perverting justice to punish him. At one point Powell refused to return their telephone calls, but Powell said Ciavarella and Conahan started calling Powell's friends and relatives. On Saturday Powell went to Conahan's house and met with the two judges on the patio: "I told them, 'I'm not going to do this anymore.' They laughed at me." Around the Fourth of July holiday, Powell took his family on a vacation trip to Italy, but when he returned the judges called him. When Powell answered, it was Ciavarella, who told him, "You can't ignore us. When I tell you we're going to meet, we're going to meet." Finally, in August, Powell made the first of four cash payments, and for the balance of 2006 he stuffed cash into

Federal Express delivery boxes and sent it to the judges. Over a period of about four months, Powell siphoned $143,500 in cash payments to Conahan and Ciavarella.

The payoffs began on August 11, 2006, when an agitated Powell ordered Patrick Owens, the treasurer of his law firm, to begin withdrawing $42,000 in cash from his bank account—in amounts under $10,000 in order to avoid attracting the attention of the IRS. Owens cashed five checks, put the $42,000 in a bank bag and brought it to Powell. Powell put the money—twenty-, fifty-, and hundred-dollar bills—into two Federal Express boxes, which were picked up on August 16 by Nicholas Callen, a court official who worked for Conahan. Callen, who was not aware of the contents, delivered the boxes to Conahan in his chambers at the courthouse.

On November 2, Powell crammed another $20,000 into a FedEx box, but this time he instructed Jill A. Moran, his law partner, to deliver the money to Conahan's house in the suburbs. She had known Conahan since childhood, and when she got there the judge and his wife insisted that she take a tour of the house. Moran did not know the contents of the box, and she left the box of cash on the seat of her unlocked car in the driveway, retrieving it just before she left and handing it to Conahan. On November 20, Powell again summoned Moran into his private office and gave her a FedEx box to deliver to Conahan. This time, again unknown to her, it contained $50,000. She telephoned Conahan to arrange the delivery to his house, but he said he was on the road and would stop at her townhouse to pick it up. Again, she left the money on the seat of her car, which was parked in her open garage, and handed it to Conahan when he arrived.

Then on December 16, Powell again summoned Moran to his office, but this time he directed her into an adjacent and windowless executive washroom. Here he began stuffing bundled fifty- and hundred-dollar bills into the box. When her face showed amazement, he said,

"These greedy motherfuckers won't let me go. Just take this thing and hopefully this is it." She took the box, which this time held $31,500, and telephoned Conahan to arrange the drop. He said he would pick it up at her home the next day. That night, knowing what was in the box, she brought it into her house rather than leaving in her car. She said when the judge took the money the next day, he was very casual and gave no indication that anything was unusual.

Had the Judicial Conduct Board chosen to look into the charges it received against Conahan, it could have stopped the bribery conspiracy sooner. This, in turn, very well might have prevented the eight-month incarceration of sixteen-year-old Stephen, who appeared before Ciavarella in October 2007 and pleaded guilty to driving without a license and presenting false identification to police. During this time the court garnished a $598 Social Security survivor's check he had been receiving since his father's death.

And perhaps thirteen-year-old DayQuann wouldn't have been pulled out of school, handcuffed, and taken in a police cruiser to PA Child Care, where he spent a three-day weekend for failing to show up for a hearing as a witness to a fight. The boy suffered from a learning disability and didn't understand the subpoena he had been handed two weeks earlier, and his mother said she was unaware of it. The first night of detention he telephoned his mother and begged her to get him out immediately. But she didn't get to see her son until the following Monday, when he was brought into Ciavarella's court in shackles. Ciavarella released DayQuann when the situation was explained. His mother expected an apology, but Ciavarella said he had no regrets and would do the same thing again because "I take court orders very seriously." His mother said when DayQuann got home, "he looked dead, like life was taken away from him. It took him quite a while to get back to normal, and then he was angry."

And had the JCB done what it was created to do, Krystal might not have spent three months at Wind Gap in 2007 for possession of drug paraphernalia. It was her first offense, but Ciavarella ordered her shackled and taken away. "It went by so quick," she recalled. "It left me thinking, 'Did that really just happen?' " At Wind Gap, "the other girls were bragging about stealing cars and beating up people. I felt so out of place. Even the officers said to me, 'What are you doing here?' " Three years later she was still troubled by the experience. It was a permanent shadow across her thoughts: "I'm constantly reminded: if there's a cop behind me, I think about it. You just have no choice but to move on, but it's always in the back of your head. I'm never going to forget about it. It's three long, hard months."

Brianna also might have been spared three months at Wind Gap. She was sixteen when she came before Ciavarella on trespassing charges involving loitering in front of a building. Her mother told the *Times-Leader* that Brianna's hearing lasted less than five minutes: "We couldn't say anything. They just took her away. They removed her jewelry and handcuffed and shackled her right in front of me." She said Brianna was changed—withdrawn and uncommunicative—when she came home. She dropped out of school: "Before she was put away, she wasn't a perfect student, but she followed rules and did what she was supposed to. She was active and outgoing and went to church." The girl was still troubled three years after her detention experience. "She has no desire to get an education or to try to better herself; she thinks everyone is out to get her."

When Bernandine was fourteen, she sent threatening messages via the Internet to another girl's web page. She admitted authoring the notes in court and spent three months in Wind Gap and at PA Child Care. Her mother said that two years after her release she was still troubled: "She's frightened all the time. She's paranoid. She can't trust nobody. You try to tell her something, she doesn't want to believe it."

And prompt action by the JCB might have prevented Jesse's ordeal. His childhood had been something short of idyllic. He was born into a household where there was neither oversight nor foresight. Things were just allowed to happen. His parents divorced when he was ten. At the age of sixteen, he fled home to live on his own. He got a job in a tire shop. But he didn't make enough money to cover the rent, so he moved in with a friend when he was seventeen. Then one of life's defining moments occurred. Jesse did the right thing. But he paid for it dearly. He volunteered to keep an eye on his friend's younger brother, who was twelve years old and often in trouble at school. When he saw the boy carrying a laptop computer, he asked where he had gotten it.

"Look what else I have," the twelve-year-old said, and he pulled a pistol out of his pocket. Jesse slapped his ward on the side of the head.

"What's wrong with you? Where did you get that?" Jesse grabbed the gun and took it away from the boy, who said he had stolen it and was going to use it to kill another youth who had been bullying him. Jesse said his first thought was, " 'What if it happened? That would have been on my conscience because

I could have stopped it.' So I did. Then, I thought, I can't just throw it along the side of the road. Someone could come along and use it to kill somebody."

Jesse said he questioned the boy, determined the owner of the gun, and tried to return it to his home the next morning. When no one answered his knocking on the door, he went to work at the tire shop and called his older cousin for advice. His boss overheard the conversation and demanded an explanation. Jesse eagerly pulled the weapon from his pocket and handed it over. His boss said he was going to give the gun to the police. Jesse felt relieved, like a weight had been lifted from his shoulders.

He heard no more until about a year later. He was a passenger in a car that was stopped by police for speeding. The police ran Jesse's name through their computer system and told him there was an outstanding warrant for his arrest on charges of possessing a stolen firearm. At first he didn't understand, but then he remembered the incident with the pistol and his friend's brother. He was arrested, taken before Ciavarella, and sent to PA Child Care to await a hearing. He knew Ciavarella's reputation for speedy justice, and so he decided to write an explanation of the circumstances by which he came to have the gun and hand it to Ciavarella at his hearing. The probation officer gave him five minutes to write, and then took the document and handed it to the judge when Jesse stepped before him.

Jesse had asked for a public defender, but no lawyer showed up, and he faced Ciavarella alone. The judge ignored Jesse's note, which was inches from his hands, listened to the charges and, peered down at the boy with nostril-wrinkling contempt, saying, "Remand him until further notice." To Jesse, Ciavarella's words sounded like the dive klaxon on a submarine, but even worse was being shackled hand and foot: "I felt like an animal."

He sat that way in a room at the courthouse for some eight hours before he was placed in a van with other juveniles for a five-hour trip to Western PA Child Care. The shackles were finally removed when he arrived. "But that place was horrible," he said. "There were some really tough guys there, and there were fights all the time. I know for sure that I didn't belong there." Jesse scoffs when his stay at Western PA Child Care is called placement: "It may have looked like a dormitory, but it was a jail because there was a lock on the door."

Jesse only spent a week there. Someone finally listened to his story and believed it. He was placed on probation and released. He was now eighteen years old. He did not return to school, but eventually got a GED diploma. The experience with Ciavarella left a wake, and three years later he was still bobbing around in it. The memory keeps coming back, like water filling a hole. Jesse has a lockjaw shyness and distrust of what he calls "the system." Like many youths, he measures events on a scale of fair and unfair. The sight of a police officer makes him nervous, and he watches his rearview mirror for flashing red and blue lights: "And if you can't trust a judge, who can you trust." It's not a question. He has trouble getting and holding down a job. "I don't want to make excuses, but the stuff I went through—all those hours in shackles—I'll never forget."

When Ciavarella heard adult cases, his courtroom had a patina of inexorability and menace. His arrogance seemed to be growing right along with his net worth. The rumors of a business relationship between the judge and Powell had oozed throughout the legal community. But no one confronted Ciavarella—even when he heard cases in which he ruled favorably for a Powell client.

Then Jeffrey B. McCarron, a Philadelphia attorney, came

before Ciavarella in a legal malpractice case in 2008. Powell was the opposing attorney. McCarron had heard many rumors about the Ciavarella-Powell relationship from members of the Luzerne County bar, and he became alarmed when, leading up to the trial, the judge claimed to have misplaced all of McCarron's motions. "He went back into his chambers and came out with a twelve-inch stack of them and said, 'I haven't read any of these, so you're going to have to tell me what's in them.' " Finally, McCarron teed up his courage (he risked being tossed in jail) and mentioned the unmentionable. The lengthy exchange is a quintessential example of Ciavarella's audacity—especially given that he had already received more than $350,000 from Powell, some of it in cash, some of it disguised as rental and fees for the Florida condo.

"Your Honor," McCarron began. "I have two issues to raise, if I may. One is, apparently there's been some considerable publicity involving Your Honor and also Mr. Powell, and I guess there's other information that suggests that—I just want to ask about whether there's a relationship between you and Mr. Powell which would present an issue to the fairness of the trial in this case by my clients. That's all." Tension hissed through the courtroom.

"What significant publicity has there been concerning me and Mr. Powell?"

"I understand there was something to do with a certain building for the county. In any event, I'm just asking the question whether there is a relationship between you and Mr. Powell which would present an issue about Your Honor sitting as the judge of this case."

"Based on what?"

"Whether there's been leisure time activities or anything of that—"

"Based on what?"

"I'm asking."

"I'm asking you, based on what?"

"I'm sorry. I'm asking the court whether there's an issue—"

"And I want to know what you're basing that on."

"The question?"

"Yes"

"I'm just basing it on—"

"Do you ask every judge that question?"

"No, I don't."

"—that you appear in front of?"

"Judge, if the answer is by—Your Honor—I'm just asking the question."

"I want to know why you're asking that question."

"Because I thought to ask it. I thought to ask it."

"Anything else?"

"There's—can I—I'm raising the issue."

"Unless you give me a basis for that question, I don't even see why it's asked."

"It's asked because I just want to be cautious about the situation. That's all."

"What situation?"

"I just want to be cautious because it's been mentioned to me a number of times."

"By whom ?"

"Well, they're privileged discussions. It's been brought—and by other lawyers. That's all. I'm just asking the question. If it's not an issue—"

"What relationship?"

"I'm sorry, Your Honor. I don't—I'm asking the question. If there's been—"

"And now I'm asking the question."

"I don't have details, if that's what you're asking for."

"Well, then, why ask the question?"

"I'm just inquiring whether there is."

"Anything else?"

"Well."

"I don't have to answer that question based upon that. Why should I answer that question based upon that? You want to present something to me, present it, and—"

"Obviously, any relationship which would impact or interfere with the case."

"There is none."

"Okay." A skeptical lilt crept into McCarron's voice.

Ciavarella said no more, but he shot McCarron a look that stuck two inches out his back.

To no one's surprise, Powell's clients won a $3.4 million jury verdict. It was overturned two years later by the Pennsylvania Supreme Court, which ordered a new trial in the case because Ciavarella did not recuse himself from hearing the case involving his longtime benefactor.

Conahan, as president judge, regularly steered key cases to his co-conspirator, even when that strategy backfired. That happened in 2006 when Ciavarella entered a $3.5 million verdict in a libel trial against the *Citizens' Voice*. The award went in a non-jury trial to a businessman who claimed he had been defamed in a series of articles involving money laundering and Billy D'Elia, the local organized crime boss. The newspaper appealed the decision, and it was overturned by the Pennsylvania Supreme Court, which ordered a new trial because Conahan had improperly assigned the case to Ciavarella. There was testimony at the trial that D'Elia had bragged he had influenced the verdict through his friendship with Conahan.

But Ciavarella was still a widely respected public figure, whose policies had broad community support. "Success stories" were reported of kids who were adrift, then came before Judge Ciavarella and straightened out their lives. Ciavarella was known to console the parents of children he had just sent to detention, go to the graduations of kids he believed he had rehabilitated, and help them get into college. Young adults recalled the days when he coached them to victory after victory on the Catholic Youth Center swim team. He was active in the community. In December 2005, the Italian-American Veterans of Luzerne County gave him its certificate of appreciation for his contributions to the post. He was a member of the board of directors and chairman of the annual family picnic.

In March 2006 Ciavarella was honored as Man of the Year by the Friendly Sons of St. Patrick of Greater Wilkes-Barre. At a dinner, the judge was introduced by his son, Marco Ciavarella, who was a freshman at Penn State University. The elder Ciavarella was moved to tears when his son spoke about the admiration that juvenile defendants had for his father. "I'm humbled, not only to receive this award, which I will cherish forever, but by the words of my son." The judge said his parents—Mark Ciavarella Sr. and Mary Cunningham Ciavarella—taught him to respect other people, his religion, and his Irish heritage. This prompted U.S. Rep. Paul E. Kanjorski (D., PA) to read a congratulation to Ciavarella into the *Congressional Record*: "Judge Ciavarella has served his community well both on the bench of the Luzerne County Court and in the many leadership roles he has undertaken with numerous civic organizations. The quality of life in the greater Wyoming Valley is made better due to the work of people like Judge Mark Ciavarella."

The following week, Ciavarella and Conahan each secretly

pocketed half of the $150,000 finder's fee from Rob Mericle for the expansion of the Pittston center, and they filed annual disclosure statements with the Pennsylvania Supreme Court that concealed the kickbacks from Mericle and Powell, which now totaled $2.7 million.

With the pesky Muroski out of the way, the rogue judges had smooth sailing in the summer of 2005. On July 20, the Pinnacle Group issued a $350,000 check to Cindy Ciavarella. She signed and deposited it in her husband's personal account. This, of course, was part of the $1 million finder's fee from Mericle that was laundered through Powell's Cayman Islands operation. Ciavarella was still winning high marks, especially from school administrators, for his draconian decisions sending kids to institutions. He rode this wave of popularity into the election of November 8, 2005, when Luzerne County voters overwhelmingly approved his retention for another ten-year term with nearly 60 percent of the votes. Ciavarella campaigned briefly and told interviewers that probation was not an effective way of dealing with juvenile offenders. He invited a *Times-Leader* reporter into his chambers and showed letters of gratitude from juveniles who had appeared before him, been sentenced, and then become responsible adults. He said the juvenile court allows him to find the most appropriate treatment facility for the youths who come before him. "It's probably the only court where you can make a difference in a child's life," Ciavarella said one week before the election. "You have the ability to put them in a treatment program that helps them get from the lowest point in their early lives to a place where they feel good about themselves."

But ten days after the election, Pennsylvania's Superior Court—acting on an appeal filed by the *Times-Leader*—overruled

Conahan's decision halting the audit of PA Child Care by the state Public Welfare Department. It was the beginning of the end for the judges. In blunt terms, a three-judge appeals court panel rebuked Conahan for abusing his discretion in stopping the audit without first holding a hearing. The appeals judges said they were baffled by Conahan's claim that the audit would reveal "trade secrets." They said the action appeared to be "nothing more than a ruse to prevent public exposure." When the hundreds of pages of documents in the preliminary audit findings were opened, there were no trade secrets.

Tom Crofcheck, the Public Welfare Department's certified fraud examiner, went back to work on the PA Child Care audit in early 2006. When their work was complete, he and his auditors concluded that the state had overpaid at least $4 million in reimbursement costs to the county for PA Child Care and Western PA Child Care. The audit team found that Powell used profits from the two juvenile detention facilities to make millions of dollars in interest-free loans to other enterprises he owned, including $140,000 in prepaid flight time on his Rockwell Sabreliner luxury turbo jet, which he bought in November 2005 for $2.6 million. Other unauthorized expenditures were $5,800 for a limousine ride to a college basketball tournament and $3,500 for a custom-tailored suit for a political friend who worked at the detention centers. In all, the Crofcheck team found more than $1.2 million in expenses that should not have been reimbursed by the state. They also found "questionable costs" totaling $836,636 in state payments for the fees of Dr. Frank Vita, Conahan's brother-in-law. Vita had earned some $1.1 million for evaluating juveniles under an arrangement with the court that was not subjected to competitive bidding. The auditors also found that Vita had submitted "cookie-cutter" evaluations—that is, they employed language that was cut and pasted from standardized material. Often the evaluations were nothing more than a new first and last page with "boilerplate" language in between. And, in one instance, the evaluation confused one child with another. It also noted that youths were often detained in PA Child Care for days or even weeks to await Vita's evaluation.

Before the final audit was released, Crofcheck went on a cruise with his family in June 2007. When he got back, he was abruptly informed by his superior that he was being removed from his position as audit director and would take on a new job, one that didn't exist until now. The new position would place him in an office very close to his home in Luzerne County and would end his 180-mile daily commute. It was very tempting as there was no cut in salary. But he knew something was wrong, and he decided to fight. Then, on June 13, 2007, he was called to a meeting with his superiors in Harrisburg and informed that he was being removed from his job because of poor performance. He was shocked, then recovered and pointed out that in his first six years he had received the highest possible ratings in his annual evaluations, and that the person now demeaning his performance had recently evaluated him as "a model civil servant" that "other state employees should try to emulate."

When Crofcheck asked for details of his alleged poor performance, he was told he should not have given the working papers of the audit to Steve Flood back in 2004. Crofcheck explained that the material had been subpoenaed by Flood, and the DPW legal counsel had told him the subpoena was legal. Crofcheck believed that the bureaucratic attitude toward audits was that the problem didn't exist until the auditor found it—and therefore the problem was created by the auditor. Crofcheck was placed on six months' probation, but he returned to his job in a few months because his superiors left state government. (He was immune to political pressure because he had civil service protection and believes that when he retires, his job will be removed from the civil service system.)

Three years after it began, the audit was released in 2007. Just before it was made public, Crofcheck met with attorneys for PA Child Care, who asked him, "Is there anything we can do to get you to not issue that report?"

"Yes."

"What?"

"Let me turn everything over to the federal inspector general," Crofcheck said, while thinking, *If they don't like me, wait 'til they see what the IG is like.*

They backed off.

In May 2010, three years after the administration of Governor Edward Rendell tried to remove Crofcheck from his job for poor performance, the same administration gave him the Governor's Award of Excellence for his role in pushing the audit of PA Child Care. In presenting the award, Rendell told Crofcheck: "As Governor of the Commonwealth of Pennsylvania, I commend you for your initiative, leadership, and strong commitment to public service. Pennsylvania state government is fortunate to have you. Citizens across Pennsylvania experience the results of your accomplishments through the services you provide. The impact of your work stands as irrefutable endorsement of the exceptional human talent and abilities of all commonwealth employees."

When Richard J. Gold became the deputy state public welfare secretary in charge of the Office of Children, Youth and Families in April 2007, he was the fifth individual to hold the post in four years. Gold was a Philadelphia lawyer with a distinguished career devoted to protecting the civil rights of children, the homeless, and the disabled. The office that he now headed, which administered Pennsylvania's child welfare system, was in need of leadership. Gold was aware that about 80 percent of the money that counties used for juvenile delinquency and dependency came through his new office. Moreover, Pennsylvania was among the worst states in terms of excessive use of placement facilities. He resolved that, unlike his predecessors, he would visit individual counties to see firsthand how the money was being spent and to find ways to curb the use of placement. He wanted to start with the counties that were spending the most money, and quickly turned his attention to Luzerne County. He noticed that not only was the placement rate higher than anywhere else in the state, but in each of the recent years county officials had been coming back to the state for more money than originally allocated. Unaware of the controversy surrounding Tom Crofcheck's audit of PA Child Care, Gold scheduled a meeting with county officials in August.

When he got to the conference room in Wilkes-Barre for the meeting, he found a very hostile group of some twenty county juvenile treatment officials—plus Ciavarella. "Everyone seemed to want me to praise them for their work," he recalled, "but I was concerned about the high placement rate and I asked what could be done to reduce the number of out-of-home cases and how the state could help to achieve this goal. I pointed out that percentage-wise, Luzerne had a higher placement rate than Philadelphia. I thought I was asking legitimate, basic questions. But their attitude seemed to be, 'How does Richard Gold get off asking us questions like this?' I kept asking about the overspending on detention and the high placement rate. I wasn't getting any answers. They wanted to talk about other aspects of their program." Everyone, that is, except Ciavarella. The judge sat at a ninety-degree angle to Gold, his face red and distorted with anger, and glared silently at him for the entire meeting. "I practiced law in Philadelphia for many years, and I had known a lot of cantankerous judges, but I had never seen anything like this. He was livid. But I was a newcomer, and I never imagined what was really going on. I figured he was a law-and-order judge and just didn't like what I was saying. At the end of the meeting, I told them, 'There's something wrong with your numbers.' No one said a word. I never expected that kind of a reception."

But an even bigger surprise awaited Gold when he returned to his office in Harrisburg. At the regularly scheduled meeting with his supervisors, he was reprimanded for upsetting Luzerne County officials. One of the rebukes came from Estelle Richman, the public welfare secretary and an appointee of Governor Edward Rendell. "She said she had received complaints—she didn't say from whom—and she wanted to know what was going on," Gold said. "I was dumbfounded. I told the secretary that I was just asking the same questions I was asking in all the other counties. She told me to be careful because I was from Philadelphia and there's a lot of distrust about the city up there. Don't rock the boat if you can help it." Gold said Richman later met with the Luzerne officials "to calm down their concerns."

7

HILLARY AND JESSICA

Laurene Transue had just shrugged her coat off on a chilly January night in 2007 when her cell phone chirped. The voice at the other end was insistent and brusque. It was a Wright Township police officer, and he wanted to speak to her about her fourteen-year-old daughter, Hillary. He said Hillary had posted something on MySpace, the social networking website, about her assistant principal at Crestwood High School. He used words like "heinous," "foul," and "disgusting" to describe Hillary's post. He said he was coming right out to arrest her on charges of terrorism and stalking on the Internet.

Laurene called up the stairs and asked Hillary if she knew anything about a MySpace page and her assistant principal. "I started that months ago, and I haven't written anything since," she called back. Then she told the officer she would not meet with him without an attorney. She remembers that he said, "That's what's wrong with you parents—you're always trying to protect your children." She thought, *Yeah, that's right. I always try to protect my children.* But she did not say it. She hung up instead.

Before the phone call, Laurene had felt drowsy. She had just driven thirty miles from Northampton County Community College, where she had taught a six-hour class designed to help welfare recipients find careers. But now she was wide awake with a swelling lump of panic in her chest. She summoned Hillary, who quickly explained she had written a satire purporting to be her assistant principal's MySpace profile. But there was nothing obscene, she said. Laurene called her mother, who told her to remain calm and call the officer back. She did. "He told me, 'If we leave the lawyer out of it, I will just charge her with harassment.' I said okay, and he said I would be getting something in the mail." The officer said the Crestwood School District wanted to discipline Hillary and make an example of her as a way to discourage students from using social networking sites to comment on faculty. He assured her that Hillary's punishment would be some form of community service and possibly a period of probation. Laurene Transue believed him.

The past few years had been turbulent for the Transue family. Laurene had gastric bypass surgery in 2002 that went terribly wrong and resulted in multiple complications. She was in a coma for three months, then bound to a wheelchair for three months, and finally needed a walker and a cane for two years. She was away from her home and family for six months and then faced a long rehabilitation. Hillary was sent to stay with an aunt and then with family friends from church. The Transues' rented home in Canadensis, Pennsylvania, was sold, and they decided to move to Luzerne County and begin a new life in the town of White Haven.

Hillary enrolled as an eighth grader in Crestwood Middle School in January 2005. She was five foot nine and towered above most of the girls and many of the boys at school. She sometimes dyed her hair deep black with streaks of pink. She stood out in other ways. Hillary was bright, brash, witty, and often acerbic. Around the faculty room she was sometimes called "The Queen of Sarcasm." That sobriquet was embellished near the end of the school year in July 2006 when Hillary created a mock MySpace profile of the assistant principal, who had a school-wide reputation as a stern, inflexible disciplinarian. Under the website's standardized heading "What Do You Collect," Hillary wrote "Johnny Depp's 'tighty whites' [underwear]." To the question, "Who Are Your Favorite People," Hillary answered, "Satan" and "Bob Barker." To accompany this "profile," Hillary drew an unflattering sketch of the school official that included a swastika armband. Finally, there was a disclaimer, branding the entire exercise a hoax that concluded by saying, "I hope that Mrs. ——— has a sense of humor."

But Mrs. ——— didn't—especially after others posted comments on the parody that were vulgar and obscene. A few months later, the vice principal filed a complaint with the local police, who went to Verizon with a search warrant and traced the posting back to a wireless account in the Transue household. Then they made the telephone call to Laurene Transue, informing her that her daughter was going to be arrested.

That was in January, and Laurene heard nothing until March, when she and her daughter were summoned to the Luzerne County Juvenile Probation Services office in downtown Wilkes-Barre. They were interviewed together and separately by the probation officer. Laurene was jarred by some of the questions. Were she and her husband intimate? Was Hillary a virgin? Was she gay? They were told that Hillary was being charged with criminal harassment, and that her recommended punishment, subject to the judge's approval, would be probation. Did Hillary need a lawyer? The officer said a lawyer would not be necessary because Judge Ciavarella usually followed the recommendations of Probation Services. But Hillary had learned of Ciavarella's reputation, and she told her mother she wanted an attorney.

Laurene told her she was being silly. Ridiculous. No one was going to send her away.

On April 17, 2007, Laurene Transue dropped Hillary off at the courtroom building and went to search for a parking place. When Hillary stepped off the elevator, she was directed to a desk to confirm her arrival with a probation officer. Did she have an attorney? No. When Laurene arrived, she was asked by the probation officer, Do you have an attorney present? When Laurene said she did not, she was told, "Sign here and sit in the waiting room through that door." She signed the form. This was a violation of Pennsylvania's juvenile court rules, which provide that only the juvenile can waive the right to counsel.

During the previous week, Laurene had coached Hillary on how to show deference and respect to the judge. The girl wore a two-piece suit and blouse borrowed from her mother. Now they waited. Finally, the bailiff stuck his head out the door and hollered, "Transue!" They stood just inside the courtroom. With rising fear, Hillary watched the vice principal she had parodied kiss the cheek of the assistant district attorney who was prosecuting Hillary. Then they exchanged friendly banter. Any hopes she had of avoiding out-of-home detention (she thought of it as "jail time") vanished. Then a voice boomed out, "Case number six, Hillary Transue."

As Hillary and her mother approached the bench, Ciavarella put his palms on his desk, leaned over, and demanded, "What makes you think you can get away with this kind of crap?" The question seemed to fill the room. The words stung. There were no introductions, no greetings. Trembling, Hillary mumbled, "I don't know." Ciavarella sat back, bright certitude shining from his glasses. "Hillary, you've been charged with harassment, how do you wish to plead?"

"Guilty."

"Based upon her admission, I'll adjudicate her delinquent. Why would you do this?"

"I have no rational explanation for that. I—"

Laurene gently placed her hand on her daughter's shoulder in a gesture of comfort and support.

"Did [the vice principal] ever do anything to you?"

"Not personally, no. I didn't take into consideration that [the vice principal] is a person as opposed to just a school administration member at my school."

"How long have you been at Crestwood?"

"A year and a half."

"What grade are you in?"

"I'm in my sophomore year, tenth grade."

"You've been at Crestwood when I've been at Crestwood?"

"Yes."

"You heard me speak?"

"Yes."

"Say 'sir,' " Laurene whispered.

"Told you what type of conduct I expected from children in that school relative to the juvenile justice system?"

"Yes, sir."

"Told you what conduct I . . . Is this—acceptable?"

"No, sir."

"What did I say would happen if you acted in an unacceptable way towards teachers and/or administrators?"

"I don't recall, sir."

"You don't recall? You don't?"

"No, sir."

"Were you sleeping?" Ciavarella bellowed, shaking his head in astonishment at his own patience with the world.

"No, sir."

"You can't remember that?"

"No, sir."

Laurene felt Hillary pressing back against her, cringing in fear.

"It's going to come back to you because I didn't go to that school, I didn't walk into that school and I didn't speak to that student body just to scare you, just to blow smoke, just to make you think that I would do that when I wouldn't. I'm a man of my word. You're gone. Send her up to FACT. Let her stay there until she figures it out.

"Thank you," Ciavarella said with a smile that never reached his eyes.

"FACT" was Female Adventure Challenge Therapy, the wilderness camp in Wind Gap, Pennsylvania.

Less than two minutes after she stepped before Ciavarella, Hillary was being led away without being able to say good-bye to her mother. As she was being handcuffed in an anteroom, she heard her mother wailing, "No, that's not fair! That's not what the officer said." Hillary pleaded with the bailiff to let her say good-bye. But all the bailiff would say was, "Just listen to what you've done to your poor mother."

Back in the courtroom, Laurene Transue screamed hysterically between great gasping sobs. Like so many other parents—Angelia's mother, Jeffrey's father—she was beset by guilt and helplessness as she watched her child taken away. She begged Ciavarella to change his mind. Her voice grew shrill and desperate. She offered to take Hillary's place. The bailiffs threatened to put her in jail or a mental hospital. Her family, so recently reconstituted, was suddenly and unexpectedly rent apart again.

And by a judge who was duty-bound to protect children and hold families together. Laurene was overcome by a crashing wave of sorrow and collapsed in the courtroom.

By this time, Hillary was in a holding cell with several other youths. After a few hours, she was placed in a van with two girls and driven to Wind Gap, some sixty miles from her home. Hillary arrived at Wind Gap about 3 p.m. It was raining and her new home looked like a desolate campground in the middle of nowhere, soaked and sodden under a low gray sky. She was allowed to make a one-minute phone call to her mother, and for the entire sixty seconds—it was carefully timed—they sobbed and apologized to each other—Hillary for causing her mother grief, Laurene for failing to protect her daughter. Then Hillary signed paperwork and removed all her jewelry and hairpins. Next she was led to a shower house where she was ordered to apply lice treatment to her hair. Her clothing was confiscated and replaced with sweatpants, a T-shirt, used underwear, and old sneakers. She felt like a convict.

Laurene Transue made it home, but a pall of wretchedness hung over her. The house was like a stage without the lead actor. She felt Hillary's absence so keenly it was a presence. She blamed herself for telling Hillary she didn't need a lawyer. She was perplexed. How could this have happened? She had worked professionally with juveniles for sixteen years. Never had she seen anything like what happened to her daughter. Sometimes she had disagreed with a court's decision, but never had she seen a judge show such disregard for the law and for the best interests of the juvenile. She felt a yoke of grief around her neck so heavy she couldn't sleep.

Then her father reminded her that before her long illness she would have been doing everything she could to rescue Hillary. The next day she was angry. Laurene Transue was different from most other parents of Ciavarella's victims. She was not a local girl. She was born and raised in northern New Jersey. She didn't buy into the Luzerne County "fear factor." Moreover, she was educated. "I learned quickly that there were basically two kinds of people here—the well-to-do and the educated were one, the uneducated and poor were the other. I fit in neither group." Laurene had a BA from East Stroudsburg University and was nearing a master's degree in education from Wilkes University. She had been trained to be a social studies teacher, but like so many others before her, she could not get a job in Luzerne County. "They told us in graduate school that to get a teaching job in Luzerne County, you had to pay $5,000 to the school board. That was the going rate, and you showed up for your interview with your teaching certificate and an envelope with the money. I couldn't afford it." So she turned to social work, and after sixteen years working as a caseworker for children in Pennsylvania—working with Head Start programs, private foster care agencies, and Children and Youth Offices—she knew without any doubt that something was deeply wrong with the treatment of her daughter. So she picked up the telephone. She called the county Public Defenders Office, the state Public Defenders Office, the Governor's Action Line, the American Civil Liberties Union, her congressman, state senator, state representative. No one was able to help. Ciavarella seemed omnipotent, untouchable. Then she contacted Sara Jacobson, an assistant public defender for Philadelphia, who in turn told her of a nonprofit organization that might be able to help—Juvenile Law Center.

•   •   •

In 1975, like many young lawyers in those days, four recent Temple University School of Law graduates decided that they wanted to change the world. It was an age of can-do optimism rooted in the belief that you could accomplish anything if you marshaled enough talent and energy. Unlike most of these utopians, Robert Schwartz, Marsha Levick, Judith Chomsky, and Philip Margolis succeeded. They channeled their idealism into a novel project—a free, walk-in legal clinic in Philadelphia to serve local youths who needed lawyers to help them negotiate the myriad legal issues they might come up against in school, their families, the courts, and on the streets. They called their experiment Juvenile Law Center. It was the nation's first comprehensive, nonprofit law firm exclusively for children.

The early days were difficult. The overwhelming majority of their clients were runaways, truants, and troubled children—kids with thousand-yard stares, kids with deep scars on their bodies and souls, kids born with plastic spoons in their mouths, kids who had made a terrible mistake when they chose their parents. Chomsky's husband was a cardiologist who had a part-time office where he did insurance examinations. This became Juvenile Law Center's first office. It was crowded, especially on Tuesday and Thursday mornings, when it served both medical and legal functions. Lawyers often used the top of an X-ray machine as their desk.

But their timing couldn't have been better. The legal rights of juveniles were expanding steadily because of a landmark 1967 U.S. Supreme Court decision involving Gerald Gault, who as a fifteen-year-old had been treated with stunning injustice by Arizona authorities. In its Gault ruling, the high court said that juveniles accused of crimes were entitled to the same due process rights as adults. These include timely notification of charges, the right to confront witnesses and, most importantly, the right to legal representation. "We were on the ground floor, and we knew it," recalls Levick.

Money was a nagging concern. Juvenile Law Center got some small grants that would run out in a year or two. They would reapply and go after new money sources. Everyone had outside jobs, writing briefs and doing legal scut work. Schwartz also picked up a few bucks as a basketball referee and baseball umpire. But Juvenile Law Center gradually gained momentum, and in the process it took each of its cases to the goal line. While defending a juvenile wronged at a detention center, it also pressed for changes in overall policies at that detention center and then all youth detention centers. This was a turning point that would transform the organization into an engine for national policy reforms.

Juvenile Law Center chalked up legal victories that resulted in more alternatives to detention for nonviolent young offenders and improvements in foster care. It played a central role in the U.S. Supreme Court's historic decision abolishing the juvenile death penalty. Pennsylvania's juvenile justice system became one of the nation's best, and in 2004 the prestigious MacArthur Foundation designated Juvenile Law Center to lead its massive juvenile justice reform initiative in Pennsylvania. In 2008, Juvenile Law Center was named the recipient of a $500,000 no-strings-attached award from the MacArthur Foundation to continue its work as a "Creative and Effective Institution."

It was Hillary's grandfather who made the first contact with Juvenile Law Center. He called the general intake number and talked to a paralegal screener, who routed the call to the voice mail of Laval Miller-Wilson, a staff attorney. Coincidentally,

Miller-Wilson had done a survey of seventeen Pennsylvania counties on the question of access to legal counsel—and the major problem area was northeastern Pennsylvania. Then he listened to the voice mail, and when he heard the name Ciavarella, it floated up in his memory like a dead fish. Was this the same Judge Ciavarella who had been slapped down in 2001 by the state Superior Court, at the behest of Juvenile Law Center, for failing to inform a thirteen-year-old of her right to counsel? It had to be. He thought, *I can't believe this guy is still doing this.*

He dialed the Transues' number in Luzerne County. Laurene answered, and immediately her eyes became glossy with tears. Finally, she had hope. Pursing her lips to make the tears stop, she haltingly told Miller-Wilson about the ninety-second hearing, that Hillary was a good student and had never been in serious trouble before, and how important her daughter was to her. He was stunned by the story, especially after Laurene told him that she was an experienced social worker and had been around courtrooms for many years.

Miller-Wilson walked over to the office of Marsha Levick, Juvenile Law Center's chief counsel. He told her about his twenty-five-minute conversation with Laurene Transue. Levick also remembered Ciavarella from the 2001 ruling. She agreed that it was time to step in. The only questions were how many resources could be invested in this case and what the extent of Miller-Wilson's personal involvement should be. Under normal procedure, Juvenile Law Center would contact outside local counsel—but the Luzerne County Public Defenders Office didn't seem like a promising avenue.

Miller-Wilson said he would handle the case, but first he had to get permission to represent Hillary. He telephoned her at Wind Gap, introduced himself, and said he'd like to seek a new trial.

Would she accept him as her attorney? She agreed immediately. She was earnest and polite, calling him "sir." Miller-Wilson was very careful to avoid getting Hillary's hopes too high.

Miller-Wilson called a strategy meeting with Levick and Bob Schwartz, Juvenile Law Center executive director. It was unanimously decided to file a motion for reconsideration and a writ of habeas corpus seeking Hillary's release in Luzerne County Court.

Miller-Wilson made the two-and-a-half-hour drive up to Wilkes-Barre with Riya Shah, a staff attorney. They first went to the Luzerne County Courthouse, where they entered an appearance and filed motions on behalf of Hillary with the clerk of courts. They notified Ciavarella, District Attorney Jacqueline Musto Carroll, and Basil G. Russin, the chief public defender. Then they walked over to the Juvenile Probation Office in the courthouse annex and asked for the file of their new client, Hillary Transue. Miller-Wilson quickly scanned the transcript. He stared at the ceiling in utter disbelief. The record of the entire adjudication hearing that separated Hillary Transue from her home and family was two pages long—331 words! Ciavarella failed to explain to Hillary the consequences of proceeding without legal representation. He failed to provide a colloquy explaining to Hillary her rights and the consequences of waiving her right to a trial. And despite the fact that she had no prior record and was convicted only of a third-degree misdemeanor, this fifteen-year-old girl was immediately dispatched in shackles to a residential treatment facility.

Events moved quickly after Miller-Wilson's filings with the court. Within a few days a hearing was held before Ciavarella. Hillary, accompanied by a FACT counselor, was brought to the courtroom from Wind Gap. Laurene, her husband, and Hillary's grandparents joined Miller-Wilson and Shah. The gathering was summoned into the courtroom, where Ciavarella quickly heard the motions and scheduled a hearing to be held in one week.

Miller-Wilson and his Juvenile Law Center colleagues spent the following weekend preparing for the trial. It was a complicated case. There were discovery issues: Hillary's name was not attached to the MySpace website in any way. Even after the police got the search warrant from Verizon and traced the spoof back to the Transue household, there was no certainty that Hillary was the author. There were four others in the same household. Miller-Wilson wanted to see if the search warrant was proper. And there was a glaring First Amendment issue: How can you criminalize what she did when she was just exercising her right to free speech?

But when they got to Ciavarella's courtroom, it was all over in a few minutes. No need for a trial. The writ of habeas corpus was granted, Hillary's adjudication was vacated, and she was allowed to return home. That weekend was Mother's Day.

Miller-Wilson had expected to spend the entire day in Wilkes-Barre. The brief proceeding with the Transues left him with time on his hands, and so he asked Ciavarella if he could stick around for the rest of the day and watch the court proceedings. "Fine," the judge said. Ciavarella was a model of jurisprudence. Juveniles were appearing with lawyers, and nothing appeared out of the ordinary. Later, he had a brief conversation with Jonathan Ursiak, an assistant public defender who was representing some of the juveniles. Miller-Wilson asked him if this was a normal day in Ciavarella's court. "No," Ursiak said, "the judge is acting very differently today." An undertow of anxiety tugged at

Miller-Wilson's brain. Earlier that day, he had asked Hillary if there was anyone else at Wind Gap who had had a similar experience before Judge Ciavarella.

"Oh, yes, sir, I know a lot of kids like that. One of them is my friend, Jessica Van Reeth."

Jessica Van Reeth was an immune-to-peer-pressure, misfit-by-design sixteen-year-old junior at Crestwood High School. Amid a sea of conformity, khakis, and polo shirts, she showed up every day in clothes that were usually black and with fingernails that were sometimes painted bright red, other times purple. She was outspoken. "You never had to wonder what was on her mind," said Bill Kane, who had her in his political science class. "She was very liberal politically while most of her classmates leaned toward the conservative side." As early as 2006, Jessica had heard bad things about Judge Mark Ciavarella. On the days he came to Crestwood for his annual warning speech, she would find a reason to be absent. "Even then I knew he was a criminal—that he was sending kids away unfairly," she recalls. "There were rumors that he owned the place he was sending them to. But no one thought this could be true. No judge could stoop that low." Jessica worked at an Italian restaurant in Mountain Top, Ciavarella's hometown. Whenever the judge came in, she would refuse to wait on him and left the job to a colleague.

In October 2006 Jessica was in the girls' bathroom at school when a friend asked her to hold on to a lighter and marijuana pipe. Just as the exchange was made, the vice principal came in the room. All four girls were escorted to the principal's office. Out of loyalty to her friend, she told the school authorities that the two items belonged to her. She was charged with possession of drug paraphernalia. The next day Jessica and her mother went to the Fairview Township Police station and asked if they could get a lawyer: "A police officer gave us the phone number for the Public Defender's Office, but we were also discouraged from calling because our family income was probably too high and we would not qualify. The Fairview Township Police also told us I would likely receive nothing more than probation."

She was interviewed in December by the Juvenile Probation Department, where she was told that because she had good grades and had never been in trouble before, the department would not recommend that she be placed in an out-of-home facility. It would, however, be necessary to appear at a hearing before Judge Ciavarella. She told her parents she needed a lawyer. They disagreed, reassuring her that she would only get probation.

Accompanied by her father, Jack Van Reeth, Jessica went before Ciavarella on January 31, 2007. She had prepared a little speech: "I have never been in trouble before, I have never been a discipline problem at school, I have a B average, and I have worked part-time as a waitress in a restaurant since I was fourteen." But when she stood before Ciavarella, fear caught her in the throat, the blood left her brain, and the words fled her lips. In a trembling voice, she pleaded guilty to the drug charges. "I thought my only option was to plead guilty," she remembered later. "So that is exactly what I did."

Ciavarella began his litany:

"Were you there when I spoke to the assembly at Crestwood?"

"No."

"Did your friends tell you what I said?"

"Yes."

"What did I say would happen if you had drugs in school?"

"That you would send us away."

"And that's exactly what I'm going to do."

It was all over in ninety seconds. Jessica was not advised of her right to counsel, nor did Ciavarella administer the required colloquy explaining the consequences of appearing without counsel. Ciavarella did not even acknowledge the presence of Jack Van Reeth, who watched stunned as his daughter was shackled by a sheriff and taken to a small waiting room just outside the court. When Jessica described this ordeal two years later, her voice cracked and she flushed with anger as she buckled an imaginary belt around her waist and snapped on imaginary handcuffs. There was no time to say good-bye to her father. Indeed, she would not see her parents for two weeks. Soon she was joined by other shackled juveniles dispatched by Ciavarella. A caseworker came in and demanded a urine test to prove she was not using drugs. It came back negative. The caseworker handed her a sheaf of papers to sign. She began reading them.

"Don't read them, just sign them," she recalls being told.

"What will happen if I don't sign?"

"The judge will sign them for you. So you might as well just sign."

Her innate rebelliousness was momentarily stifled, and she gave in. After four hours, she learned her fate from the caseworker: Ciavarella had placed her in Wind Gap for three months. With great effort, she tried to calm herself: *Everything will be all right. Don't panic!* When she arrived at the wilderness camp after a ninety-minute drive in an institutional van, she exchanged her clothing for blue sweatpants, wool socks, hiking boots, and a T-shirt with "YSA" (for Youth Services Agency) arched across the front. She was then given a lice treatment and ordered to take a shower.

That night she was allowed to telephone her parents, but because of a communication mixup neither her father nor her mother was at home when she called. She left an anguished voice mail, laced with accusations of betrayal. "I guess you were too busy to take the time to talk to me," she said, slamming the phone down. Jack Van Reeth has not forgotten that message.

Within a few days, she entered the camp's education program, which was at an alternative school designed for youths who had been suspended from their regular high schools. Almost immediately Jessica was moved to senior-level classes, which she found were the equivalent of freshman classes at Crestwood. In history class, a typical assignment might be to copy pages 56 to 60 into a notebook. Math class consisted of handing out worksheets to students. There was no formal instruction. "Stripping youth of a real education is most definitely a punishment, perhaps the worst punishment of all," she would testify before an investigating commission two years later. "With no education, most of those children have little to no chance of succeeding and are almost doomed to become career criminals."

But Jessica kept herself focused on getting out: "I knew who I was, and I coped. But kids who went there with problems, a lot of them got into more trouble. This was painful to see." Jessica served her full three-month term at Wind Gap, and just two weeks before she was released she met up with Hillary Transue, who had just arrived and was primed to be angry with Jessica; through an intermediary, Jessica had sent a jocular message to Hillary before her hearing with Ciavarella: "I'll see you at Wind Gap." Jessica had heard the story of Hillary's MySpace parody— and she knew how Ciavarella would react. But when the two girls got together at Wind Gap, Hillary was teary and still traumatized by her loss of freedom. Jessica consoled her. The two would become good friends—and within a year almost to the day they would become the lead petitioners in a lawsuit that would expose one of the worst examples of judicial misconduct in American history.

Jessica got out on April 26, 2007. She was driven to the Luzerne County Courthouse and placed on three-month probation. The terms were a 7 p.m. curfew, loss of driving privileges, six hours per week of drug counseling, three-times-a-week home visits with juvenile probation officers, and weekly drug tests via urine samples. There were other difficulties. Some of her friends shunned her at their parents' behest. To pass the eleventh grade and become a senior at Crestwood, she had to complete a research project that normally takes three months. Because she was unable to work on it at Wind Gap, Jessica had only three weeks. Moreover, her topic was the legalization of marijuana. She knew that would inflame Ciavarella, so she switched to a new one—the psychology of color. She finished and closed out her junior year with a B average.

Throughout the spring and summer she was beset by an anxiety as insistent as an alarm you cannot turn off: She imagined committing a minor infraction like jaywalking that would send her back to the legal system—and Ciavarella. Her eighteenth birthday was doubly celebrated—for reaching adulthood and for escaping Ciavarella's juvenile court. When she completed her probation, she went before Ciavarella, who kissed her on the cheek. She gave him the deferential smile one reserves for a man holding a machine gun: "I said Wind Gap was really great and, thanks to him, I was rehabbed. I didn't want any trouble getting off probation. But by this time I was talking to Laval at Juvenile Law Center, and I thought, 'You just wait, you son of a bitch, 'til the story runs in the newspaper about what you've been doing to all these kids."

Indeed, Miller-Wilson talked to Jessica several times over the summer of 2007. He noticed the similarities between how Ciavarella handled the two young women. Even his language—the same miserable string of syllables—what-did-I-tell-you-would-happen. The words had become boilerplate, insistent as a drum-roll, like a politician giving a stump speech. Miller-Wilson knew he had a pattern.

On May 29, 2007, Miller-Wilson contacted the Juvenile Court Judges Commission, a state agency created in 1959 to improve the administration of juvenile justice in Pennsylvania. One of its main responsibilities is to compile statewide statistics and issue an annual report. However, the JCJC lacked the resources to provide meaningful information on juvenile courts in individual counties. Could the JCJC, Miller-Wilson asked, come up with statistics on waivers of counsel and placements for Luzerne County alone? Ten days later, he got his answer—and the figures were breathtaking.

In 2002, counsel was waived in 7.4 percent of all juvenile cases in Pennsylvania, but the rate in Luzerne County was more than seven times higher—54.8 percent. In 2003, the numbers were 7.9 percent statewide, 50.2 percent in Ciavarella's courtroom. Then, in 2004, only 4.8 percent of all juvenile defendants in Pennsylvania waived the right, but in Luzerne County it was fully ten times higher—at 50.2 percent. Out-of-home placements were also dramatic. Ciavarella was sending kids away at two-and-a-half times the statewide average. In fact, a single judge in a county with less than 3 percent of the state's population was accounting for one in every five placements.

Back in Philadelphia, Miller-Wilson sat down with Juvenile Law Center leadership in September 2007 to assess the gravity of the Luzerne County situation. There were three disturbing pieces of information—Hillary Transue's case, Jessica Van Reeth's case, and the shocking statistics on counsel waivers from the JCJC. "What's going on here?" Marsha Levick asked. "Why are all these kids waiving counsel?" To find out, Robert Schwartz suggested that Miller-Wilson station himself outside Ciavarella's courtroom and interview parents and juveniles as they emerged. On the first "road trip," Miller-Wilson was accompanied again by Riya Shah. It was supposed to be a covert operation, but the pair—a black man and an Indian woman—were conspicuous in northeastern Pennsylvania. So, for the second expedition Miller was joined by two white law students. At both visits, they found a pattern of children going before Ciavarella without an attorney and then being dispatched to "placement" for relatively minor offenses.

Typically, the juveniles and their parents would get off the elevator at the Penn Place Building and see a table with a probation officer, who would ask,"Have a lawyer?" If the defendant said no, they would be directed to "sign here," a blatantly illegal procedure, in light of the Rules of Juvenile Court Procedure. On a statewide basis, Rule 152 had cut in half the number of juvenile court waivers. But based on their observations outside Ciavarella's courtroom, there seemed to be an ongoing countertrend in Luzerne County.

Ironically, Juvenile Law Center was at this time coordinating a celebration of the fortieth anniversary of the Supreme Court's 1967 Gault decision guaranteeing children the same right to counsel as adults. Gerald Gault himself joined juvenile justice experts from around the nation for a program entitled "Children Under the Constitution: The Fortieth Anniversary of In Re Gault" at the National Constitution Center in Philadelphia. Miller-Wilson was the moderator of a discussion panel that included Hillary Transue.

But in Wilkes-Barre, Miller-Wilson and his colleagues were having difficulty identifying children who had waived counsel in Ciavarella's courtroom. Juvenile records were sealed. Miller-Wilson began private conversations with Jonathan Ursiak, the young attorney who had joined the Luzerne County Public Defenders Office nine months earlier and was distressed by what was going on in juvenile court. Ursiak confirmed that counsel waivers were widespread in Ciavarella's court, but he refused to give the names of the juveniles. Miller-Wilson kept calling Ursiak's office and leaving urgent messages, but his pleas went unanswered. Miller-Wilson recalled: "We asked Ursiak to sign an affidavit that merely said, 'I can confirm that many children appeared before Judge Ciavarella without a lawyer.' We even offered to write it for him. But he said, 'I can't do that.' " Miller-Wilson grew frustrated: "No one is calling us to say that their kid went before Ciavarella without a lawyer. So we keep the pressure on Ursiak. But Ursiak would only confirm that unrepresented children were appearing before Ciavarella in record numbers."

Long meetings were held at Juvenile Law Center offices in Philadelphia during the winter of 2007–2008. The organization's leadership was outraged by the idea that what happened to Hillary and Jessica, and it seemed to hundreds of others, could occur in the year 2007 in the United States of America in a state like Pennsylvania, which was known for a progressive and compassionate juvenile justice system. It was fully forty years after the Gault decision gave juvenile defendants a constitutional right to legal counsel. Yet here was a rogue judge routinely trampling on the rights of children. What to do?

The customary avenue for JLC legal actions was to go into federal court and raise civil rights issues on behalf of the juveniles. But this issue was unprecedented and seemed to call for a departure from the usual. One practical matter that made this case different was that two groups who usually welcome Juvenile Law Center with open arms—probation officers and public defenders—were being uncooperative and indeed were part of the problem here rather than an aid to the solution.

At this point, Juvenile Law Center attorneys believed that hundreds of kids had been placed by Ciavarella without being advised of their right to counsel and without being advised of the consequences of pleading guilty as explicitly required by the Pennsylvania Supreme Court's 2005 rules. What Juvenile Law Center needed was some means of identifying these defendants so their adjudications could be vacated and the records expunged.

Marsha Levick had a long-standing fascination with what she called "obscure writs"—meaning little-used legal devices that went to the heart of the legal system and often had their roots in old English common law. One of these time-honored devices was a King's Bench petition, which in Pennsylvania allowed the state Supreme Court to vacate the decisions of lower courts in extraordinary circumstances where the interest of justice overrode normal procedures. The center studied a 2005 case in which the King's Bench device was used successfully in a case involving an art gallery.

After weeks of discussion, a decision was reached. JLC would ask the Pennsylvania Supreme Court to exercise its King's Bench powers, take immediate jurisdiction, and issue an order "to end the practice of the Luzerne County Common Pleas Court of conducting delinquency hearings without counsel for children—or without lawful waivers of counsel." With Hillary Transue and Jessica Van Reeth as lead petitioners, Juvenile Law Center filed suit on April 29, 2008, asking the state's highest court to exercise its "King's Bench Power or Power of Extraordinary Jurisdiction."

The petition charged that inordinate numbers of youths were unrepresented because Ciavarella had been routinely violating Rule 152 for two and a half years by failing to advise juvenile defendants of their right to counsel. It asked that the Luzerne County Court be ordered to identify every case since October 1, 2005 (the effective date of Rule 152), in which the child defendant did not have an attorney. These child defendants should have their punishments vacated and their records expunged. JLC still believed there were several hundred of these cases to be nullified.

The petition said about half of all juveniles who came before Ciavarella in 2005 and 2006 did not have lawyers—nearly ten times the statewide rate. And of these unrepresented children, 60 percent of them received punishments that involved being placed away from their homes. Joining JLC in the lawsuit as friends of the court were the State Attorney General's Office and the Pennsylvania Department of Public Welfare, whose chief counsel alleged: "The practices in Luzerne County are likely having a harmful effect on the court-involved juveniles, their families and, in turn, the Luzerne County community."

Ciavarella's immediate reaction was anger. He told the *Citizens' Voice* that all juveniles were informed of their rights in his court. "I don't have an obligation to get them a lawyer. That's their business. I don't know why that percentage is what it is. I am not going to spoon-feed people." He said his sentences were nearly always merely affirmations of recommendations by the county probation department, and that neither the general public nor Juvenile Law Center understood how the system worked. "I don't make the decision that a child gets placed. I just affirm the decision that a child gets placed."

However, three weeks later Ciavarella changed his tune and resigned as juvenile court judge, though he remained on the bench. Now well aware that he was under an intense federal investigation, Ciavarella claimed he was stepping down for the good of the court: "The focus is no longer on the juveniles, the focus is on the judge and that's just not right. It's a treatment court, it's a court where you're trying to help kids, not trying to hurt kids, and the focus is no longer on helping the child, the focus is on me, and that's not a good thing in any treatment facility."

That same day he telephoned Miller-Wilson in Philadelphia and barked, "Okay, I'm off the bench. What the hell do you want from me now? Why are you breaking my balls?" Miller-Wilson hung up.

Ciavarella's exit prompted Luzerne County District Attorney Jacqueline Musto Carroll to announce her opposition to Juvenile Law Center's petition, contending it was moot now that Ciavarella was no longer on the bench. Musto Carroll also challenged the accuracy of the statistics from the Juvenile Court Judges Commission and denied there was any wholesale violation of children's rights in the court. She did not, however, address the issue of all the children who had improper criminal records as a result of Ciavarella's actions and were having trouble getting jobs, getting into college, getting into the military, and otherwise carrying on with their lives. It was not a moot point for them.

8

DISGRACE AND INFAMY

As soon as Rob Mericle heard that Mary Ciavarella, the mother of his good friend Mark Ciavarella, was ill and hospitalized, he went to the judge's chambers and was ushered into his office. "Hi, Mark," he began in a voice heavy with concern and sadness. But Ciavarella pressed a cautionary finger to his lips, sat down at his desk, took a sheet of paper from a drawer, and pushed it across the desktop. The note said, "Wired? Yes. No. Circle One." Mericle, astonished and bewildered, circled "No." Still silent, Ciavarella gestured him into the adjoining courtroom, which was empty. They sat at a table. Still taken aback by the note, Mericle was staggered by what came next.

Ciavarella informed him that a federal grand jury was investigating the financing of the PA Child Care and Western PA Child Care facilities and that there might be "a problem" with the $2.1 million Mericle had paid in three finder's fees. When Mericle interjected that the payments were legitimate business transactions, like hundreds of other similar commissions he had paid out over the years, the judge said there was a problem if the money had been first paid to Robert Powell because that would show an attempt to conceal the true recipients of the money, the two judges. Ciavarella said he knew he was vulnerable, but he was not sure how vulnerable he was. "If the money went from you to me, I could get a slap on the wrist. But if it went from you, to Bob Powell, to me, I could go to jail," Ciavarella said. The judge then asked his friend to go back to his office and "review" the finder's fee documents to be sure that the payments did not go through Powell. Ciavarella, of course, knew very well that the money had gone through Powell because it was he who had requested that the payments be made that way. Nevertheless, as Mericle was leaving, Ciavarella said, "Don't lie to the FBI and don't obstruct justice."

Mericle returned to his office, checked the three transactions, and confirmed the payments had gone to Powell. As he was about to leave and return to Ciavarella's chambers, he was intercepted by his secretary, who told him there were people waiting outside to meet him. They were agents of the Internal Revenue Service, who questioned him about the $2.1 million in payments. He said they were intended for Powell. He lied to the agents because he didn't see a choice. "I didn't want to be the person to lay Mark out," he said later. Three weeks later, Powell's wife answered a knock at the door. She found IRS agents with a subpoena. "May we come in?" they asked.

Meanwhile, Ciavarella's long-standing concerns about Conahan's relationship with Billy D'Elia, the mobster, were well founded. D'Elia had come under the scrutiny of state and federal investigators as soon as he took over as organized crime boss in northeastern Pennsylvania upon the death of Russell Bufalino in 1994. The investigators learned that D'Elia often served as a mediator in disputes among mob families in New York, Philadelphia, and Pittsburgh. In 2001, raids were conducted on the homes of several northeastern Pennsylvania racketeers, including D'Elia, by the Pennsylvania State Police, U.S. Postal Service inspectors, and agents of the Internal Revenue Service. D'Elia escaped prosecution, but indications of extensive gambling operations led New Jersey officials to ban him from all Atlantic City casinos. Finally, in May 2006, federal authorities charged him with money laundering the proceeds from illegal drug sales. Five months later he was charged with attempting to have a prosecution witness in the money-laundering scheme killed. D'Elia eventually pleaded guilty to reduced charges of witness tampering and money laundering, but nearly two dozen other counts were dropped because he cooperated with federal authorities. Right up to the time of his arrest, D'Elia kept meeting with Conahan to share omelets and information at Perkins restaurant—sometimes as often as three times a week. Now Chester Muroski's suspicions about Conahan, Ciavarella, Mericle, and Powell didn't seem so far-fetched. The U.S. Attorney's Office and the IRS joined in a grand jury investigation into the financial dealings among the quartet.

When the grand jury subpoenaed Powell, Mericle, and Barbara Conahan in early 2008, the judges went into full panic. They demanded a nighttime meeting with Powell and instructed him to wait for them in a parking lot behind Crestwood High School. They arrived in a car Powell did not recognize as belonging to either of the jurists. They asked to see his cellular telephone and then instructed him to leave it in his car. They said federal investigators could track his whereabouts, and therefore theirs, through the phone. Conahan was driving, Ciavarella in the front passenger seat. Powell got in the back. They told Powell that Mericle had "lied through his teeth" before the grand jury and testified that the payments to them were totally Powell's doing. They said the three of them "need to get our stories straight" and suggested a strategy of discrediting Mericle and Jill Moran, Powell's law partner who had delivered the cash in the Federal Express boxes. As Powell recalls the conversation, Ciavarella said, "We'll take care of Mericle. Bobby, you've got to hold the water here. You've got to say those boxes never came to us." They drove around for about ninety minutes without coming to a final agreement. Besides, Powell had other ideas. A few weeks later, he agreed to cooperate with prosecutors and secretly record conversations with the judges.

On July 30, 2008, Powell, Ciavarella, and Conahan gathered in the model unit of The Sanctuary, a townhouse the three were developing south of Wilkes-Barre. Unlike Rob Mericle nine months earlier, Powell *was* wearing a wire—a tiny microphone taped to his chest that was sending a recording to FBI agents parked in a van nearby. But Ciavarella didn't ask his now-former friend if he was wired. Conahan did inquire about the cellular phone, and Powell reassured him that he had left it in his car. By this time, all three had been subpoenaed to appear before the grand jury, and there were eddies of fear all over the townhouse.

The goal of the meeting, as far as the two judges knew, was to devise a defense strategy, and Powell began the conversation with a warning that Jill Moran had cleaned out her office at Powell's law firm, had not picked up her paycheck, and was now communicating with him only via BlackBerry. "She's the weak link." Powell said. "That's why she's not here tonight. I think Jill is off the fuckin' reservation." Powell reminded them that she had seen him stuffing cash into the Federal Express boxes. Both judges replied that they would deny ever receiving the cash and warned Powell that he must back up their stories. "The problem Jill has is she never gave me anything," Conahan said, crocheting lies and facts into an exoneration before the grand jury. "If anything was given to her, she has it." Ironically, Conahan expressed concern that Moran might show up at a meeting wired by federal investigators. "The problem with Jill is you just don't know what she is going to be wearing," he said to the wired Powell.

Powell's justification for calling the meeting was his concern that his business partner in PA Child Care and Western PA Child Care, Gregory Zappala, had become suspicious of the way the money was being handled in the two businesses. This was true. Powell had brought the companies to the brink of financial ruin because of his payoffs to the judges, and he feared that his partner might file a lawsuit against him. When Ciavarella suggested that Zappala would be placated by being paid off, Powell said it would be futile: "For Greg, it's not about the money." It was decided that Powell would sell his interest in both of the centers, because that might enhance the judges' ability to lie about the cash extortion payments. Ciavarella volunteered that he was going to deny any knowledge of the cash payments delivered to Conahan through Jill Moran or about Powell's condo rental payments to companies owned by the judges' wives.

Nevertheless, Ciavarella launched into yet another tirade about the profits going to the two juvenile centers. "They're making a shitload of money," he complained bitterly. Ciavarella went on to claim that he did not believe there was anything wrong with accepting the finder's fees from Mericle. "When he said to me, 'I want to pay you a finder's fee,' I said, 'You're kidding.' I would never approach Rob Mericle to ask him for a finder's fee. I didn't even know there was such a thing. Never in my wildest dreams did I ever imagine this was illegal money."

Suddenly, Ciavarella stood up. "Shhhhhhh!" he said, walking slowly over to a kitchen window. He had spotted the FBI van. He pointed to it. The trio went outside.

"We better get the fuck out of here," Powell said.

"Mark, do me a favor—would you go check that," said Conahan, his voice high with nervousness. Terror bled into the room as Ciavarella left and walked quickly over to the vehicle. He looked in the windows, but they were tinted and the inside of the van was not visible. He tugged at the sliding passenger door. Then at the rear door. Both were locked. Inside, Agent James Glenn and a colleague had been monitoring the conversation and videotaping the townhouse. When they saw Ciavarella headed their way, Glenn turned off the equipment lest the electronic hum alert the judges to the surveillance. When Ciavarella returned to the townhouse to join Powell and Conahan, they resumed recording.

Now fear blossomed into full panic. Before Ciavarella reached them, Conahan and Powell had a whispered conversation.

Powell: "Listen, this is my story. I never got any boxes. We're going to both have to stick to that because she's going to testify otherwise."

Conahan: "She's going to testify that you gave her boxes, one box filled with cash. She doesn't know what's in the other one."

Powell: "It's going to be our word against hers."

Conahan quickly outlined a plan to explain away the kickbacks: "Listen, you paid me rent for my condo. You didn't pay me rent for my condo to shut the juvenile detention center down or fix cases. And I got no boxes from Jill. Nobody gave boxes to Jill. If somebody gave boxes to Jill, she still has them. The only thing Mark knows is the conversation with Mericle. He doesn't know about the rent to the condo. He knows you paid me rent. He doesn't know about any boxes. That's why he is our most credible witness."

Then the three got in their separate cars and drove away. The agents waited fifteen minutes and left.

• • •

While Wilkes-Barre might have been firmly fixed in the public mind as a provincial dying coal town, it had something that was absent in Pennsylvania's largest urban centers, Philadelphia and Pittsburgh—two rollicking, competitive newspapers. The *Times-Leader*, a broadsheet, and the *Citizens' Voice*, a tabloid, had been dueling since 1978, when striking *Times-Leader* staffers broke away and started their own newspaper. It was a bitter strike that lasted nearly four years, and when it was over, the *Citizens' Voice* opted to keep publishing. The papers have changed owners several times, but the rivalry has remained. In 2006, Wilkes-Barre was the nation's smallest competitive newspaper market—good news for readers, bad news for crooked politicians. The *Times-Leader* had a slight edge in circulation—40,000 to 33,000—but the papers were battling to a virtual draw in attracting local advertising. And demographics didn't hurt—an older population meant more newspaper readers. Reporters, editors, and photographers from both dailies were frequent award winners in the annual state newspaper contests. The battle was very real, and there were frosty relations between some of the top reporters.

The *Times-Leader* had produced a first-rate, widely ignored series on Ciavarella's sentencing practices in 2004, and late the following year it was on the receiving end of the leaked documents outlining the damaging findings of the state Public Welfare Department's audit of PA Child Care. As the federal investigation picked up steam, reporters at both papers pored over documents and relentlessly questioned courthouse sources. On May 29, 2008, the *Citizens' Voice* published a story on the financial ties between the two judges and Powell. "Two Luzerne County judges who played key roles in closing the county's juvenile detention center in 2002 have financial interests in a Mountain Top real estate project linked to Robert J. Powell, an investor who has reaped millions by leasing a private juvenile center that he co-owns to the county," began a story by Dave Janoski, the paper's projects editor. Janoski was back one week later with the first story on the investigation by the FBI and the IRS. The revelations piled up about the judges' Florida condo and Powell's use of the adjacent boat slip. When the FBI seized the juvenile probation records in August, it became evident that the two juvenile detention centers somehow were involved in the probe.

By autumn the judges were done for and were working with the feds on a plea bargain. Conahan had retired from the bench and was hearing cases on a part-time basis in drug treatment court, and Ciavarella had resigned as juvenile court judge though he was still on the bench full-time. The FBI already had carried cartons of documents out of the Probation Office. In addition to Powell, Rob Mericle and Jill Moran were cooperating with the U.S. Attorney's Office. Despite all the payments from Mericle and Powell, Ciavarella was again desperately in debt. He had borrowed $265,000 from Conahan to cover credit card balances, college tuition, and household expenses. Even when Ciavarella was aware of the federal investigation, Powell said the judge tried to persuade him to give him another $40,000. And just a few weeks before he would plead guilty to corruption charges, he borrowed $50,000 from a local attorney.

While the feds' focus was on the two judges, dozens of other Luzerne County officials were under investigation. Around the courthouse, there was a feast of rumors festering into fact. Indictments were dropping like cinder blocks, and there was talk of a "culture of corruption." County officials, school administrators, school board members, and government contractors resigned and pleaded guilty, hoping for leniency. Yet there was a ho-hum attitude on the part of much of the public. This was northeastern

Pennsylvania, after all, and this was how things were done. Politicians helped each other out, gave each other jobs, gave their relatives jobs, and then stayed quiet. Everyone had to pay for a job. Why let someone else take it? Why be a sucker? Payoffs and nepotism were okay so long as everyone was treated equally.

So what if the court administrator stole $70,000? If the superintendent of the Pittston Area School District took a bribe in exchange for a contract? That a member of the Wilkes-Barre Area School Board took payoffs to influence the hiring of teachers? That a magisterial judge stole $5,000 from the Wyoming Valley Sanitary Authority? That a member of the Wyoming Valley West School Board took money for getting a contractor approved for a tax-forgiveness program? So corrupt were the schools that eventually the FBI would make an amazing appeal that was carried by newspapers and broadcast media throughout northeastern Pennsylvania: "If you are a teacher, prospective teacher, employee or prospective employee of any kind who has been required to provide money, or anything else of value, to any individual in connection with being hired at any public school in northeastern Pennsylvania, you are requested to immediately contact either Special Agent Richard Southerton or Special Agent Joseph Noone in the FBI's Scranton office."

Almost immediately, the telephones were ringing.

Back at Juvenile Law Center headquarters in Philadelphia, there was an uneasy expectancy. The Pennsylvania Supreme Court was not responding to the urgent King's Bench petition that was filed by Juvenile Law Center in April 2008 asking the state's highest court to end the abuse of the rights of child defendants in Luzerne County. Laval Miller-Wilson, Robert Schwartz, and Marsha Levick all waited with unraveling nerve endings to hear from the court. Just a week after the petition was filed, Levick took a call from an FBI field agent, who asked a lot of questions. It was clear to her they were investigating juvenile court in Luzerne County. Juvenile Law Center lawyers were hoping for an immediate and affirmative reaction from the Supreme Court, but realistically they expected to hear by September. Spring came and went, then summer ebbed and rusted into autumn. Nothing.

Finally, in December 2008—nearly eight months after the original King's Bench petition was filed—Juvenile Law Center filed an amended petition that added more cases of injustice in Ciavarella's courtroom and urgently asked the Supreme Court to intervene. But on January 8, 2009, came the shocker. The Supreme Court, without comment or explanation, rejected the petition in a single sentence. Schwartz and Levick were aghast. How could Pennsylvania's highest court ignore its own statistics? Kids were appearing without lawyers ten times more often in Luzerne County than in the rest of the state! They were being taken out of their homes at two-and-a-half times the statewide rate! In a single year, Luzerne County—with about 3 percent of the population—was responsible for 22 percent of all placements in Pennsylvania. Miller-Wilson never recovered. He had already been planning to leave Juvenile Law Center to pursue a career in public health, but this accelerated that process. He resigned, effective February 1: "I was disillusioned by the Supreme Court's disregard for this massive injustice. I thought this case was my best achievement and my biggest failure, I didn't want anything more to do with the juvenile justice system." Levick and Schwartz began looking at options.

But over the Thanksgiving-Christmas holiday period, local lawyers and courthouse insiders in Luzerne County were speculating that two or more judges, including Ciavarella and

Conahan, were in trouble. The near-unanimous assumption was that the wrongdoing involved fixing cases, especially arbitration cases. Ciavarella's harsh treatment of children was well known, but his no-nonsense stance was still very popular among a large portion of the population. The idea that two judges had been taking millions of dollars in bribes from a private juvenile detention center was known only by the federal investigators and a few others, like Chester Muroski, the judge who was now cooperating fully with the feds.

January 26, 2009, dawned sunny and cold in Wilkes-Barre. It was only sixteen degrees outside when Muroski stood somberly before a news conference in Wilkes-Barre and announced that Ciavarella had resigned as president judge. Muroski released copies of a single-sentence letter from Ciavarella to Governor Edward Rendell: "Please accept this letter as my official notice to you that I am resigning effective immediately from my position as President Judge of the Eleventh District." Muroski said that as the judge with the most seniority, he would take over running the courts until a successor was elected by the full bench. He added pointedly, with an arch of his bushy brows, that he and his colleagues would attempt to restore public confidence in the courts by "acting the way judges should act."

Two hours later, at the federal building in Scranton, U.S. Attorney Martin C. Carlson held a news conference that elicited inhalatory gasps from many of his listeners and left others staring at the ceiling in disbelief. Terrie Morgan-Besecker of the *Times-Leader* and her media colleagues had come prepared for something big—something to do with case-fixing, PA Child Care, or kickbacks. But nothing like this. Carlson, in a matter-of-fact tone, said Ciavarella and Conahan had agreed to plead guilty to "a scheme to defraud the citizens of Luzerne County and the people of Pennsylvania." They had "abused their positions and violated their fiduciary duty by secretly deriving more than $2,600,000 in income in exchange for official actions and anticipated official actions. The actions from which they derived improper income included directing that juvenile offenders be lodged at the juvenile detention facilities operated by PA Child Care and Western PA Child Care." In some cases, Carlson said, Ciavarella ordered children into detention even when juvenile probation officers did not recommend it. Added Deron Roberts, chief of the Scranton office of the FBI: "They sold their oaths of offices to the highest bidders." The elaborate kickback scheme was detailed in a twenty-two-page list of charges (called an "information") that did not name Mericle or Powell, but instead referred to them as "Participant #1" and "Participant #2."

Among the witnesses to the news conference was Jack Van Reeth, the father of Jessica, who said, "We feel that it's a great day for the young people and the youth of this area to see the system really does work, the system really isn't rigged against them. It's just wonderful to see that the scheme of jailing-for-dollars has come to an end. Jessica is extremely happy. She said this is better than Christmas."

At Juvenile Law Center in Philadelphia, Schwartz and Levick had been alerted by Marie J. Yeager, the center's public relations consultant, that a major development was about to occur in Scranton. Carlson's news conference was streamed live, and they watched with mounting amazement as the story unfolded. Then, wide-eyed, they went online and read the list of charges. This wasn't about five hundred cases. This was about thousands of cases! The amounts of money were huge and the scheme was brazen. Carlson connected the dots between the payoffs and the constitutional violations—a quid pro quo! This meant that from the time PA Child Care opened, Ciavarella had a financial incentive to place kids. *All* cases before Ciavarella were tainted!

A hailstorm of phone calls and emails ensued from the media, parents, and other juvenile lawyers. For the next two days Yeager took calls from all over the world: the networks, cable news, the *New York Times*, the *Washington Post*, *Time*, *Newsweek*, the *Economist*, newspapers in Britain, France, and Australia. So many aggrieved families were contacting the center that it hired additional attorneys to handle the calls.

Schwartz and Levick decided immediately that it was time to give the King's Bench petition another try. This time they attached to it the federal information outlining the kickback scheme and amended it to challenge cases going back to 2003, when money first was exchanged between the judges and Mericle via Powell. The petition was re-filed on Thursday, three days after the Carlson news conference. The following Monday the Supreme Court, without outward sign of what could only have been an infinity of embarrassment, put out a press release saying it would take jurisdiction as Juvenile Law Center had suggested some ten months earlier. Another belated joiner of the anti-Ciavarella-Conahan bandwagon was the Judicial Conduct Board, which said it would file a petition seeking the immediate suspension of the two judges. This came two years and five months after it received the anonymous complaint against Conahan. Before the JCB could get around to acting, the Supreme Court stripped the two judges of all judicial power.

Facing jeering, booing, hooting, hissing citizens and a gale of cameras and reporters from the local and national media, the two judges (who would resign in a few days) were back at the William J. Nealon Federal Courthouse in Scranton on February 12. Before going into the courtroom, they were fingerprinted and posed for mug shots. Then they sat at separate tables with their lawyers and listened to U.S. District Judge Edward M. Kosik, who said he wanted to be sure that, "regardless of the sophistication of the defendants," each of them fully understood their rights. Each wore a dark gray suit. Ciavarella was slightly slouched in his chair. Conahan drummed the tabletop nervously with his fingers. Finally, Kosik asked, "How do you plead?"

"Guilty, Your Honor," said Conahan.

"Guilty, Your Honor," said Ciavarella.

Under the terms of the plea bargains with federal prosecutors, the felonious judges agreed to serve eighty-seven months in prison, resign within ten days of their plea, and consent to automatic disbarment. Kosik released them on $1 million bail that was secured by their Florida condominium, which was legally owned by their wives and had served as the laundry for most of the kickbacks from Powell. At the rear of the courtroom, Ciavarella stopped to answer a question. "How do you think it would be?" he answered incredulously. "It wasn't fun." Then the co-conspirators strode out of the courthouse to a waiting car. One woman shouted, "Burn in hell!" That night on the CBS News, Katie Couric intoned, "Two judges in Pennsylvania pleaded guilty today to taking huge payoffs to send teenagers to privately run detention centers."

Among the courtroom spectators was Kevin's mother, who admired Judge Kosik's handling of the drama: "You felt like you were sitting in a place that was being fair and that he was being fair. It went as it should be. He was very forward in explaining things, in making sure they understood, in making them answer, in making sure that they understood what was happening." She did not feel Ciavarella had extended the same consideration just

ten months earlier when her seventeen-year-old son had appeared before him on a simple assault charge growing out of a
fight outside a concert hall with a friend. Her frustration began
when she tried to persuade court officials to change the date of
Kevin's hearing because she had to attend an important meeting
involving her daughter's education as a dental hygienist. Unable
to resolve the conflict, she asked her seventy-five-year-old father
to accompany Kevin to the courtroom. Since it was Kevin's first
offense, she was told by probation officials that her son did not
need an attorney. Kevin admitted that he punched the boy, but
when he tried to explain, Ciavarella cut him off and dispatched
him to Camp Adams for ninety days.

Kevin's trauma began when he was handcuffed and leg-
shackled, taken to a side door and placed in a van. After a ten-
hour drive to Camp Adams, Kevin felt out of place with juveniles
who were there for violent offenses involving guns and drugs.
He was allowed to telephone only his parents, so whenever he
called, his mother would run down the street with the mobile
phone handing it to his friends so they could talk with her son
for a minute. About a dozen of his classmates at Hanover Area
High School organized a protest with T-shirts that said, "Free
Kev." They counted down the days until July 22, 2008, his scheduled release date. The *Times-Leader* and the *Citizens' Voice* ran
articles. Parental visits were limited to one hour on Sundays. "It
was heartbreaking to watch Kevin in battered-up clothes, shoes
that were too big, filthy, oversized sweats, sores on his feet, heavy
boots in the middle of summer. It was just a horrible feeling to
see your son unshaven with long hair. I couldn't believe that
they weren't taking care of him in a better manner up there," his
mother said. She added that twice he was beaten by other boys
out of range of the Camp Adams surveillance cameras.

Juvenile Law Center intervened with an appeal to the state Superior Court asking that Kevin's adjudication be overturned because Ciavarella failed to fully question him to ensure he understood the possible consequences when he opted to admit to participating in the fight. He was released in June after fifty-seven days at Camp Adams by Judge David W. Lupas, the former district attorney who had taken over from Ciavarella as juvenile judge.

Among those most appalled by the revelations out of Scranton was Judge Arthur Grim, who was in his office in Reading, Pennsylvania, on February 12 when he received an unexpected telephone call from Ronald D. Castille, the chief justice of Pennsylvania. Was he aware of the Luzerne County situation? Yes, he said, painfully so. Would he serve as a special master to review Ciavarella's cases for the Supreme Court? Grim hesitated. It shouldn't take much time, Castille reassured. Grim said he needed to talk it over with his wife, but he already knew his answer. There was no way he could turn down a request like that. Grim had been a juvenile court judge for twenty years, and he was serving as chairman of Pennsylvania's Juvenile Court Judges' Commission and as a member of the Juvenile Justice and Delinquency Prevention Committee to the Pennsylvania Commission on Crime and Delinquency. He called Castille back the next day and accepted. The task would occupy and obsess Grim for most of the rest of the year, and his painful findings would be permanently lodged in his memory like a thorn.

Five days after his initial phone call from Castille, Grim and a law clerk assigned to him, William Ehrlich, drove to Wilkes-Barre and met with a group of key officials that included Muroski; David W. Lupas, the former district attorney who was now a county judge; Jacqueline Musto Carroll, who succeeded Lupas as district attorney; and Basil G. Russin, the chief public defender. It was agreed that Grim would begin with the cases that were most likely to be expunged because they involved minor offenses. Grim and Ehrlich took the files back to the judge's office on the third floor of the Berks County Courthouse and began their reviews. It wasn't long before Grim felt a seeping, molten anger threatening to wash over him. In Ciavarella's courtroom, the constitutional rights of children were nonexistent. Vulnerable kids were being coaxed by adults into waiving their right to an attorney and then advised to plead "guilty"—a word that wasn't even supposed to be used in juvenile court. Kids and their parents were advised by probation officers that getting a lawyer would "only make matters worse." When Grim sat as a juvenile judge, cases lasted for several hours. But in Ciavarella's courtroom, the average case lasted about four minutes. One of the first transcripts he read involved an eighth-grade girl who was brought to Ciavarella by school authorities for possessing a small amount of marijuana.

Ciavarella: "It says here that you have been charged with violation of the Controlled Substance, Drug, Device and Cosmetic Act. How do you wish to plead?"

Juvenile: "Guilty."

Ciavarella: "Based upon her admission, I will adjudicate her delinquent. Where did this occur?"

Juvenile: "School."

Ciavarella: "What grade are you in?"

Juvenile: "Eighth."

Ciavarella: "Were you at the school when I was there?"

Juvenile: "Yeah."

Ciavarella: "What did I say about drugs in school?"

Juvenile: "That you're going to get—well, you're going to get arrested in school."

Ciavarella: "What else did I tell you?"

Juvenile: "That you will get arrested and get charged."

Ciavarella: "What did I say I will do?"

Juvenile: "Send us away."

Ciavarella: "Did you think I was kidding?"

Juvenile: "No."

Ciavarella: "Very good. She will be remanded. Send her to [Wind Gap]. Let her stay there until she learns her lesson. I mean what I say. Thank you."

It was the same in case after case. Ciavarella was sending away kids with a routine that seemed coded in his brain. Not a single word about the right to counsel. Grim discovered early in his review of cases that Ciavarella often read probation reports about a child's alleged offenses, past behaviors, and social circumstances before he held the hearing to determine whether or not they were guilty of the specific offense. This was an egregious violation of law and procedures that are designed to keep a judge impartial in reaching a decision. A juvenile judge, Grim believed, was supposed to follow the rules with the best interests of the child, the community, and the victim in mind. Ciavarella was perverting this idea in ways Grim had never imagined possible. Grim quickly realized that the abasement of constitutional guarantees was pervasive. Ciavarella didn't just sometimes fail to protect kids' rights, or even most of the time. He violated the law in every single case.

The review of these easier cases—Grim called them "low-hanging fruit"—took a month. In his initial recommendation to the Supreme Court, Grim noted that Rule 152 forbade the court to accept a waiver of counsel from a child unless the waiver is "knowingly, intelligently, and voluntarily made" and only after the judge "conducts a colloquy with the juvenile on the record." With that preface, Grim wrote in his initial report to the Supreme Court: "My preliminary investigation points to the conclusion that a very substantial number of juveniles who appeared without counsel before Judge Ciavarella for delinquency or related proceedings did not knowingly and intelligently waive their right to counsel. My investigation also uncovered evidence that there was routine deprivation of children's constitutional rights to appear before an impartial tribunal and to have an opportunity to be heard."

Grim also concluded that if these children had had competent lawyers, they would not have been adjudicated delinquent and would have received lesser sanctions, such as consent decrees that in effect provide juveniles with a second chance. Since these youth would not have had juvenile delinquency records, as they now did, Grim said these cases should be vacated and the records expunged. The Supreme Court agreed two weeks later, and the long process began to wipe out the records of about 360 kids.

Grim now turned his attention to the more serious cases. Since a hundred of the easy cases had taken a month, Grim and Ehrlich knew they couldn't plow through each individual case. So they asked the court officials for a cross-section. Even then, they knew they could not examine the entire file of the selected cases, so they focused on the charges, transcripts, findings, and dispositions. A realization came quickly to Grim: Every case heard by Ciavarella between 2003 and 2008—perhaps three thousand of them—must be vacated and the records of the juveniles expunged. He made his recommendation for universal expungement on August 7. He said no child who appeared before Ciavarella could have had an impartial hearing because of the bribes and the routine denial of constitutional rights. On October 29, the Pennsylvania Supreme Court, which ten months earlier had refused even to consider the denial of constitutional rights in Luzerne County, adopted Grim's recommendations in a nine-page order.

There was a dimension to the Luzerne County tragedy that went largely unnoticed by the general public, but Grim was gravely sensitive to it: there was a large group of citizens who would be upset by universal expungement—those who were real victims of juveniles who came before Ciavarella. Many of the youths whose records were cleared did commit serious offenses against innocent people. They would now have clean records. Some of them even were paying court-ordered restitution to their victims. This would now be stopped. Grim said he understood how the victims felt, but the unfortunate situation was unavoidable. "The bottom line is when an order is vacated and a record expunged, it's over. There is no ability for anyone in the court system to require anything further of these kids," he said.

But many, like Karen, were not consoled. On a subzero night in 2005, when she had just turned forty-one, Karen was working as a pizza deliveryperson in Wilkes-Barre. "It was very dark. I was making a delivery on New Street. I got out of the car, and suddenly four kids wearing hoodies were running at me. One of them pulled out a hunting knife and screamed, 'Give me your money!' I reached in my pocket to get the money, and another kid hit me in the lower back with a baseball bat. I didn't know he was behind me, and I went to my knees. Then he swung at my head. I managed to block it, but then they started kicking me, and I shouted, 'I can't get to the money if you keep kicking me.' I gave one of them about twenty-two dollars. They ran off. I wasn't sure I could stand up, but I managed and got back in my car and dialed 911. They told me to stay where I was, but I was terrified and wanted to get away. Somehow I drove back to the restaurant, staggered in the door and fell on the floor. The ambulance came and took me to the emergency room."

Karen had suffered two herniated disks in her lower back, multiple contusions, and bruised ribs. Pain tore through her body like a jackhammer. Part of the attack was caught by a surveillance camera at a convenience store, and her assailants were arrested the next day. They were boys aged fifteen, sixteen, seventeen, and eighteen. The three youngest went before Ciavarella, pleaded guilty to assault charges, and were incarcerated for about a year. Karen had to identify them in the courtroom: "I didn't understand how difficult it would be until I had to do it. I had to be in the same room as those people who had brutalized me. Now that I know what it's like, I'm not sure I could ever do it again."

She said once the attackers were identified, her son and her husband wanted to go after them in retribution. "I said, 'No, the court system will handle it.' I swore to them that the courts were going to handle it." She underwent physical therapy for about a year, and long after that she continued to suffer mental anguish. She was afraid to turn her back on anyone, even someone she knew: "I was phobic about going outside the house. Even today, if I see kids going down the road with hoodies, I get panicked. I am easily startled by loud noises and quick movements."

Then, in October 2009, she was stunned when she learned of the Supreme Court's expungement order. "Okay, a lot of these kids were sentenced unjustly, but the guys who went after me deserved what they got. Expunging a criminal's record is very un-validating to the victim. To just say it didn't happen makes me feel like I don't matter. I will carry this incident with me for the rest of my life, but the criminals who attacked me will not have to do the same."

Following their guilty pleas, Conahan withdrew into seclusion, but Ciavarella made some headlines. When ABC's *20/20* did a twenty-five minute segment on the scandal in March, he was intercepted outside his home by reporter Jim Avila and a camera crew. He gave an angry, finger-pointing performance in which he denied that the payoffs had influenced dispositions of young defendants. "You take a look at their file and you look to see if this was the first time they had a run-in with the law," he snarled at Avila. "It might have been the first time they were in front of me. You may be surprised that it's not going to be as clear-cut as they would like you to think."

The *Citizens' Voice*, which had been on the losing end of a $3.5 million libel verdict in a case heard by Ciavarella in 2006, asked the Pennsylvania Supreme Court to review the ruling in light of the corruption allegations. The high court ordered an unusual evidentiary hearing in nearby Lehigh County that was held on July 1 and 2. In a remarkable appearance on the witness stand, Ciavarella admitted to being a "corrupt judge" in the libel case, and he unabashedly admitted that he took the money from Mericle and Powell in connection with the construction and operation of the two juvenile detention centers. But he insisted that he did not think the payments were improper. "I did not consider what I did to be illegal," he testified. "I did not consider the money that I was receiving to be illegal mob money. I was told it was legal money. I was told it was something that I was entitled to. And for that reason, I did not have a problem with where that money went or how it came to me." He said he didn't report the payments, which totaled about $1.4 million, to the Internal Revenue Service because he thought Conahan had paid the taxes. He said the federal charges about the kickbacks were the result of a "misunderstanding" on his part. And, most emphatically, he denied the payments had anything to do with his decisions to send children to the two juvenile centers.

This was too much for Judge William H. Platt, who ordered a new trial in the libel case and in a scorching opinion wrote: "Ciavarella's admissions that he was a corrupt judge while presiding over the [libel] case, that he did not report outside income on the annual financial disclosure form for judges, that he lied when completing the form, and that he failed to properly report income on his tax returns are sufficient basis to conclude that he violated his fiduciary duty to the citizens of the Commonwealth of Pennsylvania, that he violated his duty to refrain from conduct that constituted a conflict of interest, and that he failed in his obligation to recuse himself in cases in which he had a conflict of interest. The conclusions alone are sufficient to create the appearance of impropriety to serve as judge for any matter in the case. Tellingly, former Judge Ciavarella, a witness called by [the plaintiff], was, because of his demeanor and lack of remorse, one of *Citizens' Voice*'s best witnesses."

Platt was not the only judge troubled by Ciavarella's testimony. For Edward M. Kosik, the federal judge who was weighing the plea bargain orchestrated between prosecutors and the two judges after months of negotiations, the testimony was the last straw. Kosik had watched with mounting distress as Ciavarella denied there was any connection between his decisions in juvenile cases and his huge payments from Powell and Mericle. Kosik also believed that Conahan was not cooperating as much as he should with federal authorities. On July 31, Kosik rejected the pleas because the two defendants had not accepted responsibility to a degree sufficient to justify the eighty-seven month sentence. Both the federal prosecutors and the judges' defense lawyers tried to get Kosik to change his mind, but he refused. On August 24, Ciavarella and Conahan withdrew their guilty pleas and became innocent citizens. Al Flora, Ciavarella's attorney, told reporters: "At this point, Mark Ciavarella has not been convicted of any crime. He is entitled to the full presumption of innocence provided under the Constitution of the United States. Now the next step has to be taken by the government and the case will proceed accordingly."

Powell pleaded guilty to charges of failing to report a felony and being an after-the-fact accessory to a tax-avoidance conspiracy. As part of his plea, he forfeited his ownership of the fifty-foot fishing yacht, *Reel Justice*, and his corporate jet. He also continued his cooperation with the U.S. Attorney's Office. Mericle pleaded guilty to lying about the payoffs to the judges and failing to report the tax conspiracy. As part of the agreement, he contributed $2,150,000—the total of his finder's fee payoffs to the judges—to be used for "programs for the health, safety and general welfare of the children of Luzerne County." Two months after Kosik tossed out the plea bargains, federal authorities filed a forty-eight-count indictment charging Ciavarella and Conahan with racketeering, bribery, and extortion. Both pleaded not guilty, but Conahan would later change his plea to guilty.

The opportunities presented by the scandal were not lost on the nation's trial lawyers, who scented multiple opportunities in Luzerne County. Attorneys as far away as Florida took ads in the *Times-Leader* and the *Citizens' Voice* soliciting clients. One local attorney represented himself as the "Juvenile Justice Center," capitalizing on the now sterling reputation of Juvenile Law

Center. Several class-action suits were quickly filed, including one by Juvenile Law Center. All charged that Ciavarella had done great harm to the young plaintiffs by incarcerating them improperly. As a result of their incarcerations, Juvenile Law Center argued, many of the teenagers suffered emotional damage, were unable to attend school, lost scholarships, were refused military enlistment, and attempted suicide. In addition, they and their parents were forced to pay probation fees, evaluation costs, and had their wages garnished by the court. Also named as defendants were Powell, Mericle, and various county officials. The suits were consolidated by the U.S. District Court. The suits asked that the youths, whose convictions had been invalidated as "a travesty of justice" by the state Supreme Court, be repaid for actual financial losses and as compensation for emotional suffering at the hands of the two judges and others involved in the scheme.

However, U.S. District Judge A. Richard Caputo ruled that Ciavarella and Conahan could not be held liable for actions in their own courtrooms under the seventeenth-century doctrine of judicial immunity, which is designed to give judges freedom to rule without fear of legal retribution. But Caputo left the door open to liability for actions outside the courtroom, such as Conahan's order that closed an existing county-owned juvenile center and the signing of the secret agreement guaranteeing that the child-defendants would be sent to the new private center. Caputo also held that county officials—commissioners, the District Attorney's Office, the Probation Department, and the Public Defenders Office—were not liable in the civil action.

As the details and scope of the massive injustices in Luzerne County came out in the spring of 2009, representatives of all three branches of state government met in Harrisburg and decided to propose legislation that would create an eleven-member study commission, the members of which would be appointed by the Governor's Office, the Supreme Court, and the Legislature. Despite an ongoing state budget crisis, the Legislature acted with uncharacteristic swiftness and passed the bill six weeks after it was introduced.

9

THE TRIAL

The trial of former Judge Mark Ciavarella on thirty-nine counts of racketeering, bribery, and extortion opened on February 7, 2011, two years and two weeks after the original charges were announced by the federal government. It was a cold day with bright sun that whitewashed the four-story limestone William J. Nealon Federal Building and U.S. Courthouse in Scranton. The proceeding took nine and a half days, including a day to select a jury and a day and a half for that jury to reach a verdict. In seven days of testimony, prosecutors presented twenty-four witnesses, and the defense called six, including Ciavarella. At the end, Ciavarella received what few if any of those who had come before his court ever received: a fair trial.

Day One

Laurene Transue arrives an hour early at the courthouse and stands outside the main entrance. It is meat-locker cold, and she is shivering. But she has waited a long time for this moment. It has been nearly four years since she collapsed in Mark Ciavarella's courtroom as her daughter Hillary was whisked away by bailiffs and driven to the juvenile detention camp at Wind Gap for making fun of her assistant principal on MySpace. Hillary is now a college student in New Hampshire studying for a final, but Transue wants to be here to represent her. She is not alone. TV and radio reporters are buzzing around like pollinating bees. Three or four other parents of kids dispatched by Ciavarella show up, and a handful of curious citizens. They huddle against a stiff wind that has snow on its breath, and as they talk excitedly they exhale vapor from their mouths and nostrils. They all wait for one person. Ciavarella is finally going on trial for the PA Child Care scheme. Conahan has already pleaded guilty to similar charges, and it is widely supposed that he will testify against his co-conspirator.

However courthouse officials, concerned about security, have allowed Ciavarella and his two attorneys to use a back door, and everyone at the front door eventually gives up and hurries inside, where jury selection is about to begin. Transue, disappointed at her failure to see Ciavarella but grateful for the sudden warmth, rides the elevator up to the second floor. The door opens with a ping, an electronic voice says "second floor," Transue steps off—and almost bumps into Ciavarella. Panicked, she brushes by him, but after a few steps, she steels her nerves, does an about-face, and walks right past him. He gives her a smirk she has come to hate, says, "Hello," and turns away. She doesn't say anything. For the next two weeks, Transue will drive two hours a day from her home in White Haven to attend the trial. She sends text messages to Hillary during breaks in the testimony, and calls her with a report each night. "I want justice to come as swiftly for him as injustice came for Hillary and the thousands of other children and their families," she says.

A cathedral hush comes over the courtroom and everyone stands for Judge Edward M. Kosik, a sprightly cricket of a man who used to be an avid runner and once trekked in the Himalayas. He has slowed his pace at the age of eighty-five, but he still strides out briskly, and today he is wearing treaded hiking shoes. Kosik was appointed to the federal bench by President Ronald Reagan in 1986 and has been a judge for forty years. Ciavarella's defense team has argued that Kosik should not hear this case because he had shown bias in throwing out the guilty pleas of the two judges. But Kosik has refused to remove himself. Kosik settles in his high-backed chair, and jury selection begins. There is speculation that jury selection could take up to a week, but Kosik makes it clear he wants the jury in place by the end of the day.

Ciavarella, natty in a gray suit, light blue shirt, and black and gray tie, is at a table flanked by his attorneys, Al Flora and William Ruzzo. Flora, the fifty-nine years old son of a Baltimore boxing promoter and a veteran defense attorney with high-profile cases in the Wilkes-Barre area, is a portly man, wearing a wrinkled herringbone sport coat. When making an argument in court, he tends to stand with his hands on his hips, arms akimbo. Ruzzo, sixty-seven, didn't become a lawyer until he was nearly fifty years old. He said he was inspired to become a lawyer after being arrested for bookmaking and placed in a probation program. He is gaunt, needle-thin, and speaks out of the side of his mouth in a raspy voice. Flora and Ruzzo are both on leave from their part-time jobs as public defenders in Luzerne County. Flora was named by county commissioners to succeed Basil G. Russin as chief public defender, while Ruzzo was named an assistant public defender. These dual roles—public defenders and private attorneys for Ciavarella—drew some sharp criticism. One of the critics, George D. Mosee, the Philadelphia assistant district attorney, said, "If you are representing a judge who has been accused of violating the rights of juveniles, then you can't be representing juveniles. It's a very obvious conflict."

At the prosecution table is the lead U.S. attorney, Gordon

Zubrow, who has been a federal prosecutor for thirty-one years and has special experience in cases involving organized crime and the sexual exploitation of children. Zubrow, with close-cropped hair, has a Clark Kent earnestness about him. His assistants are William Houser, a sixteen-year veteran of the U.S. Attorney's Office, and Michael Consiglio, who became a federal prosecutor in 2008.

Under Kosik's relentless pressure on both sides, the prospective juror pool of ninety is whittled down to thirty-six and finally to sixteen: a panel of twelve jurors—six women and six men—plus four alternates. All day long, Kosik is a study in impatience, flicking with annoyance at an unruly lock of white hair, pushing his glasses up the bridge of his nose, licking his thumb as he rapidly turns pages in documents. Sometimes he calls the five attorneys to sidebar conferences, turning on a staticky white noise device intended to prevent everyone else in the courtroom from hearing the discussions. Sometimes the masking device is insufficient, as when Flora animatedly insists that he be allowed to question each prospective juror for possible bias. Kosik refuses and, in exasperation, finally says, "If I'm in error, I'm in error. I made my decision and will stand by my decision. Now let's go!" Around 4 p.m., the group of sixteen is led to another courtroom for final instructions before being sent home for the day. Kosik says opening arguments will be held tomorrow.

Day Two

Ciavarella gets to courtroom 2 early, accompanied by his wife Cindy and two married daughters, Nicole Oravic and Lauren Stahl. Ciavarella exchanges hugs with two men who are standing in the rear, then makes his way to the defense table inside the rail.

The three women sit in the front row. Near the bench, standing across from each other like captains at a football coin toss, the five lawyers shake hands and wish each other luck. The air is prickly with tension, which is broken when an unrobed Kosik sticks his head out the door and proclaims, "I'm a little late because I've just shoveled the snow off two driveways." He is in his chair a few minutes later, and the jury is sworn in at 9:14 a.m.

Zubrod goes first and outlines the government's case. "Mark Ciavarella and his co-conspirator Michael Conahan were engaged in racketeering activity. In other words, they turned the Court of Common Pleas into a criminal enterprise, using their judicial positions to take bribes, kickbacks, using the mails and wires to put the criminal scheme into effect to extort money, using the power of their office to conceal the payments of bribes and kickbacks and extortion by making illegal payments look like business transactions with other individuals knowing that the money will eventually wind up in their pockets. Now, how did Mark Ciavarella and Michael Conahan abuse their positions of trust to enrich themselves in violation of law?" Zubrod points directly at Ciavarella and asks, "How did Mark Ciavarella turn the office of judge, the high office of judge, into a cash cow, into a moneymaking machine where he and Michael Conahan illegally took in millions of dollars and hid it from public scrutiny?" Ciavarella makes a temple of his fingers, but he appears aloof and emotionless.

Here, Zubrod, using a chart, begins explaining the complicated money-laundering scheme. Kosik fidgets from the bench, seeming to be looking for a more comfortable portion of his anatomy to sit on. Finally, he leans toward his microphone: "Excuse me. I hate to interrupt you, but I'm not sure all of the jurors are seeing what you're pointing to. And I'd appreciate it if you talk to the jurors instead of the exhibit." Zubrod says, "Yes, sir, I will," but he seems annoyed and thrown off stride. Several times Zubrod shows the jury unflattering photographs of Ciavarella and Conahan that look like police mug shots. Near the end of his forty-minute opening, Zubrod comes to one of the government's key arguments—that the $733,500 Robert Powell paid to the judges was extortion: "Powell knew if he refused to pay, he wouldn't get any children from Luzerne County. If he refused, he knew that Mark Ciavarella and Michael Conahan could ruin him. In addition to running PA Child Care and Western PA Child Care, Robert Powell was also a very active trial lawyer in Luzerne County and judges have enormous power in determining the outcome of a case. He paid the money."

In the defense opening, Ruzzo ridicules the idea that Ciavarella, who stands at five foot seven, could intimidate Powell: "Robert Powell is not a man to be extorted. He was a Division 1 basketball player, big guy, six-five, six-six, maybe 250, 240, athletic, assertive lawyer. He's not a man to be easily extorted." The money from Powell, Ruzzo avers, was for rent on the condominium owned by the judges' wives. And he says Ciavarella did not realize that the $2,086,000 Robert Mericle paid him was either against the law or against judicial ethics, but instead thought it was a legitimate finder's fee. Ruzzo describes the genesis of the first payment: "Bob Mericle comes in and says, 'I'm going to take care of you, I am going to give you a finder's fee.' Mr. Ciavarella wasn't even familiar with the process. He says, 'What are you going to give me?' He says, 'I'm going to give you a finder's fee for alerting me to the project. I'm going to take care of you.' Mr. Ciavarella says, 'Could you do that? Is it legal for you to do this?' And Mericle says, 'I do it all the time.' Bob Mericle will come in here and tell you he did it all the time. And Mark Cia-varella is pleased, I'm going to get money, it's a finder's fee, it's for recommending a friend, my friend is going to make money on the project. He's going to cut me—he's going to give me a finder's fee."

"There's no question he should have used better judgment on the bench," Ruzzo concedes. Several jurors look puzzled, an-other skeptical. Laurene Transue rolls her eyes.

Robert Mericle sits in the witness stand most of the afternoon. He says his testimony is part of a plea agreement that requires him to cooperate with prosecutors, who in return are to recom-mend he serve a reduced prison term for lying to federal authori-ties about the payments to Ciavarella. Asked what his company does, he says, "We construct buildings, we own buildings, we manage buildings." He testifies he had known Ciavarella since he was sixteen, considers him a "big brother," and gave Ciavarella ever-more-valuable Christmas presents after he became a judge. Mericle tells the jury he considered his initial $997,600 finder's fee payments to Ciavarella a normal part of the real estate busi-ness. "If anybody deserved the referral fee, it was Mark." He says he initially lied about these payments because "I did not want to be the person to lay Mark out." Near the end of the day, Laurene Transue leans forward and taps a television courtroom sketch artist on the back. 'You've got Ciavarella's eyebrows all wrong," she complains.

Day Three

Mericle's matter-of-fact admission that at Christmas he gave Ciavarella $5,000 in cash in an envelope wrapped in a travel magazine leaves several jurors with little expressions of amazement flash frozen on their faces. Most of the jurors intently follow Mericle's account of visiting Ciavarella and getting the first inkling of impending disaster: "It was November 1, 2007, and I went to his office. The first room that I walked into was dark. It was a typical business day. I was surprised. I went around the corner to where his office was, and Mark was standing behind his desk, and it was dimly lit. And I walked in, said, 'Hi, Mark.' And he said, 'Hi,' and put his finger to his lips as if to be quiet. He opened his desk drawer and sat down and wrote out in—with a pen—wired, yes, no, circle one."

"And when after he wrote this down, did he show it to you?"

"Yes, he did."

"How did you indicate?"

"I circled no."

"After you circled no, what happened?"

"He waved me to move into the courtroom, and we sat down at one of the tables in the courtroom."

"When you sat down at this table, what does Mark tell you?"

"Mark told me that there was a grand jury investigation going on and that—I believe a secretary of Michael Conahan was already interviewed, and that he [Mark] might be in trouble and that he [Mark] needed to talk to me."

After four hours on the witness stand, Mericle comes across as a sympathetic, soft-spoken, almost contrite figure.

Robert Powell, on the other hand, seems to displace a large portion of the room when he enters and sits in the witness chair. He is six foot six, with shoulders as broad as a buffalo's. He is at least three times as big as Kosik, who jokingly asks if Powell was with the Pittsburgh Steelers. As an experienced trial lawyer,

Powell is courtroom savvy, with a basso profundo voice, and he looks directly at the jury when he testifies. Under questioning from Zubrod, Powell recalls a meeting with Ciavarella and Conahan in the autumn of 2003 when he says he first learned that the judges also expected *him*, not just Mericle, to pay them.

"I was called to a meeting at Judge Ciavarella's chambers. Judge Conahan was there. And I was told specifically by Judge Ciavarella how well he thought the PA Child Care facility was doing financially and that it was now time for me to give him and Mike Conahan money. And I said, 'Are you telling me that you guys blew through a million bucks already?' And they both kind of laughed and said, 'You guys are doing very, very well.' Specifically, Judge Ciavarella had on a piece of paper some numbers written down on an account and said, 'I know what's going on up there, I know what's happening, I want a part of it.' "

"Do you know what the numbers represented?"

"It represented his calculation of how many kids had been sent there."

"Sent by whom?"

"By him and by others, other counties. So it was a rough calculation of approximately how many kids we had at the facility on a daily basis, what our basic costs would be, and how much was left over."

Powell says he protested that Ciavarella's statistics were misleading because they failed to take into account large start-up costs associated with the new center. "Ciavarella was very adamant. He said he didn't care, 'I know what's going on and I want to get paid.' " According to Powell, Conahan was less adamant, but he too insisted that Powell pay them money.

Several times during Powell's account of the meeting,

Ciavarella, seated across the courtroom at the defense table, folds his arms, exhales in disgust, and shakes his head negatively.

Powell describes how he paid the two judges $590,000 that was disguised as rental fees for the Florida condo owned by Barbara Conahan and Cindy Ciavarella. He says he only actually used the facility on two occasions, both in July, because when he asked for it during the winter it was never available. When Zubrod points out that the monthly checks often seemed to be paying for the same things with overlapping months, Powell explains: "There's only so much you can write to make things up, and now it looks foolish." He says part of this money was masked as rental for a boat slip that the judges didn't even own: "This had nothing to do with my boat. They didn't have a slip. I had to pay a real marina fee to keep my boat there. This was just another way to conceal the payments."

Courtroom technology is easing the prosecutors' task of explaining complicated financial transactions to the jury. Gone are the days when attorneys would have to hand documents to jurors, who would then pass it around to each other. Here, the exhibits—checks, contracts, charts, and even handwritten notes—appear on monitors positioned between each pair of jurors. There are identical monitors at the prosecution and defense tables, and larger monitors on either side of the spectator gallery. On the other end of the technology scale, Laurene Transue has been taking extensive handwritten notes, scribbling furiously, filling notebooks with handwriting like unlaced shoes. She wants to get it all down. She doesn't want to miss a word.

Day Four

As Powell returns to the witness chair, the morning sun angles through the window in a way that illuminates Ciavarella's face at the defense table. Zubrod presses Powell on why he paid the phony condo rentals to the two judges: "What was the obligation? Why did you have to pay them now? What was the quid pro quo?"

"It was extortion, it was a kickback. They wanted money because they said, 'Look, you're in this business, we helped you get into it, you're making a lot of money, you're going to give us some.' It's what it was, pure and simple. Mr. Zubrod, I wasn't paying them for any services rendered, I was paying them because they demanded it in their position of authority and I was going to do it. They weren't helping me run the business, they weren't helping me in my law practice, they weren't taking the calls, putting up with the press that was related to the running of the facility, it was pure and simple. They thought we were making money, they thought they were entitled to it because of their position of power and authority, and they wanted it. They had gotten used to, Mr. Zubrod, a lifestyle of two and a half million dollars by this time. I don't know what their salaries exactly for judges were, but at $120,000 or whatever they were making, when you start to add two and a half million dollars to somebody's appetite, the lion was out of the cage and I was the bait."

Zubrod asks Powell about Ruzzo's comment in the defense opening that Powell was too big physically to be intimidated by Ciavarella and Conahan. "These were the two most powerful men in Luzerne County," Powell scoffs. "They ran the show. I could have been Shaq [basketball player Shaquille O'Neal] and it wouldn't have mattered. They knew politicians, and they knew mobsters, and they flaunted their relationships with both of them."

Powell describes trying to escape from the judges and their demands for more money with trips to Costa Rica and Italy. When they persisted, he decided to cooperate with federal authorities and wear a wire to a meeting with Ciavarella and Conahan. After a morning break, the prosecutors play the tape of the July 2008 conversation in the model for a townhouse complex called The Sanctuary. Zubrod frequently stops the tape to allow Powell to explain the meanings of certain statements. The tape records the trio devising the scheme they will use to defend themselves against the federal grand jury investigation of the PA Child Care and Western PA Child Care juvenile detention centers. They will discredit Mericle and Jill Moran, Powell's law partner who saw him stuffing cash into Federal Express boxes and then delivered them to Conahan. When Powell warns that Moran is "off the fucking reservation," Conahan says he will simply deny that she ever brought him the boxes. "The problem Jill has is she never gave me anything. If anything was given to her, she has it," he says. They will stick with the tale that Powell's payments were to rent the condo. "Listen," says Conahan on the tape, "You paid me rent for my condo. You didn't pay me to shut the juvenile detention center down or fix cases."

Flora, wearing a greenish tie that disagrees vehemently with his blue sport coat, begins his cross-examination of Powell by challenging the statement that Conahan and Ciavarella were the two most powerful public figures in Luzerne County. He runs through a list of offices—district attorney, county commissioner, State Police, state attorney general—and each time Powell responds that the judges were more powerful to him than these individuals. Finally, Flora gestures toward Zubrod and asks, "Is it your testimony, sir, that they were more powerful than the prosecutor sitting here at this table?"

"No, he's the only guy that scared them," Powell shoots back.

In this exchange, Flora is clearly the second-best attorney. He often frames a question that contains a statement and then asks, "Is that not correct?" Powell responds that it is not correct and then amends the statement. Flora appears to be off balance, and his questions ramble and zigzag. At one point, Powell becomes hoarse and appears tired. He mistakenly talks about "putting the box into the cash." But then he rallies. When Flora asks Powell why he stayed at the condo if he was being extorted by the judges, he answers as though explaining something obvious to a child: "That was part of the ruse here. If I didn't use the condo and pay $590,000 it would have made no sense, and I would have put myself in that pickle. There was other places I would have preferred to have been than Florida in July, but to write those checks and say rent, rent, rent and not use the condo would have been doubly foolish on my part. It was foolish to do it, it would have been more stupid not to use it to say that I was there."

The cross-examination ends abruptly after one hour and twenty minutes. When Powell is excused by Kosik, he steps from the witness stand and stalks past the jury, out of the courtroom, looking like a man who has just lost his law license, is burdened with millions of dollars in debts, and faces jail for failing to report a felony and abetting tax evasion.

The jurors, several of them sipping bottled water, are amused when FBI agent James Glenn recounts how he and a colleague were in a surveillance van that was spotted by Ciavarella during the taped conversation at the model unit. "We could actually hear him approaching, the footsteps, closer, closer to the van, grasping the handle of the front passenger door trying to get in. Moving around the van to the back door, trying to get in, the side door, to the front door, but he was unsuccessful. He returned to the area where Michael Conahan and Robert Powell were situated."

Patrick Owens, the former treasurer of Powell's law firm, recounts writing and cashing sixteen separate checks, each for less than $10,000 to avoid scrutiny by the Internal Revenue Service, to come up with the $143,500 that Powell gave to the judges in 2006. According to Owens, Powell was normally very relaxed and easygoing around the office. "But during this time frame, he just became very short-tempered, demanding. He was acting paranoid. We had the building swept for listening devices at one point."

That set the stage for the day's final witness—Jill A. Moran, Powell's former law partner who transported the cash payments in Federal Express boxes to Conahan. She is a study in black—high-heeled black boots, black skirt, black top, black blazer, jet black hair. Moran says she didn't realize what the boxes contained in the first two deliveries. But, her voice taut with melodrama, she depicts a scene in Powell's private washroom before the third and final delivery: "Bob's office has all windows around it, and the bathroom does not have any windows in it. He summoned me into the bathroom, and at that point, he began stuffing the FedEx box with banded bunches of money."

"This was cash he was stuffing in this box?"

"Yes."

"What was Bob's demeanor when he was doing this?"

"He was very agitated, he was mumbling, he was, you know, saying certain things to me as he was putting the money in the boxes."

"What did Bob say?"

"He made a comment, just mumbling as he was putting them

in, just, Greedy, and then some expletives after that, and then he just kept saying, This is the last one, if anyone asks you, this is the last one."

"What did he do with the box, after it was all done being filled with cash?"

"He sealed the box and he gave it to me, and he again told me to call Mike Conahan and to give the box to Mike Conahan."

"Did you do that?"

"I did."

Day Five

The day begins with a pretrial lightning bolt. The *Citizens' Voice*, citing "an attorney familiar with the prosecution case," reports that the feds will not call Conahan to testify. The source says Conahan is considered "too big a liability" as a witness. In pleading guilty to a racketeering charge in July 2010, Conahan was not required to agree to testify against Ciavarella, but Zubrod had said earlier that Conahan was willing to testify. Neither Zubrod nor Conahan's attorney will comment. Laurene Transue is uneasy at the news.

All week long, Flora has been increasingly dismayed by Kosik's rulings, and the issue boils over when the defense attorney, as part of his ongoing attempt to discredit the idea that Powell was vulnerable as the judges' extortion target, tries to question Moran about Powell's political connections. Kosik leans forward. "Excuse me. What's this got to do with this case? What's this got to do with her direct examination?"

Flora, a rosy spread of indignation flooding his face: "Your Honor, the Government has portrayed Robert Powell as a weak individual who had no one to turn to when this alleged extortion was taking place. We have every right to challenge this."

"You certainly have. But all she said was that there was a falling-out and he was very upset. That does not open the door for what you're pursuing."

"Judge, I will note for the record that this is about the second or third time when you've raised objections to my question on your own, without any objection by the Government."

"You are an experienced defense counsel. Are you suggesting that a judge cannot intervene, if the evidence is not being presented according to the rules, even though there's no objection to it?"

"Yes, I am."

Kosik shoots Flora a look that could peel paint off a battleship: "I have a right to move this trial, whether the Government objects or not, and you don't have a right to waste time in this trial, unless you're pursuing an appropriate subject under the rules."

"In light of this Court's remarks to me, Your Honor, I move for a mistrial at this point."

"Your motion is denied." Kosik closes the subject and sits on the lid.

Three attorneys who had appeared before Ciavarella in cases involving Powell or Mericle testify they were never advised of the financial relationship between the judge and the two men. They say if they had known of the connection, they would have asked Ciavarella to withdraw from hearing their cases. The day and the week end with testimony from two accountants and a bookkeeper who worked for Conahan and Ciavarella. Using the courtroom monitors, the prosecutors track the various payments involved in the money-laundering scheme.

Day Six

It's Valentine's Day, and five of the six women jurors appear in bright red tops. Kosik peers at them from the bench as they walk in, then surveys the rest of the courtroom and says, "Only the jury has dressed in the spirit of Valentine's Day."

The next-to-last prosecution witness is Brian Berntson, a money-laundering expert from the Internal Revenue Service. Zubrod poses "a hypothetical question"—which is in fact the scheme used by Ciavarella, Conahan, Mericle, and Powell— and asks, "Would that be consistent with money-laundering?" Berntson says it would, but on cross-examination from Ruzzo he agrees that if the payments were legal—as the defense claims—it would not be money laundering. The twenty-fourth and final prosecution witness is another IRS agent, Ray Eppley, who testifies that between 2003 and 2006 Mark and Cindy Ciavarella under-reported their income by some $720,000 and should have paid an additional $231,000. Zubrod carefully takes Eppley through the four federal tax returns and asks each time if they were signed by the Ciavarellas "under penalty of perjury." Each time Eppley says they were. Throughout most of the morning, Ciavarella has been looking toward the ceiling, boredom baked on his face, eyebrows arched in semipermanent superciliousness. Laurene Transue keeps looking at him with annoyance. "Are you kidding me?" she murmurs to no one in particular. "You're on trial here. You're accused of horrible crimes."

At 10:44 p.m., Zubrod says, "Your Honor, at this time the United States rests." Transue is aghast. What about Hillary? What about all the kids? They were supposed to be the focus of this whole proceeding. They have not even been mentioned!

This trial has been about a judge on the take, not about children being sent away when it was not in their best interest nor in the best interest of the entire community. Where was the outrage? She had sat here for six days, waiting for validation of the injustices committed by Ciavarella and Conahan in pursuit of their own personal enrichment. What about all the probation officers and their boss, Sandra Brulo. Why weren't they called to testify? This was called the "kids-for-cash" scandal, but nothing has been said about Ciavarella filling a private juvenile detention center by jailing kids on minor charges, denying their right to counsel, and pressuring probation officers to recommend harsh punishments. During a recess, she tells the *Citizens' Voice*, "I've been at this trial every day, and I knew that the main focus was not going to be on the children, but what I'm surprised at right now is that it seems like it has been totally excluded from the trial. That makes me feel very emotional." Zubrod's boss, U.S. Attorney Peter J. Smith, who has attended the trial, declines to explain the prosecution's strategy.

The defense begins with three of Ciavarella's family members—Brian Stahl, his son-in-law; Nicole Oravic, his daughter, and Marco Ciavarella, his son. They all attempt to discredit Powell's critical assertion that he was extorted by the judges. Stahl says the relationship between Powell and his father-in-law was always "very cordial." Oravic testifies that she worked for Powell's law firm during part of the alleged extortion and Powell was always very complimentary about her father: "The way he spoke about my dad was with the utmost admiration and respect." Son Marco remembers that the two men were neighbors and "very friendly," often sharing drinks and cigars at the Ciavarellas' home. During a recess, Ciavarella is asked about his son's name. He warms to the question and becomes a stand-up comic: "While he was being conceived, Cindy kept saying, 'Oh, Mark! Oh, Mark,' and we got it backwards." Laurene passes by right at the punch line and creases her brow in disapproval.

The day's last witness is a surprise—Gina Carrelli, a Hazleton restaurateur with political connections, who has been subpoenaed by Flora. She is clearly a reluctant witness. Swaying nervously in the chair, she tells the jury that she witnessed Powell giving two envelopes of cash to a prominent state official at the Hazleton airport in the fall of 2006. She declines to name the official. In his cross-examination, Consiglio starts a question with, "So you claim." Carrelli snaps back at him, "Excuse me. I don't claim anything. I'm here to tell the truth. It's a fact, not a claim."

It's been a good beginning for the defense. If any of the jurors thought Powell left the courtroom last week with a halo, it's no longer there.

Day Seven

Ruzzo stands, buttons his jacket, and clears this throat. "Your Honor, we call Mark Ciavarella." His voice is limp, without intonation, as though he is reciting the alphabet. As the defendant walks to the witness chair, his wife Cindy replaces him at the defense table. After Ciavarella swears to tell the whole truth, Ruzzo says, "Mr. Ciavarella, I will ask you to state your name."

"Good morning." Ciavarella says looking directly at the jurors, launching a smile and keeping it afloat. "My name is Mark Ciavarella. I am sixty-one years old, former judge of Luzerne County Court of Common Pleas."

Ruzzo interjects: "And I will take the liberty of calling you

Mark. I think I earned that privilege over the last thirty, thirty-five years."

Ciavarella gives Ruzzo a one-ha laugh, smiles faintly, and nods his head in agreement. "Absolutely."

"Tell us about your family background so the jury will get a picture of you."

"Sure. I was born in the east end section of Wilkes-Barre, predominantly Irish section of town. I lived on a little street called Hillard Street. To show you how Irish it was, nineteen O'Brien kids were living on that street. The only way that I think my father was allowed in the neighborhood was—obviously his last name is Ciavarella—was if my mother was Irish and my grandfather owned the home my father bought." In a well-rehearsed recitation, Ciavarella rifles through the closets and drawers of his childhood memories. "It was a great neighborhood to grow up in, just a wonderful place to be raised. Everybody was very close. Every door was open in the neighborhood. You were allowed to go in and out of people's houses. Everybody looked out for everybody." He looks at the jury wistfully. "My dad, he was a—worked in Stegmeier Brewery. He worked at Stegmeier's from roughly 1946 until they closed in 1973. After Stegmeier's closed, he went to work for the street department." Ciavarella is turned in his chair so he faces the jury directly. Often his eyes go wide with his recollections. "We lived in a little house, three rooms down, three rooms up and bathroom on the second floor. I was the middle child. I had an older sister and younger sister." He tries to blink sincerity into his words.

Ciavarella tells the jury about his college and law school days, his marriage, his children and grandchildren. When Ruzzo asks him what he's been doing since he stepped down as judge two years ago, he says he first served as a babysitter for his granddaughter while getting his commercial driver's license. He took a job driving a truck in northern Pennsylvania, but this didn't work out because the owner was reluctant to entrust him with an expensive vehicle. "Then I came back obviously without a job. And a friend called me and asked me if I wanted to paint apartments. I gladly said yes. I went to an apartment building he owned. So for about three or four weeks, I painted apartments and also delivered flowers. I used to get in maybe twenty-five to thirty hours a week." Several jurors foreheads have sympathy lines, and Ciavarella seems encouraged and continues his riches-to-rags story. "And eventually a friend of mine called me and asked me if I would be interested in a job that paid a little more and would give me more hours. That was with a cleaning company. I said, yes, I will do anything, didn't matter to me. I just wanted a job, wanted to be able to provide for me and my wife. And I went to the cleaning company. I began working there. I stripped floors, waxed floors, cleaning offices, cleaned bathrooms, run vacuum cleaners, dust, mop, whatever the company needed, that's what I did. And I would get in approximately forty hours a week, which is good. And I was able to provide a little bit for me and Cindy to help pay the bills."

Ciavarella says that soon after he became juvenile court judge, he visited the existing juvenile detention facility on River Street. "When I walked through the front door, the first thing that I noticed was that the place absolutely reeked. There was no ventilation. The building was old. It was decrepit. And the probation officers—their offices were the old cells. It used to be a women's jail facility. And the probation officers were meeting with parents, children and anybody else that they had to meet with in an old jail cell. When I walked through the facility back into the kitchen area, the kitchen area consisted of a kitchen table that we would have in our kitchen. It had a stove with four burners, an oven. And lunch that day was hot dogs and beans. They took me on a tour of the facility. The facility was in deplorable condition." Ciavarella's eyebrows descend and nearly unite in disgust. "Ventilation was terrible. The place needed to be painted. The plumbing wasn't adequate. The place had two showers. The place had three toilets. It just shocked me as to how bad this place really was. When I walked out of that building on that day, the only thing I can think of was how I would feel if my kids—one of my kids had to be placed into that facility. And because of that feeling, I decided right then and there that these children—these children needed a better place to be housed. They needed a better place to be detained. It just wasn't a type of facility that we should be putting children in."

But Ciavarella laments that he got nowhere in his attempts to persuade county officials to build a new facility, and finally he enlisted the help of Conahan to find private sources to build a for-profit center. He is animated in his earnestness and outrage, looking directly at the jurors, placing his right hand over his heart, jabbing with his finger for emphasis. He introduces his justifications with phrases like "I truly" and "Just so the record is clear." Throughout most of his ninety-minute direct testimony with Ruzzo, Ciavarella appears confident, sometimes even cocksure. A few attempts at lightheartedness fail. He tells the jury that he and his wife disagreed on a Florida condo. "I wanted to be on a golf course. Cindy wanted to be on the water. So the joke was that we'll get a place on a water hazard on a golf course." His mouth crevices into a chuckle, but the jury sits stonily, faces empty of sympathy and judgment. He admits filing false tax returns, and he says he should have recused himself from hearing cases involving Powell and Mericle. He looks to his wife at the defense table, and his children in the first row of the spectator's area and says, "The thing that bothers me is not how it hurt me, but how it hurt my family." Several times Ciavarella shrugs as though to say he can't believe he's here and can't understand why.

Ciavarella's aplomb quickly vanishes under cross-examination from Assistant U.S. Attorney William Houser who, unlike any previous interrogators, has a microphone clipped to his red-and-black striped tie that allows him to move freely about the courtroom rather than stand at the podium. A fifty-two-year-old career prosecutor, Houser is angular, marathon-lean, as he ranges back and forth from the jury box to the prosecution table to the witness. He keeps his hands clasped behind his back, and sometimes asks a question with his back to Ciavarella, then whirls and waits for an answer, alert as an exclamation point. Ciavarella now is avoiding eye contact with the jury. Whenever Houser wants to call the jurors' attention to a response, he pauses, walks over to the prosecutors' table, and sips from a bottle of spring water.

Ciavarella says when Mericle offered him the first finder's fee of $997,600, he assumed it was perfectly legal: "I never considered the money Rob Mericle paid to me was illegal. Never in my wildest dreams did I consider that money to be a kickback."

Houser pauses for dramatic effect, then asks, "Who told you that was legal money?"

"Rob Mericle."

"Anybody else?"

"No."

Houser looks to the ceiling and reminds the jury that Mericle is not an attorney and, indeed, Ciavarella had been Mericle's lawyer. "When did you start to turn to Rob Mericle to give you legal advice?" Houser asks. Ciavarella licks his lips and answers lamely, but the question itself is devastating to the defense. Houser is sipping his spring water.

Using charts, Houser runs through the intricate money-laundering web the two judges used to conceal the payments they received from Mericle and Powell. The questions come in crisp bites. "Every penny of that money, you and Michael Conahan took steps to conceal," Houser says, facing Ciavarella directly, "but you thought it was legal money?" Ciavarella says he did and reiterates his insistence that he hid the payments and did not report them on his income tax returns as a way of avoiding public embarrassment rather than to conceal a crime: "I just wanted to avoid all this. How'd I do?" He spreads his hands and looks around in mock irony. There's not a trace of a smile in the jury box, and juror no. 6 fixes Ciavarella in the crosshairs of her glare.

As a way of suggesting one reason that the former judge chose not to question the legality of the finder's fee, Houser introduces exhibits of bank account and credit card statements showing that the Ciavarellas were massively in debt just before getting the money from Mericle. When the finder's fee money started flowing in 2003, Ciavarella immediately used $310,000 of it to pay off debts, mostly credit cards. Much of the credit card debt involved cash advances. The witness, as well as his wife at the defense table, are uneasy and fidgeting. Houser notes that at the end of 2003, Ciavarella had only about $4,000 in the bank. Ciavarella, whose annual judicial salary was $158,000, concedes that he hadn't been "living within my means."

And just in case the jury missed his point, when Ruzzo objects and asks Kosik why the financial information is relevant, Houser responds, "It shows motive for the crime, Judge." Houser sips.

Houser points out that Powell paid some $70,000 for "rent" on the judges' Florida condo while it was still a shell without fixtures or furnishings and could not be used, and then he asks, "Would you consider that a sweetheart deal?" Ciavarella testifies he did not. He also denies that he ever received any of the $143,500 in cash that Jill Moran delivered to Conahan in Federal Express boxes in 2006. Thereupon Houser produces a receipt showing that Ciavarella had paid $27,000 in cash for a new Audi sedan not long after Moran handed the cash to Conahan. This leads Ciavarella to admit to a crime he isn't even on trial for by saying he had other sources of ready cash at this time, including $20,000 he had raised while running for reelection as judge in 2005. State law forbids the use of campaign money for personal expenses.

Houser grills the defendant for about three hours. Leaving the courthouse at the end of the day, Ciavarella is asked by a television reporter about his admissions on the witness stand. "You admit to what you did and fight like hell what you didn't do," he snaps.

Day Eight

Kosik, his face as stern as a book of rules, leans down and tells Zubrod and Flora to limit their closings to one hour. They nod in agreement. Each will take only forty-five minutes. Zubrod's outfit is a careful orchestration of red (tie), white (shirt), and blue (suit). The part in his hair is as precise as the crease in his trousers. He stands, straight as a British brigadier, at the lectern placed right in front of the jury: "I said during the opening statements that this is an important case. It is important to Mr. Ciavarella." Zubrod turns and looks at the defense table. Once again the morning sun has placed a rhomboid of light on Ciavarella's face. Zubrod's voice rises. "He's been accused of some of the worst acts that could ever be laid at the door of a public official who is a judge. He stands accused of betraying the trust by the very people who elected him. It is charged that he sold himself and used his high office as a judge for personal gain. It is charged that he took money through bribes, kickbacks, rewards, and extortion for doing his job as a judge.

"And in the process, as I mentioned to you in our first statement when I appeared before you a week and a half ago, that he hid that money, he turned his office into a cash cow, into a money-making machine, and he then hid that money to avoid public and law enforcement scrutiny. It is important for Mr. Ciavarella to have his day in court. I told you in the opening statements that it's also important to the citizens of Luzerne County and the Commonwealth of Pennsylvania because their lives and the lives of their children should only be put in the hands of public officials who have honor and integrity as their lodestar, who wouldn't think of taking a bribe or extortion or harming one of their own children. I told you that it was important to the victims in this case, particularly the victims that did not appear today but who appeared before Judge Ciavarella when he sat as juvenile court judge and used his pawns and schemes to enrich himself." Laurene Transue arches two eyebrows that say, *Finally, somebody mentioned the kids.*

Several jurors tilt their heads attentively, and Zubrod warms to his task. "Let's look at a series of remarkable coincidences that surrounded Mark Ciavarella in this case. From the time Mark Ciavarella became a judge, became the juvenile court judge in 1996, he complained to anyone who would listen about the deplorable condition of the Luzerne County Youth Detention Center. He complained to the commissioners. He said it was unfit for children. We heard in court that it was dangerous to put children in there. Using the authority of his office, he set in motion the movement to build a new youth detention center.

"A juvenile court judge has the absolute power to stop sending children to the county detention center, to send them instead to any contract facility that he chose. But he didn't do a thing until January of 2003. Why? By July 2001 Robert Mericle had told Mark Ciavarella he had a whopping payday coming as a finder's fee as a reward for getting the contract for building PA Child Care. Mark Ciavarella immediately went over to Michael Conahan and offered to split the money with him. Why? Because Mark Ciavarella needed the power and authority of the president judge to force the closure of the county-run facility."

Zubrod says that while Robert Mericle voluntarily paid the $2,086,000 to the judges, Robert Powell's $733,500 in payments was extorted: "It was a demand. Powell was told explicitly if he didn't make the payments he wouldn't get the children sent to PA Child Care." He sneaks a quick glance at this watch and then decides to conclude. "When I began this trial, I told you that Mark Ciavarella appears before you cloaked in the presumption of innocence, that he doesn't have to prove a thing to you, that the burden is at all times upon the United States to prove every element beyond a reasonable doubt. Well, that cloak has been removed. That presumption is gone."

Flora, by contrast, is a study in disheveled sartorial nonchalance. Seizing on the prosecution's unexplained failure to call Conahan to the witness stand, he introduces a conspiracy theory to strengthen Ciavarella's claim that he was unaware of the $143,500 that was handed to Conahan in Federal Express boxes: "If there was something going on, I suggest to you it was a back-room deal going on between Robert Powell and Michael Conahan. Mark Ciavarella had no idea."

Calling his client "a lowly judge in one Pennsylvania county," Flora dismisses as "ludicrous" the prosecution's claim that Powell was the target of continued extortion by the judges: "I suggest he can't be extorted. They want you to believe that Robert Powell is this meek man who couldn't stand up to anybody. He was no man to be extorted under any circumstance. Robert Powell wants you to believe that Mark Ciavarella or Mike Conahan had the ability simply to pick up the phone and call somebody and all of a sudden he would just lose all this business, all these contracts would be canceled. He would be put out of business? That makes no sense under any circumstance." Flora notes testimony of a warm relationship between Ciavarella, Powell, and Conahan. "He gives graduation presents to Mark Ciavarella's children while he's being extorted? It makes no sense."

Flora, widening his eyes to feign amazement that anyone could ever believe otherwise, says Mericle's payments were legitimate business transactions rather than kickbacks. He says Ciavarella's actions in promoting the construction of PA Child Care were not done in his official capacity as judge. "When someone is elected a judge, that doesn't mean they're a judge twenty-four hours a day, that they don't have a private life, that they can't refer someone for a job.

"When he was elected in 1995, he had one motivation, one goal, one dream, and that motivation, goal, and dream wasn't dictated at that time by Robert Mericle or Robert Powell. They weren't even heard of at that point. And that was to argue publicly for the development of a new juvenile detention facility to be owned by the county. That's what he wanted. There was no conspiracy at that point. There was no claims of finder's fees. None of that existed back then, and that is what he continually argued for and got nowhere."

Flora reminds the jury of testimony that the existing juvenile detention facility was rodent-infested. Indeed, Flora reasoned, far from victimizing the children who appeared before him in his courtroom, Ciavarella was acting in their best interests: "That request was pure. That request was innocent. There was no evil motive or intent in that purpose whatsoever." Flora bristles at the injustice. Laurene Transue's face balls up like a fist.

Kosik's charge to the jury is a two-and-a-half-hour monotonous monologue about burdens of proof. It covers eighty-six pages, and there are legal distinctions for each of the thirty-nine counts. About halfway through it, he interrupts himself with a coughing spasm that seems to rattle the windows. He turns to jurors apologetically and manages to wheeze, "I hope I make it." The jury receives the case about 2:45 p.m. Kosik instructs them to begin by choosing a foreperson and organizing the documents they will need for their deliberations. Thirty minutes later, they tell Kosik they are organized and want to adjourn for the day. Kosik tells them to return at 8:30 tomorrow morning.

There is a lone protester pacing the sidewalk around the federal building who identifies himself as Bill Clark. He is dressed as Chewbacca, the character in the *Star Wars* movies, and he's carrying a handwritten sign: "Send Them on a Jet to Planet Jupiter Prison. I'm the Boss—Real Chewy Justice." Clark says the costume is merely intended to attract attention: "If you just walk up and down in regular clothes, nobody cares." He says he cannot forget the day several years ago that Ciavarella sentenced his sixteen-year-old son to six months in juvenile detention for a minor offense: "I was there when they had the kids with the orange jumpsuits and the belt, the hook, the cuffs, and the shackles, and he sent them right away. And I asked, 'What's going on here?' and he told me I can't talk. So now I'm talking."

Day Nine

The jury deliberates all day without a verdict. Ciavarella, his wife, and his family members spend part of the time in a witness waiting room just off the courtroom. But frequently he emerges and paces up and down the corridor that overlooks a glass-and-steel atrium connecting the original 1931 courthouse building to a 1999 annex. Occasionally he stops, leans over the railing, looks down to the lobby below while chatting with local reporters. "I'm just trying to stay calm and keep the butterflies out," he tells them. Laurene Transue is also edgy: "I feel like a little kid on a long car ride. Are we there yet? Are we there yet?" About 4 p.m., Ciavarella leaves for the day through the front door, and as his transition lenses darken in their steel frames, he stops to talk to reporters. Someone asks Cindy Ciavarella how she's doing. "I'm doing OK. Holding up. Supporting my husband. It's the worst nightmare that you can ever imagine. It's horrible for your family. I don't wish it on anybody, that's for sure." The words knife through the air to Laurene Transue. She starts to speak, then decides not to and walks away. "It's a nightmare for her!" she fumes. "Her husband gets to come home every night. He doesn't go off to jail in handcuffs. Not yet." But Cindy Ciavarella's lament is carried on the evening news, and one of the viewers is Sandy Fonzo, who blames Ciavarella's incarceration of her son as a juvenile for depression that eventually led to his suicide. That night, she can't sleep for the rage.

Day Ten

Back in Wilkes-Barre, fifteen miles southwest of Scranton, the Circles on the Square delicatessen is offering a menu of Ciavarella-inspired sandwich specials that includes "Judging the Judges" (rosemary ham served on a hot wrap with melted provolone), "Fudging Ethical Bounds" (turkey breast on pumpernickel with Cheddar cheese), and "The Perp Wore Prada" (spiced, hot chicken breast with melted Jarlsberg cheese). The morning's *Times-Leader* carries a story headlined, "Mayor's Son Gets Teacher's Position." It's buried on page three. Nothing new here.

The jury announces about 1:30 p.m. that it has reached a verdict. Within minutes the courtroom is filled with media people, spectators, and federal workers from other offices in the building. Ciavarella hugs his wife and walks to the defense table. The six men and six women of the jury take their seats. The room crackles with tension as the foreman hands the verdict slip to a clerk, who passes it up to Kosik. The judge licks his thumb as he pages through the document.

Finally, the clerk asks, "Ladies and gentlemen of the jury, have you reached a verdict?"

"Yes, we have," replies the foreman.

"In the United States District Court for the Middle District of Pennsylvania. The United States of America v. Mark A. Ciavarella Jr. Criminal number 09-272. Verdict?"

"We, the jury, make the following findings in the above captioned matter: Count 1. Racketeering. On the charge of conducting and participating in the conduct of the affairs of an enterprise, through a pattern of racketeering activity, in violation of U.S. Code, we find the Defendant Mark A. Ciavarella Jr., guilty."

Ciavarella sits at the defense table, hands clasped in front of him on the defense table, face empty of emotion.

It's a mixed verdict, and it takes nearly thirty minutes to complete the recitation. The jurors believed Mericle, but they did not believe Powell. They find Ciavarella guilty of multiple counts of racketeering, money laundering, conspiracy, and tax evasion for accepting the initial finder's fee of $997,600 from Mericle. But they acquit him of bribery, extortion, and racketeering charges connected to Powell's payments of $733,500 to the two former judges. The box score is that Ciavarella is guilty on twelve counts, not guilty on twenty-seven counts.

Houser asks Kosik to order Ciavarella into immediate detention: "This jury's verdict demonstrates that Mr. Ciavarella is not a man of his word. Mr. Ciavarella has little to lose at this point by leaving, by fleeing, that his word to appear does not give rise to confidence on the part of the Government that he will appear. An ankle bracelet and home detention are not sufficient. Flight is as easy as cutting off the ankle bracelet and going."

Ruzzo counters: "While Mr. Houser says Mr. Ciavarella has nothing to lose, I want you to take a look right there in that first row. He has daughters, his son was here, his son is in law school, his son-in-law, his family and friends have been here supporting him, Your Honor. This man would rather go on the gurney and get injected than leave his family."

After fifteen minutes of wrangling, Kosik rules: "There's no question that these are serious offenses. The attitude of the public has been apparent to all of us, whether we are associated with this case or just the ordinary citizen out on the street. But there's a time for everything, and in this case, in light of the fact that this defendant has complied with all of the rules, we feel that there's no reason to believe that he would flee, and to ensure that, in addition to the conditions that have been placed on him at this time, as well as the unsecured bail, we put the condition that he will be placed in the custody of his pregnant daughter. To that extent, he can leave."

On the courthouse steps, Flora declares victory: "The jury rejected ninety-five percent of the government's case. The government really got hurt today on this entire case, and it stands for the proposition of what Mark Ciavarella said all along was true: he never took a kickback, he never took a bribe, and he never extorted Robert Powell. This is a major victory for Mark Ciavarella. This was not a cash-for-kids case, and we hope somebody starts getting the message."

His words ignite simmering rage in Sandy Fonzo, the mother of Edward, who committed suicide after a long history of criminal activity that began when he was sent away by Ciavarella on a drug paraphernalia charge at the age of seventeen. Pushing her way through the crowd, her forehead knotted in fury, Fonzo reaches Ciavarella, who is facing the other way: "Do you remember me? Do you remember my son? He was an all-star wrestler and he's gone. He shot himself in the heart." A sorrowful huskiness creeps into her voice. "You scumbag. You ruined my fucking life!" Ciavarella turns to face her, but already federal marshals are escorting her away. "He was my son. I don't have kids now. I don't have anything. I'm not a mother. I'm not anything." Her eyes overflow, and her bottom lip quivers.

Ciavarella's face is frozen into a mask of indifference: "I don't know that lady. I don't know what the facts and circumstances are concerning her son." There is an I-don't-give-a-shit shrug in his voice. Minutes later, Ciavarella tells reporters he feels vindicated by the verdict: "I absolutely never took a dime to send a kid anywhere. If that was the case that would have been in this trial. You don't think the government would have put me on trial for that if that was the case? Never happened. Never, ever happened. This case was about extortions and kickbacks. That's what this case was about, not kids for cash."

Almost simultaneously, U.S. Attorney Peter J. Smith is deriding the claims of a victory for Ciavarella: "The defendant, and this should be noted by everyone, has been found guilty of racketeering, one of the most serious offenses in the criminal code, originally intended to be aimed at thugs and street criminals. It is no small thing, no right thing, for any public official at any level of the government to stand convicted by a jury of the crime of racketeering. I find it interesting that a man just convicted of racketeering is claiming any sort of victory out there today. I wonder what he would consider a defeat."

Laurene Transue is nauseated by the fact that Ciavarella was allowed to leave the courtroom. "Do you understand how vastly different this is from what my daughter experienced?" she asks a TV journalist. "They put the handcuffs on my daughter before she left the courtroom. Boom! She disappeared. All I asked for was please, could I give her a hug. But no, they threatened to arrest me or put me in a psych ward." She is also dismayed at the prosecution's scanty presentation of how Ciavarella violated the rights of children: "Even if they could find him guilty of every single count, it still wouldn't answer to what happened to these kids. It still wouldn't be him saying, 'I abused the children of Luzerne County.' It's not about for how long he's going to jail; it's about recognition of how he abused our children."

Transue tells the *Times-Leader*, "I knew the main focus was not going to be the children, but it seems like they totally excluded them. That makes me feel very emotional." At home that night, she realizes that her dream of seeing Ciavarella being hauled off in handcuffs, as Hillary had been, was not a realistic one. Most courtrooms don't operate like that. At the insistence of her husband, they went out to dinner to celebrate. But they came home early because she didn't feel there was anything to celebrate.

Another disgruntled onlooker is Erica Michaliga, whose son spent nearly five years in juvenile facilities after a run-in with Ciavarella when he was thirteen years old. As she watches Ciavarella walk away from the courthouse, she tells Terrie Morgan-Besecker she was stunned when the federal prosecutors failed to call a single one of Ciavarella's child-victims: "Not only is this kids for cash, this is kids forgotten."

But the prosecutors made a simple strategic decision: Rather than convolute an already convoluted case with evidence of their indictment's claim that Ciavarella routinely sent kids to PA Child Care for minor offenses because of the kickbacks, they would keep it simple by focusing on the kickbacks. But money-laundering is a hard sell for any prosecutor. It's all smoke and mirrors, and lacks a human dimension. Interviews with jurors in ensuing weeks showed that they were perplexed by the government's failure to call Conahan as a witness. Conahan's absence was so deep it became a presence over the two weeks of the trial. Smith would say only that the decisions about which witnesses to bring before the jury were based on "very good legal and evidentiary reasons." All of the jurors came from outside Luzerne County, and at least two of them said they were unaware of the kids-for-cash aspect of the case until they saw post-trial news coverage.

Sentencing

The days and weeks and months passed. Winter released its grip on northeastern Pennsylvania, and bare limbs silver plated with freezing rain gave way to the slow, green fireworks of spring. Summer came early with humid, syrupy air. The temperature was near 100 degrees in Scranton on July 21 when a one-page order came down under Kosik's signature, consisting of three energetic, incomprehensible loopings of black ink. "USA v. Mark A. Ciavarella. Criminal 09-272. The above case is listed for sentencing on Thursday, August 11, 2011, at 9:00 A.M."

Flora, Ruzzo, and the prosecutors had sparred for months over an appropriate sentence. The stakes were high since the U.S. Probation Office determined that Ciavarella qualified for life imprisonment under federal sentencing guidelines. Zubrod contended that the children incarcerated by Ciavarella could be considered victims of his crimes since he failed to disclose that he had a conflict of interest in sending them away. The defense contended that the juveniles should not be part of the sentencing considerations since their client was found guilty of only twelve counts that had nothing to do with the kids-for-cash scheme. Indeed, they objected to the phrase itself because it had never been proven in federal court. They also argued for a lighter term because their client faced possible retaliation in prison.

Kosik, saying he wanted to avoid a "circus," resisted entreaties that the former juvenile defendants and their parents be allowed to testify at the hearing. Instead, he said they could write letters. He received about two hundred letters from parents describing their shock at unexpectedly seeing their shackled children being hauled out of Ciavarella's courtroom and the psychological harm their children suffered from detention. Flora said he had received more than one hundred letters from Ciavarella supporters, but his client told him not to submit them to the court. "He did not want the people who wrote the letters on his behalf to be subjected to public ridicule, condemnation, or scorn," Flora explained.

But letter writing was not enough for some of the juveniles and their parents. Sandy Fonzo ordered one hundred T-shirts with photographs of her late son on the front and varied slogans ("How Much Is Your Child Worth?" and "Cash for Kids Is an American Travesty") on the back. At a rally two days before the hearing, Fonzo distributed the shirts to the members of a support group she had organized. "Even if we can't speak, Ciavarella will have to see us," she said.

At 7 a.m., nearly two hours before the start of the hearing, a line that would build to nearly four hundred people forms outside Kosik's courtroom. Not surprisingly, Laurene Transue is in it, but today she is joined by her daughter, Hillary, who is now twenty years old. Hillary worked until 3 p.m. the previous day at her job in Vermont, then drove more than four hundred miles, reaching home around 2 a.m. "I thought we were going to be late," Laurene says, "but Leadfoot Hillary got us here on time." Hillary is anxious about seeing Ciavarella, whom she last beheld four and a half years ago when he was the judge and she was the defendant. "No one is going to drag Ciavarella away from his screaming mother, as I was, and he won't have to wonder what's happening to him, as I did. I just want to see justice done here today," she says.

The spectator area of the courtroom is quickly filled, and the overflow is directed to a second courtroom to view the proceedings on a live video feed. Cindy Ciavarella and her family are seated in the front row. Three rows back, wearing a T-shirt with her son's picture, is Sandy Fonzo. She is surrounded by perhaps twenty-five others, all wearing the shirts. Standing every few feet all around the courtroom perimeter, trying to be vigilant and appear inconspicuous, are federal marshals. Sitting behind the Transues are Marsha Levick and Lourdes Rosado of Juvenile Law Center.

As Flora walks to the microphone, Laurene begins a nervous foot tapping that will occasionally abate, but never stop entirely, during the ninety-minute hearing. Flora says two reports—Judge Grim's recommendation that all of Ciavarella's cases be expunged and the report of a special study commission—should not be taken into consideration in arriving at a sentence. Zubrod, wearing a black bow tie he apparently thought better of when appearing before the jury at the trial, stands and points at Ciavarella: "He is not standing before you today to be sentenced for what he did to particular juveniles. He's being sentenced today because he engaged in a racketeering activity in relation to his job that inevitably involved juveniles. In essence, it seems to me that Mr. Ciavarella's argument is that, 'I was not selling kids retail.' And we agree with that. He was selling them wholesale." Applause is mimed in the T-shirt brigade.

Zubrod makes more legal arguments, then suddenly Ciavarella stands: "Can I take the podium, Your Honor?" Kosik assents, and the defendant walks to the podium. "Your Honor, I'm going to read most of what I have to say because I don't want to miss anything that I have to say and I don't want to misstate anything that I have to say. Even though I have privately apologized to my family, I believe it is important to publicly apologize to my wife Cindy, children Lauren, Nicole, Marco, and their spouses and fiancée for the hurt and embarrassment I have caused them by my irresponsible acts. I will also thank them for standing by me at the most difficult time in my life. I will be remiss if I did not also express to my sisters Roseanne and Mary, my uncle Joe, my in-laws, Jerry and Helen, my brother-in-law and sister-in-law John and Debbie, and friends how sorry I am for the pain and hurt my conduct has caused them to endure." Ciavarella continues, apologizing to the community, the Luzerne County bar, other judges, and probation officers. He labels himself a hypocrite who failed to practice what he preached. "I blame no one but myself for what happened." Laurene is shaking her head, wondering about an apology to her and her daughter.

Then, without warning, Ciavarella launches an attack on Zubrod, whom he says unfairly labeled the case kids-for-cash: "Those three words made me the personification of evil. They made me the Antichrist and the devil. Those words caused hurt and agony for me and my family. They made me toxic and caused a public uproar the likes of which this community has never seen. He uttered those three words knowing full well there was little or no evidence of me receiving a dime to send children into placement."

Ciavarella calls Robert Powell "a liar and self-centered individual who would say and do anything to protect himself." He insists there was no relationship between the payments and his adjudications: "There was no connection between the money I had received and the children I placed at PA Child Care. I tarnished the once-proud name of Ciavarella to the point where my son can't even consider returning to this area to practice law. I lost my job, and I'm financially ruined. I am about to lose the physical presence of my family, a loss which is almost unbearable to shoulder. But I will never lose my will to fight against individuals who say I took cash to put children in placement when I never did. I was convicted of receiving a kickback for the construction of a building. The money was paid before the PA Child facility was even opened. This payment had nothing to do with the sending of the children to that facility."

Kosik peers down, waits to be certain that Ciavarella has

finished, then says, "I appreciate your remarks, but I have one question."

"Sure."

"You apologized to everybody except to those people that the Pennsylvania Supreme Court has said you denied rights when they appeared in your court. You probably don't agree with the Supreme Court's assessment, but that's what the Supreme Court of Pennsylvania said, and that is a matter that this court has a right to take into consideration in assessing your character for sentencing purposes."

"Your Honor, I will respectfully disagree with that Supreme Court opinion. I never violated one child's right. There's no hard-core evidence that that ever happened. Your Honor, my courtroom was conducted—and it was always conducted in a fair and reasonable manner. Those children were not denied their rights." There is an audible disbelieving gasp from the T-shirt area, but Ciavarella appears not to hear it. "They had the right to counsel. They had the right to confront witnesses. They had the right to make whatever statements they wanted to make, and they also had the right if they chose—and their families chose—to waive counsel. I did not deny them that right." Hillary stifles a scream, and Laurene reaches over and pats her arm. "I think the misconception here, Your Honor, is that there was an obligation on me to do something that I didn't do. I did everything that I was obligated to do to protect those children's rights. I never violated any of their rights." Sandy Fonzo has reddened and is trembling.

Zubrod stands, fingers his bow tie, and starts to address the issue of whether Ciavarella's character should be considered in the sentencing. But then he seems to sense the tension in back of him: "I first wish, Your Honor, to acknowledge the presence in the courtroom and in the spillover courtroom of a number of persons who were victims of Mark Ciavarella's criminal conduct." There is a palpable release of tension in the spectator rows. Zubrod continues, and concludes: "One aspect of Mr. Ciavarella's history outweighs all others. That is his failure to accept responsibility for the jury verdict, to accept the responsibility for his actions. From almost the day of initiation of charges against him to the day the jury found him guilty of accepting bribes and kickbacks, he has consistently and pro-actively refused to accept responsibility for his crimes."

Zubrod sits down, and Kosik looks to the defense table. There is silence as the judge clears his throat: "Okay. I've been doing this forty years. I can under oath say that it has never been a pleasant task. Everything about this case has already been said, addressed orally, in writing by individuals, judicial and otherwise including the media. So we will get right down to business." The Transue women are holding hands. "Pursuant to the Sentencing Reform Act, it is the judgment of the court the defendant is committed to the custody of the Bureau of Prisons to be imprisoned for a term of 336 months." There is a nanosecond pause while the entire room divides 336 by 12 and comes up with 28. Someone shouts, "Woo-hoo!" from the back row. Hillary looks at Ciavarella and says, "Bye-bye." Laurene is teary. "Do you know what this means? Do you know how much this means?" She answers her own question. "There's a Russian journalist who keeps wanting to interview me. From the tone of her emails, I know she wants to make America look bad. I'm avoiding her because I don't think what happened to these kids is typical of our country. But if we hadn't made Ciavarella answer for this—not for the bribery, but for the injustice—then the whole world would have thought this is how it's done here."

It is one of the longest sentences ever handed down by a

federal court in a public corruption case. In addition to the prison term, Kosik orders Ciavarella to pay restitution of nearly $2.2 million that includes the first payment from Mericle and his judicial salary between 2000 and 2007. He also owes the Internal Revenue Service $207,861 in back taxes.

There is an outbreak of hugging. Among the Ciavarella family, it is grief based. Among the T-shirt contingent, it is joyous. The happy ones soon spill out into the hallways and then outside the building, where the morning has ripened into meteorologic perfection—sunny and seventy-two degrees. Sandy Fonzo tells microphones and cameras, "The judge was wrong. What he did to my son, what he did to all the families, was wrong. Today proves that." Hillary Transue is asked about Ciavarella's comments just before the sentencing. "I was sickened and disgusted," she says, bitterness buzzing in her voice. "This entire time he has been adamant about denying he did any of those things to children. It was despicable that, with the victims sitting in the room, he would dare deny what he did."

Flora is trying to tell reporters that he will appeal both Ciavarella's conviction and his sentence, which he said violates the constitutional prohibition on cruel and unusual punishment. "You had a guy who was acquitted of twenty-seven counts and found responsible for receiving one payment and to get twenty-eight years? I've represented people who committed third-degree murder who have gotten seven to eight years. It's quite a shock." But most of his words are drowned out by chants of "Kids for Cash, Kids for Cash."

Peter J. Smith, the U.S. attorney, calls Ciavarella's complaint about the lack of trial evidence in the kids-for-cash scheme legal hairsplitting: "The juvenile justice system is the responsibility primarily of the state of Pennsylvania. We can't decide or rehear juvenile cases in a federal criminal proceeding. It is fair to say that there was no evidence presented regarding a specific cash payment to Ciavarella or Conahan for any particular individual juvenile sent to facilities owned or controlled by Powell or Mericle, but the facts showed clearly here that it was the overall corrupt scheme that contaminated the entire system." Zubrod chimes in that Ciavarella's pre-sentencing behavior was typical of the intimidation tactics he used in his own courtroom: "I think that's his way of doing things. Never retreat. Always go on the attack. Always blame somebody else. Always get them to back off. He tried it with this judge. It didn't work."

Back in the courtroom, a handcuffed Ciavarella is escorted by marshals to a waiting black van with tinted windows. It will transport him to a federal holding center in Philadelphia to await assignment to a permanent prison. He is entered into the federal inmate database as prisoner 15008-067.

In May 2012, Ciavarella asked the Third U.S. Circuit Court of Appeals to overturn his conviction on the grounds that Kosik should have disqualified himself because of pretrial statements he made to the media and because the evidence at the trial failed to support a conviction.

Mark Ciavarella was undergoing a thirty-day orientation at the Federal Correctional Institution in Pekin, Illinois, when his co-conspirator, Michael Conahan, came into federal court in Scranton on September 23, 2011, for sentencing. He arrived more than an hour early, holding hands with his wife Barbara, who wore a forced smile, as though the corners of her mouth were being tugged by wires. Conahan's tan suit jacket was slung over his left arm and his tie was loosened. Between two fingers he held a typewritten statement. Before entering the courtroom, he donned his jacket and tightened his tie. Inside he was greeted by some two dozen family members and friends, including several of his eight siblings. The Conahans had no children. As the clock ticked toward 9:30 a.m., Conahan sat at the defense table, upright as a genteel dinner guest, and reviewed the typewritten pages.

Michael Conahan did not dispatch a single child to undeserved detention, but the scandal would not have been possible were it not for his behind-the-scenes political manipulations, secret agreements, and money laundering. He had been free on bail since July 2010, when he pleaded guilty to one count of racketeering conspiracy in the scheme. Recently he had been living in Florida in a house his wife purchased in the summer of 2011.

Kosik entered the courtroom precisely on schedule and told everyone to sit down. He invited Philip Gelso, Conahan's attorney, to address the court. Gelso said his client had begun seeing a psychologist in December 2009 in an effort to understand his illegal behavior in the kids-for-cash scandal: "Through the process, what became apparent was that Mike had to confront demons that were revealed in the psychological testing, that was confirmed in the conversations with his siblings, and locked away by years of repression. We found out that, despite his outward persona of confidence, Mike suffered from insidious feelings of inadequacy and insecurity. He comes from a family with a patriarch who drove his children to success and used money as a barometer of that success. He was taught the ends justified the means. And due to these deep insecurities and inadequacies, he used repression and alcohol as a defense mechanism to keep those insecurities in check and help him ignore the consequences of his actions."

Gelso claimed that Conahan's father, a powerful politician and businessman, "beat him mercilessly" when he was an adolescent, once because he forgot to stoke the furnace fire in the family-run funeral home. Gelso then attacked Conahan's co-conspirator, whom he pointedly referred to as "Ciavarella" without any first name or honorific title: "Your Honor, this pathway walked by Michael is in stark contrast to the road traveled by Ciavarella. As Ciavarella continued to deny responsibility for his actions and the disastrous consequences of the same, Michael accepted it. As Ciavarella made public statements antagonizing the juveniles and antagonizing the public who were hurt by his criminal conduct, Michael remained quiet, with the hope that his silence would somehow begin the healing process. Your Honor, as Ciavarella challenged the government, the court, and the public concerning his criminal conduct, Michael challenged himself to understand why he committed these crimes. He also met with the government, forfeited his pension, and offered to forfeit any remaining asset that he could to pay restitution."

Next, Conahan, his hands shaking slightly, read from his typed statement: "Your honor, this has been a long road for me. It has been difficult, embarrassing, damaged my reputation beyond repair. I've lost everything that I worked for my entire life, and I'm about to go to prison. Your honor, I deserve these consequences because of what I've done.

"First, please allow me to apologize to the children and the families of the children that appeared in juvenile court in Luzerne County. You are the vulnerable people of our society and are entitled to have decisions based upon what is in your best interests. I let you down the most. My actions undermined your faith in the system and contributed to the great difficulty in your lives. As the president judge, I owed you better. I'm grateful that the Supreme Court overturned your findings of delinquency and expunged your records. I am sorry you were victimized."

For five more minutes, Conahan apologized to the citizens of

Luzerne County and every group affected by the scheme: "The system was not corrupt, I was corrupt. I did not perform my duties as I should. I did not have integrity."

Houser rose from the prosecutors' table and agreed with Gelso there were a number of factors that weighed in favor of leniency for Conahan. "In contrast to Mark Ciavarella, Mr. Conahan has, in fact, accepted responsibility. Your Honor must consider the need for the sentence imposed to reflect the seriousness of the offense, to promote respect for the law, to provide just punishment for the offense, and to afford adequate deterrence to criminal conduct. The serious offense committed by Mr. Conahan warrants a serious prison sentence. To afford adequate deterrence to others, the government asks the court to impose a prison sentence that sends a clear message that when a person abuses one of the highest and most trusted positions in our society for criminal conduct, for personal gain, he must pay a very dear price with many years of his life spent behind bars."

Before sentencing Conahan, Kosik said he had read the former judge's psychological report. Kosik cleared his throat and raised his voice an octave: "One sister told the psychologist, 'Michael was like his father, he sees a lot of gray.' And that's a very important word. Another sister more succinctly said that he also sees a lot of gray. She alluded to the fact that when her father was mayor, there was an occasion where he was charged with some ethical violation, which he didn't consider an ethical violation, and couldn't understand why people considered it an ethical violation, because he was awarding a contract to a friend, because he thought that friend's work would benefit the community. She said their father never understood this. He couldn't see what the problem was. 'In some ways, I think Mike looked at the juvenile center in the same way, in that everyone was going to benefit and that no one was going to get hurt.'

"I don't exclude myself when I say that is one of the greatest dangers of public office," Kosik said, "particularly if we serve in that public office for a period of time. We conclude that different standards seem to apply to us than to the average person on the street. We see that day after day after day, and it's not uncommon in this area.

"When I was a child, those practices were accepted. A school board member could have coal delivered to his home, even if it was being paid for by the school board, people were aware of that and they said, 'Well, he's not getting any salary, and in those days, it was perfectly all right.' It's the gray area, in my mind, that led this defendant to his fate today."

Kosik then peered directly at Conahan: "A lot has been said about this case, and there's no point to extending it or attempting to lecture a defendant who sat in a role similar to this one, and he knows what my job is, and I suppose I'll have to do it.

"So pursuant to the Sentencing Reform Act, it is the judgment of the court that the defendant is committed to the custody of the Bureau of Prisons for a term of 210 months"—Conahan blanched at the defense table as hope became a doused fire—"We find the defendant has an ability to pay a fine, so it's ordered that he pay to the clerk of court the sum of $20,100, consisting of a special assessment of $100 due immediately and a fine of $20,000 payable to the clerk and interest is waived. Further, that the Defendant shall make restitution in the amount of $874,167."

The entire proceeding took only thirty-one minutes. For a few seconds, Conahan stood by himself, sad and lonely. Then federal marshals took the fifty-nine-year-old former judge into custody. He was entered into the federal inmate database as prisoner 15009-067. Before going to the Philadelphia holding center to await assignment, he was allowed to say good-bye to his family and friends. The courtroom was empty within fifteen minutes.

Three days after Christmas 2011, Robert Powell reported to a minimum security federal prison in Pensacola to start an eighteen-month sentence for his role in the kids-for-cash conspiracy. Robert Mericle faced twelve to eighteen months in prison for lying to federal investigators, but his sentencing was delayed because he was expected to testify in another, unrelated public corruption case.

10

THE HEARINGS

A few weeks after it was authorized by the state legislature in 2009, the Interbranch Commission on Juvenile Justice was formed and making plans to investigate Luzerne County's juvenile justice scandal. Its goal was to recommend reforms to prevent recurrences there and elsewhere. It was a remarkably able, industrious group that included a state judge, two county juvenile judges, a magisterial district judge, a prosecutor from Philadelphia, a public defender from Philadelphia, a victims' rights advocate from Erie, a juvenile justice researcher from Pittsburgh, a former county commissioner, the district attorney of rural Susquehanna County, and a former president of the Pennsylvania Bar Association.

The chairman was John M. Cleland, a judge on the Pennsylvania Superior Court, a silver-haired, wizened, and wise intermediate appellate tribunal official. The commission held its first hearing in Harrisburg on October 14, 2009, in the Pennsylvania Judicial Center, a handsome nine-story limestone building that had opened the previous year to accommodate state courts and administrative offices. This hearing, like the others that would follow, was carried live by PCN, Pennsylvania C-SPAN. Cleland, flanked on either side by five fellow commission members, made an opening statement:

This morning our Commission begins its public hearings to assess the breathtaking collapse of the juvenile justice system in Luzerne County. Two judges stand criminally charged for conduct that had the unmistakable effect of harming children. Whether they are guilty or innocent of any specific criminal charge brought by the United States Attorney is not for this Commission to decide. But there is little doubt that their conduct, whether criminal or not, had disastrous consequences for the juvenile justice system that must be understood and prevented from happening again. Our concern, however, is not only the action of two Luzerne County judges. Our concern is also the inaction of others. Inaction by judges, prosecutors, public defenders, the defense bar, public officials and private citizens—those who knew but failed to speak; those who saw but failed to act.

One of the first witnesses was state Senator Lisa Baker, a Republican from Luzerne County and sponsor of the legislation that created the commission, who cited an "atmosphere of intimidation that permeated the courtroom and the courthouse." However she added that the judicial breakdown was not an aberration: "We cannot write off this as a horrible situation unlikely to recur. The lesson is that someone has to keep an eye on things. As the public understands the current situation, the Supreme Court, at the top of the pyramid of the unified judicial system, does not have the capacity to keep watch over sixty-seven county courthouses. The state bureaucracy does not have time to sift through whatever data is being produced to check for warning flags, insufficiencies, and inaccuracies. Do we really want a commonwealth where we rigorously track every dollar that moves

through casinos, but where we casually lose track of the constitutional rights of thousands of kids?"

The main witness was Judge Muroski, who outlined the conspiracy and described his clash with Conahan over funding for
dependency court and his subsequent demotion in 2005. As he
recited the details, the expressions on the commission members'
faces went from anger to disbelief to shock. They appeared most
distressed when Muroski told them of the mainstream support for
Ciavarella's zero-tolerance policies: "At the beginning of every
school year, he spoke at assemblies held in most school districts
within Luzerne County and, in effect, promised institutional
placement for school-related infractions. He was true to his word
and became even more popular when he followed through with
placements sometimes for minimal offenses. In attempting to an-
alyze the alleged, ever-increasing placements, I have found that
pressure for placements by school administrators of allegedly
disruptive students is not uncommon; however, with Ciavarella
very little encouragement was necessary. A lot of people admired
what Ciavarella was doing. Many people knew how quick these
proceedings were, but they supported them. School administrators, teachers, and police supported and applauded Ciavarella's
efforts to get disruptive youths out of the classroom and off the
streets."

Muroski was tense, and there was a wrinkled edge of stress
between his eyes, which were puffy and sleep-deprived. His
testimony seemed to galvanize the commission. They had read
about the scandal in the newspapers and in a briefing book, but
here was a live person sitting in front of them telling the story
from the perspective of someone who had been there. Indeed,
several commission members pressed Muroski on why he and
other Luzerne County judges hadn't done more to stop Conahan

and Ciavarella. "We knew there was something not right," he said. "But the scheme was so contrived and had so many laby-rinths that at first we didn't know money was involved. Our main concern was the high incarceration rate." When the possibility of financial misdeeds began to emerge, Muroski said there was "disbelief" on the part of his colleagues: "They thought, 'That really can't be.' " Muroski said the nepotism in the courtroom itself provided a "protective shield" for Conahan and Ciavarella.

For the next nine months the commission members held hear-ings and meetings and then came up with forty-three recom-mendations for legal and procedural changes. But in the process they heard some astonishing testimony from officials directly re-sponsible for the breakdown of justice in Luzerne County. It was an orgy of denial that had everything except a straight answer. Always, there was the unmistakable sound of the buck being passed.

Among the first witnesses was David W. Lupas, who was dis-trict attorney for much of Ciavarella's tenure—from 2001 to 2007. Lupas replaced Ciavarella as the juvenile judge in 2008, and in his opening testimony he outlined the reforms he had set in place, including a requirement for on-the-record explanations of the consequences of waiving the right to a lawyer. Lupas's ap-pearance was one of the critical points of the entire inquiry, but he seemed indifferent to the surroundings and the situation, like a prize-winning sheep at a county fair. He appeared unaware that on his watch thousands of adolescents had been locked up, often for minor crimes after hearings in which they were effectively denied lawyers. None of it seemed to pertain to him.

Commission member Dwayne D. Woodruff, a former Pitts-burgh Steeler cornerback who is now a juvenile court judge, noted that more than half of the children brought before Ciavarella did not have lawyers. "Would you expect your assistant DAs to come to you with that?" he asked.

"No one came to me," Lupas said.

Woodruff pressed on. "I understand that they didn't, but would you *expect* them to?"

"On its face as you're saying it, yes. But I think I can understand, like I explained the situation with the written colloquy, where perhaps they didn't perceive that. Again, I'm only trying to put myself in their mind, but perhaps they didn't see that so much as being a deprivation of their right to a waiver because they were waiving it, although they were doing it in writing not on the record by an oral colloquy from the judge. So perhaps they didn't see the need to raise it. I don't know. I'm only surmising."

Woodruff looked away, bewildered.

Another juvenile judge on the commission, John C. Uhler of York County, asked if the juvenile court was considered "kiddie court" and less important than adult court. Lupas replied: "I don't know if it was a lesser court. There may have been some of those attitudes. Unfortunately, I see some of those attitudes today as a judge. There are limited resources. I guess there were times, because of lack of resources, that it maybe didn't get the priority maybe that it should have."

Cleland, marinating in impatience, pressed Lupas on how he could have been unaware of what was transpiring in Ciavarella's courtroom: "Your testimony was that you never heard it discussed among any of your assistant DAs, defense lawyers, public defenders, or anyone involved in the system. A case here, a case there, maybe. But thousands of cases over year after year after year three days a week of juvenile hearings, and no assistant district attorney, public defender, or defense lawyer ever raised a question? Now, either there was incredible incompetence, which

I find it hard to believe among that many lawyers and professionals, or there was an awful lot of intimidation about reporting and discussing what was going on. Which was it?"

Lupas, eyes glassy with indifference, answered. "There were times—not as often, but there were times where perhaps an Assistant DA was disappointed with the outcome of a case because he went the other way and maybe dismissed a petition or threw something out. So—but it was—it was basically he—Ciavarella ran the courtroom. That was—that was the way it was."

Next came Jacqueline Musto Carroll, who succeeded Lupas as district attorney and served as his first assistant for seven years before that. She acknowledged that she, like Lupas, had never set foot in juvenile court. Kenneth Horoho, a former president of the Pennsylvania Bar Association, went through a litany of questions trying to determine why Musto Carroll was not aware of the long-standing problems and finally ended by saying, "The bottom line is that zero tolerance went unchallenged by your office." Musto Carroll said that she was not aware that more than half of the teenagers going before Ciavarella were unrepresented.

"If the purpose of this commission is to make sure this never happens again," Musto Carroll said, "and I don't mean to be smart about this, but you tell me how not to have a judge who's a criminal? That's the bottom line here."

Cleland, his face torqued with anger, interrupted: "You report them, Ms. Musto Carroll! You report them. That's the answer. That's the simple answer!"

But Musto Carroll, unintimidated, kept digging a deeper hole. Under questioning from Robert L. Listenbee, chief of the juvenile unit of the Defender Association of Philadelphia, she blurted, "I need to be completely honest here. I have heard many cases that say that Judge Ciavarella—what he did was helpful, and he saved a lot of these kids' lives. Now, I know that that is not popular, and I know that no one wants to hear that. But I have heard people say, here's a Ciavarella success story. The kid was out of control. The parents brought him into the courtroom. Or the teacher brought him into the courtroom and said, do something with this child, and he sent the child away. I've heard stories where the kids have joined—joined wrestling teams at these different facilities, have gone on to get scholarships and have college degrees and come out—have come out of those institutions and are better for it."

Listenbee interjected. "Ms. Carroll, one of the fundamental issues is that you are sworn to uphold the Constitution of the United States and the Constitution of Pennsylvania. The constitutional rights of these children is what we're talking about here."

Musto Carroll was reprimanded several times for rambling, long-winded answers, and the commission was particularly dismayed by her insistence that the main issue was the kickbacks rather than the denial of juveniles' rights. When Woodruff pressed her on her lack of awareness of what was happening in juvenile court, she said: "But—but I know you don't want me to say more than I need to, but let me just say this. Even if all these colloquies and the law and everything was followed in the courtroom and he was a procedural stickler for rules, even if that had all occurred, is there anyone saying on the other hand that he wouldn't still have gotten kickbacks from the people who built this PA Child Care?"

"Ms. Carroll, I understand," Woodruff said.

"I think that's an important question, sir. And I . . ."

"I do not agree with that. Because my position is that without the kickbacks there are rights being violated of these juveniles."

Thomas J. Killino, who worked under Lupas and Musto Carroll as an assistant district attorney, said he took the job in 2004 because he wasn't getting enough courtroom work in his private civil practice and wanted to get trial experience. Was juvenile court considered important? "It certainly didn't appear to be number 1 on the list of things going on to be very honest with you." Was he bothered by the judge's failure to advise children on waivers of counsel? "I came into a very fast-paced environment. I observed my colleagues handle that environment in the same way as I came to handle it. And, again, it was an established practice by the court. And the trust factor there that if the court is satisfied in proceeding in that manner that was the manner it proceeded." Did he ever question the placement of a single juvenile? "You're trusting that the court is looking at that file, that the evaluation is performed by whatever is required based on the specific circumstance of the evaluation."

Commission members were further exasperated by testimony from Sandra Brulo, who headed the county probation office through much of Ciavarella's tenure. County probation officers under her supervision obtained the illegal waivers of counsel from juveniles and their parents outside Ciavarella's courtroom. Parents would be met at elevators and urged to sign unsanctioned waiver-of-counsel forms because their child's offense was minor and would probably result in probation. Brulo was questioned by Mosee, a deputy Philadelphia district attorney, who asked: "Don't you think that it's problematic for a probation officer to go over a legal document with a juvenile whose very liberty is in jeopardy?"

"We did what the judge instructed us to do," Brulo replied. She added that she had concerns about Ciavarella's actions, had brought them to her immediate supervisor, but had not received a response. Ronald P. Williams, one of three non-lawyers on the commission, threw up his hands and asked, "Don't you think you should have taken it further when you didn't get any satisfaction from your supervisor?"

"I took it to my boss," Brulo replied. "That's as far as I thought I should go."

Brulo was not implicated in the bribery scheme, but she had already pleaded guilty to altering a court record involved in the scandal. She changed the document to indicate she had recommended probation for a juvenile when she actually had recommended placement. Brulo was subsequently sentenced to two years' probation.

Basil G. Russin, who had been chief public defender in Luzerne County since 1980, painted a picture for the commission of overwhelming caseloads, inadequate offices, and hand-me-down computers. He was interrogated by Mosee, who asked: "I know that you're a bright guy, probably a good attorney. You're not a chief public defender for the money. You're a chief public defender because you want to do something for kids and for people who have been charged with whatever in our system; isn't that right?"

"That's my purpose," Russin agreed.

"Well, as the chief public defender why wouldn't you confront a mishandling, a misapprehension of something like zero tolerance?"

"Well, the dispositions in juvenile court are within the judge's discretion. The judge can decide what he wants to do with kids, and this was the way he did things. This was the way he disposed of cases. Unlike in the adult system where we have guidelines and reasons and so forth, in juvenile court the judge can just say, you're going to Pennsylvania Child Care, and off you go."

Mosee squirmed, his patience slipping away, but he rallied and asked why zero tolerance was tolerated. Russin answered with rising exasperation, "Because everybody loved it. Everybody loved it. The schools absolutely loved it. They got rid of every bad kid in their school. When I was in school if you threw a spitball, maybe you went to the principal's office and sat for a couple periods. Last couple years if you threw a spitball, they got the police, and you ended up in juvenile court and got sent away. Schools got rid of all their problems. Parents, parents who had problems with the kid at home, they called the police. Police said, you want us to take him away? Sure. I can't control the kid anymore. Away the kid would go. Parents loved it. Police loved it. They knew every arrest they made the kid would get sent away. And despite what you heard this morning, the DA loved it because they were getting convictions. They were never losing cases."

Mosee, brows down in anger, asked if Russin knew that young clients of his attorneys were being sent to PA Child Care merely to be evaluated by Dr. Vita.

"I'm aware that he would detain people for evaluations. I didn't know what those evaluations entailed. I assumed the psychological workup," Russin replied.

"Did you find that problematic?"

"Did I? Certainly that could have been done as an outpatient. Everybody that came before him went away."

"I don't want to editorialize again, but that meant that the juveniles' liberty was taken away from them just so that they could be evaluated?"

"That's correct. It was very troubling, but he's the judge. You have to assume the judge, this is his philosophy. He's honest. I've always respected judges. Maybe that's a false assumption, but I have the utmost respect for the judicials, no matter on what level. And if he said you're going away until this evaluation's done, I have to respect him that he's an honest person."

Jason Legg, the small-town district attorney on the commission, took over and followed up on Russin's earlier statement that his office didn't pursue many cases on the assumption that there was a proper written waiver of counsel.

"Do the rules allow for a written waiver of counsel?" Legg asked.

"I'm sure they don't."

"Okay. So how could it be a proper written waiver of counsel?"

"I said it would be a written waiver. Now, whether it's proper within the rules or not would be decided at a future time. . . ."

"But you had watched proceedings and saw that there were no oral colloquies?"

"Oh, I knew that. There was no oral colloquy."

"And you knew the rules didn't allow for written waivers?"

"That's correct."

"So at that point in time you knew whatever was occurring wasn't proper?"

"It wasn't proper. There's no question it wasn't proper."

"And is it fair to say that that assumption was motivated, at least in large part, by your desire to keep your caseload down? You said you don't solicit business?"

"I keep my caseload down. I keep it so we can at least represent people, manage it."

"Would it be fair to say that you really didn't want to know what was going on?"

"No, that's not fair."

"Would it be fair to say that you should have known what was going on?"

"In hindsight I should have known."

The commission heard from Judge Arthur E. Grim, who had vacated some 3,000 of Ciavarella's adjudications. He told the panel that justice had been perverted in Luzerne County "in ways that I would never have dreamed possible," and children were trapped in a scheme that grew out of "unfettered power, greed, opportunity and intimidation."

Grim defended his decision to recommend expungement of all cases despite the estimate that only about 25 percent of the placements were in the two centers connected directly to the kickbacks: "Any time that there is an obscene amount of money paid to a judge or judges by a facility, in this case a juvenile justice detention center, there is not only the appearance of impropriety, there is, in fact, such impropriety that it would make it impossible for this individual to be impartial. There was never any disclosure, never any indication of any conflict, perceived or otherwise, by this judge in any of his deliberations or any of his proceedings. And yet, although not every child was sent to Pennsylvania Child Care, a good number were. Now, does that also cloud his determinations with regard to other proceedings? In my opinion it clearly—it clearly does. You can't be just a little bit unethical. You're either an ethical judge or you're not."

But there was moving testimony from Carol L. Lavery, the head of the state's victim advocate program, who called attention to "the original victims"—meaning those who had suffered at the hands of juveniles who came before Ciavarella. She said this was a group that had been overlooked in the anguish over the scandal, and many of them were distressed that their attackers would have their records expunged. Lavery said she had talked to parents whose children had been victimized by other juveniles:

They said, "We stepped up and did the right thing. We wanted to make certain there was a record of this event in the event that the defendant assaulted someone else in the future. Now there will be no record of the assault on our child. Now this individual can be near our child." They had felt that the system had worked for them and their child. They're no longer sure that that child is safe at school.

They asked, what about the victim? That same sense of futility has been echoed many times from parents of child victims who have reached out.

To each of these parents, their efforts to do the right thing in seeking justice in the juvenile justice system now seems to have been in vain. Many of the victims talked about the fact that the juvenile did have an attorney present, and many talked about learning in the courtroom that the child had a previous history of criminal behavior. For these victims, as well as those who said that the juvenile was never placed in a treatment facility, they find the fact that the cases are being vacated and expunged as incomprehensible.

One mother spoke about her child who was severely beaten during an attack at school by a group of juveniles who had notified other students ahead of time to come and watch the assault. The mother felt the juveniles did not receive a harsh enough sentence. For their cases to be expunged, she said, what does that say to my child and every other child that is assaulted or bullied? I hope someone takes into consideration the hurt, the fear, the pain my child had to endure at the hands of these juveniles that are very, very troubled juveniles.

Many of the victims talked about not having received their restitution, and many, many of them were very angry about that. Many victims talked also about their frustration over the loss of not only restitution, but personal and irreplaceable items of sentimental value. They talked of burglaries of family heirlooms, the grandparents' jewelry, of coin collections that were never recovered. They spoke of personal items saved to pass along to their own children, war medals and work and retirement mementos destroyed in burglaries and in arsons. And for some victims the lack of any recognition or remorse or apology from the juvenile has increased the harm once these cases have been vacated and expunged.

At the end of Lavery's testimony, Cleland assured her that the commission was aware of the plight of the original victims: "So I'm glad that we have finally been able to give an opportunity, even indirectly, for them to have a voice and for us to hear the very practical and personal consequences of this juvenile justice tragedy. I don't believe that there is anything that any of us on this commission can do to make it right. If we knew what to do, we would certainly do it. But I think that we all can say that we're sorry that it happened to all of these victims, particularly that it happened to them at the hands of a system that we care about so deeply and that affected them so horribly."

One of the later witnesses was Juvenile Law Center's Robert Schwartz, who said the Luzerne County tragedy was ironic because Pennsylvania had one of the nation's most progressive juvenile justice systems:

> There are many reasons that Pennsylvania has been held in high regard. The state as a whole has had a relatively low rate of incarcerating youth. Our county-based system, tied to highly creative funding incentives, has encouraged local innovation. By giving broad powers to juvenile court judges, Pennsylvania created a system that is, in theory, highly accountable. Juvenile courts can order a delinquent

youth to receive any service that is available to abused or neglected youth. Our laws place a premium on using the least restrictive method for achieving their goals, and there are many opportunities to divert youth from the system, or from placement within it.

The commission spent an unexpectedly large amount of time, including its entire final hearing, trying to unravel the mystery of how the Judicial Conduct Board fumbled the 2006 complaint about criminal and unethical actions by Conahan. Joseph A. Massa, the board's chief counsel, conceded to the commission that he sat on the complaint for nearly eight months before he informed the board about it in a memorandum that did not include a copy of the complaint. The memo also omitted key information, including Conahan's relationship with Ciavarella. But the memo did contain detailed allegations of wrongdoing that the board never acted on. There were no interviews, subpoenas, or document reviews. Patrick Judge, the Luzerne County businessman and Conahan business partner who was board chairman in 2006 and 2007, testified that he recused himself when the memo was brought up in June 2007. The rest of the board voted to defer action until October, but the complaint was not on the agenda for that meeting and dropped completely off the radar. Indeed, the board didn't even turn over the information to federal investigators until they were asked to do so in April 2008. Throughout the testimony of various board staff and members, it became clear that the members—all unpaid, part-time appointees—knew very little about the agency's activities. In the end, Massa said he had simply allowed the matter to get lost in the bureaucratic shuffle, like an unpaid utility bill. "I hold myself accountable," Massa testified. "It was on my list. There was nothing nefarious or in terms of a subterfuge at all. I am accountable."

The final report concluded that Ciavarella was most responsible for the "tragic events in Luzerne County." As an example, the report cited Ciavarella's fines court—the practice of rounding up juvenile defendants and, if they had not paid their fines, ordering them into detention at PA Child Care. It called the practice "Dickensian" and said it amounted to "effectively using the county detention center as a debtor's prison for children." But the commission found many other culprits: "The failures of the juvenile justice system do not stop with Ciavarella. The Interbranch Commission on Juvenile Justice found a far more complex and nuanced picture in which many individuals may be seen to have shared the responsibility. Silence, inaction, inexperience, ignorance, fear of retaliation, greed, ambition, carelessness. All these factors played a part in the failure of the system. Prosecutors, defenders and probation officials witnessed and participated in proceedings in Ciavarella's courtroom."

The report leveled direct criticisms at some individuals. It said Lupas and Musto Carroll, the two district attorneys, "incredibly conceded that they had never set foot in a juvenile court throughout their entire careers" and "demonstrated no initiative, interest, or concern with what was occurring in juvenile court." Russin, the chief public defender, did not properly monitor the activities of his assistants. "Through his silence and the silence of the juvenile defenders on his staff, Russin became complicit in the zero-tolerance policies instituted by Ciavarella and the routine placement of children for minor offenses."

The commissioners adopted the forty-three reform recommendations at a meeting that lasted only twenty-three minutes.

11

OUR LOCK-'EM-UP SOCIETY

For several months after the Interbranch Commission released its recommendations, John Cleland struggled with a nagging question: Was what happened in Luzerne County merely a singular, bizarre departure from judicial normalcy? Or could it happen again elsewhere? The former possibility was widely believed, especially within the legal community. Indeed, addressing ceremonies celebrating the centennial of the Luzerne County Courthouse, Justice Max Baer of the Pennsylvania Supreme Court said the juvenile justice scandal that unfolded there was so far beyond anyone's experience that no one could have foreseen it. A few months later, Cleland fired back at a statewide judicial symposium: "The hardest, and cruelest, lesson of Luzerne County is this: Given the structural and administrative limitations of our present justice system, to conclude with absolute assurance that what happened in Luzerne County could not happen anywhere else in Pennsylvania is not much more than wishful thinking."

In addition to the recommendations of the Cleland commission, Juvenile Law Center came out with a set of remedies for Pennsylvania's juvenile justice system that sometimes paralleled and sometimes exceeded the Interbranch Commission's. Some three years after the huge injustices and attendant bribery in Luzerne County came to light, many of the most important recommendations have become law. They were shepherded through the Legislature by state senator Lisa Baker, the freshman Republican from Luzerne County.

In addition, the Pennsylvania Supreme Court, which had been so indifferent to the scandal before the kickbacks became public, had adopted a series of rules that embody most of the recommended reforms.

Perhaps the most pressing area of reform was waiver of counsel. Currently, only three states—Texas, Iowa, and Illinois—totally forbid juveniles to decline legal representation. Pennsylvania had given juveniles the right to defense counsel at all phases of proceedings against them, but had also given them a broad right to waive that representation, which was exploited by Ciavarella. Under a new law signed by Governor Tom Corbett in April, 2012, only juveniles older than thirteen are allowed to waive counsel, and only under very limited circumstances. Baker called the measure "the cornerstone of reform and the surest remedy to ward off wrongdoing."

The experience in Luzerne County showed clearly that neither kids nor their parents are very dependable arbiters over the question of the need for legal representation. This situation was aggravated when probation officers actually advised children to decline legal representation—even told them that it would "make matters worse." If parents were brought in, they were subjected to the same coercions plus the "why waste money on an attorney" argument. Additionally, it was sometimes the parents themselves who initiated the legal actions against their children. At other times parents were angry with their children for being arrested. In either case, having parents decide whether to waive counsel presents an inherent conflict of interest.

The importance of legal representation in protecting the basic rights of children is starkly illustrated by the fact that of all the kids who went before Ciavarella with a lawyer, only 22 percent were incarcerated. Among those who did not have a lawyer, the figure jumped to 60 percent. Juvenile Law Center's Robert Schwartz adds another reason that lawyers are important: "Children place great value on fairness. There is a growing body of literature on procedural justice, explaining that youth more readily accept what happens to them if they feel they are treated fairly. This is something that parents understand. So should juvenile courts. Fairness includes giving kids and their witnesses a meaningful opportunity to be heard. It includes court orders that are proportionate to the offense. Fairness is at the heart of justice, and fairness begins with the right to counsel."

Baker's reform package also implemented the commission's recommendation that there should be no income measure for appointing public defenders and that all juveniles should have access to legal counsel in all phases of a proceeding. Many of the Luzerne County child-defendants, like Jessica Van Reeth, requested representation by public defenders but were denied because their parents' income was too high to qualify them for free counsel. Under the new law, all juveniles will be presumed indigent, regardless of their parents' income, for the purposes of public representation. Many of Pennsylvania's sixty-seven counties, including recently Luzerne County, already automatically assign public defenders to juveniles, but this is not a legal requirement.

The commission also recommended that state funds be made available to help counties finance public defender offices. Currently, Pennsylvania and Utah are the only states that do not provide state funding for juvenile defense. The money also is needed to provide other key elements of quality legal representation, such as investigators, expert witnesses, social workers, and para-legals. This funding change was not implemented.

In nearly all of the cases where Ciavarella ordered out-of-home placement, he never bothered to explain his reasons for doing so or how it furthered the stated goals of "balanced and restorative justice" in the Pennsylvania juvenile system. Part of the Baker package requires juvenile court judges to make on-the-record statements justifying their sentences. The commission supported the change, saying it would add a level of transparency to juvenile proceedings, without opening them up to the public and media. And it would "serve as a reminder that out-of-home placement should occur only when there is a clear necessity to remove the child from the home." The Pennsylvania Supreme Court also adopted a rule requiring these explanations of disposition.

The court also adopted an anti-shackling rule stating that "the use of any restraints, such as handcuffs, chains, shackles, irons, or straitjackets, is highly discouraged" except to protect the accused and maintain courtroom security. The Florida Supreme Court approved a similar rule in 2009, citing a study by the National Juvenile Defender Center that found shackling to be "repugnant, degrading, humiliating, and contrary to the stated primary purposes of the juvenile justice system and to the principles of therapeutic justice."

However Baker said the restrictions on shackling should be given the weight of law, and Juvenile Law Center agreed: "Children should only be placed in shackles when there is an essential state interest, such as a flight risk, public safety threat, or a disruption to the courtroom that cannot be managed in other ways. Indeed, countless Pennsylvania courts do not use shackles or cuffs. They find that sheriffs, police, probation officers or court personnel can easily manage risk 99 percent of the time." The JLC noted that adult criminal defendants are less likely to be shackled than children in Pennsylvania. Baker's bill was signed into law in May 2012.

There was considerable national attention on shackling juvenile defendants following a 2007 article in *USA Today* which showed that juvenile courts in twenty-eight states regularly shackled youths at their hearings. Many states subsequently restricted the use of such restraints, and at least five of them—California, Illinois, New York, North Dakota, and Oregon—give defendants the right to a hearing on whether they should be shackled.

The Legislature acted quickly on the commission's recommendation for the establishment of a special fund to compensate the "original victims" of juvenile crimes who were denied restitution because of the mass expungement order. A $500,000 Special Juvenile Victim Compensation Fund was created, and payments began in July 2011.

However other recommended reforms had not been enacted more than three years after the scandal came to light. None is more controversial than open juvenile court hearings.

Among the important elements of the "perfect storm" that struck the Luzerne County juvenile justice system was Pennsylvania's requirement that court hearings be closed to the press and public for all but the most serious offenses. The good intention is to protect the privacy of the youths, but the undesired by-product is that there is no outside monitoring to protect their rights. Juvenile Law Center has recommended that juvenile proceedings be opened, while giving any party the right to close them for good cause. "There's a reason that the Bill of Rights includes a right to a public trial," says Schwartz. "Citizens have an interest in how justice is dispensed, and defendants don't fare well in a star chamber. Juvenile courts have traditionally been closed to the public to protect privacy. Unfortunately, that provision offers little or no outside monitoring to ensure that youths' rights were not violated." Juvenile Law Center added that there should be strict safeguards to limit the distribution of sensitive information by the media. In many states, including Florida, Tennessee, Texas, and New York, juvenile courts are open to the public unless good cause is shown as to why the public should be excluded.

However, the Interbranch Commission said the present restrictions closing most juvenile proceedings should be continued because it would be impossible to adequately protect the privacy of the children brought before an open court, thereby "exposing them to the possibility that the facts surrounding childhood misconduct could be perpetually maintained in news clippings, and now even on the internet." Instead, the commission said the best protection against abuse of judicial power was to strengthen the appeals process in juvenile cases and toughen the mechanisms for disciplining errant judges.

Although appeals of convictions and sentences are common in adult courts, currently there are few appeals from juvenile courts decisions in Pennsylvania because many cases involve guilty pleas and because court-appointed attorneys have high caseloads and lack resources.

The commission recommended a streamlined appeals process under which youths could seek prompt relief from unfair adjudications. It noted that many of the parents of children treated unjustly by Ciavarella went to great expense and effort to free their children from detention—usually to no avail. "Parents should not have to exhaust their resources and search throughout the United States to find ways to protect the constitutional rights of their children. Additional steps should be taken to ensure that juveniles understand their appellate rights and are able to take advantage of the right to appeal."

Juvenile Law Center said the case of Hillary Transue was a good example of the need for an effective, fast-track juvenile appeals process. Ciavarella found Transue guilty of harassment for her MySpace parody of the assistant principal and ordered her into juvenile detention for ninety days. It was an imprecise application of the harassment provisions of the Pennsylvania Crimes Code that many lawyers would have refuted, and Hillary would have had an excellent chance of getting her adjudication and placement sentence reversed. But Hillary, who did not have an attorney, admitted to Ciavarella that she did the parody. There was no clear avenue of appeal open to her.

"If juvenile courts are to be truly accountable, there must be a fast track for appeals, a qualified right to a stay pending appeal, and a standard of review that provides meaningful oversight of juvenile court dispositions." Schwartz said. "In addition, of course, there also must be knowledgeable lawyers available to work on appeals."

The commission rejected Juvenile Law Center's proposal that a state ombudsman office be created in the executive branch to monitor juvenile court practice and investigate possible wrongdoing. Currently, no state has such an agency, although there are ombudsman offices in Alaska, Maryland, and New Jersey that monitor courts in some manner. Juvenile Law Center said such an independent watchdog might have analyzed available statistics and detected the unusual number of counsel waivers and out-of-home placements in Ciavarella's courtroom. But the commission said the new office was an unnecessary addition to the state bureaucracy and that "the resources that would be needed to create and maintain the office of ombudsman could be put to more productive uses."

With the help of the Annie E. Casey Foundation's Juvenile Detention Alternatives Initiative, Clayton County, Georgia, has developed a model program for blocking the "school-to-prison" pipeline. Juvenile court judge Steven Teske sat down with police and school officials and developed specific guidelines for what types of behaviors would be handled within the schools. Teske said that the changes have resulted in dramatic decreases in school-based court referrals and juvenile felony rates while raising graduation rates by about 20 percent. "Now, instead of automatically arresting youth, school police have a variety of options, including giving students up to two warnings and referring them to a conflict skills class," according to Teske.

Because it believed the issue was beyond the scope of its authorized inquiry, the commission did not tackle the difficult issue of private juvenile detention facilities that operate for profit, such as PA Child Care. Pennsylvania, like most other states, maintains a network of state-operated facilities for juveniles who are taken out of their homes by the court and, to use the approved euphemism, "placed." But most of these young people end up in private facilities, the overwhelming number of which specialize in such problems as learning difficulties, drug and alcohol abuse, and emotional instability. The nonprofit centers, subsidized by government funds and licensed by the state, are the backbone of the detention system.

However, a few of these "providers" are for-profit businesses, and therefore interested mainly in making money. This goal can be met only when they operate at or near capacity. Juvenile Law Center said there should be a law forbidding the use of for-profit, non-treatment detention centers such as PA Child Care. "It is axiomatic that for-profit programs are in the business of making money. While detention centers provide some short-term services to youth, their primary mission is control. At their core, detention centers ensure that a youth will show up at trial and not commit a crime prior to trial. For-profit detention centers make their profit based on a headcount. While public detention centers will stay in business even if their populations are low, for-profit detention centers cannot afford low populations."

The commission cited the failure of Pennsylvania's Judicial Conduct Board to investigate serious and detailed complaints against Conahan. It said the JCB lacked sufficient oversight, and its existing confidentiality provisions prevent any meaningful accountability. It noted that the board already has revised its internal operations, but said a study of its entire operating procedures was needed. The commission recommended that the Supreme Court review courthouse hiring practices and set guidelines because of the fact that Conahan and Ciavarella filled the Luzerne County Courthouse with their relatives and nurtured the overall corruption. "Court employees were less likely to speak out against judicial misconduct if they had personal ties to the judges engaging in misconduct."

Juvenile Law Center noted that few parents of Ciavarella's victims were aware of the board's responsibility to move against rogue judges, and it said the Legislature should study ways to amend the state Constitution to increase the effectiveness of the board and to raise public awareness of it as an avenue of relief from wrongdoing by judges.

In Pennsylvania, district attorneys prosecuting juvenile cases have the obligation not only to protect the public and crime victims, but also to weigh the needs of the young offender, emphasizing rehabilitation over punishment. The commission said the prosecutors working in Luzerne County juvenile court had failed in this responsibility, and it recommended better training for young assistant district attorneys. But it added: "While training provides an appropriate foundation, there must be vigilance by all concerned regarding the importance of the mission of the juvenile justice system. All too often during the commission's hearings, there were references to 'kiddie court' and the juvenile court in Luzerne County being considered a training ground for prosecutors and defenders. Officials at the state and county levels must emphasize the importance of balanced and restorative justice, and must see to it that the individuals who fill the roles in juvenile justice possess the integrity, the desire and the commitment to the goals and values of the system. Attitude reflects leadership, and the system will not function properly if it is simply a training ground, or an unwanted stepchild of the entire justice system."

A basic question emerges from the Luzerne County tragedy that cannot be addressed by any law or regulation: Were it not for the millions of dollars in bribes, how much of a public outcry would there have been against the actions of these two judges? What voices would have been raised if the only wrongdoing was Ciavarella's everyday denial of the basic rights of children? It is unsettling to speculate.

Before the whole world became aware of the kickbacks, it was clear to anyone involved, directly or indirectly, that Ciavarella was running a kangaroo court, something even Charles Dickens might have had difficulty imagining. Yet no one objected effectively. Lawyers, elected officials, police, school administrators, teachers, probation officers, prosecutors, and civil servants charged with protecting children all remained silent. The

Pennsylvania Supreme Court ignored Juvenile Law Center's entreaties to step in until the bribery was revealed. The Luzerne County Bar Association has never commented, even to this day. The FBI and IRS originally were interested in Conahan's organized crime associations.

Perhaps most disturbing is the fact that the *Times-Leader* published a series of articles in 2004 outlining in detail what was going on in juvenile court. It generated very little reader interest. The calamitous events in Luzerne County, Pennsylvania, manifested a widespread public misunderstanding of the juvenile justice system, which is legally unique and not merely a version of adult court for children. Part of this popular confusion has to do with the stereotype of youthful offenders—hardened, old-before-their-time, violent "predators" that need to be removed from society. Only about 5 percent of all juvenile arrests are for violent crimes such as homicide and rape. Most of them are for property crimes, vandalism, and drug and alcohol abuse.

In its final report, the Interbranch Commission said, "it appears the public does not always understand how the juvenile justice system works and has conflicting ideas about what it is expected to accomplish." It added:

> Some erroneously believe the system should be punitive in nature and emphasize punishment; others believe the system should be protective and emphasize education and socialization. Understandably, these potentially conflicting approaches can lead the public, lawmakers, judges, and attorneys to a muddled conclusion about what exactly the juvenile system does and should do.

On the one hand, society expects juvenile courts to be places where children learn the consequences of engaging in unlawful conduct and to be places where punishment is a reality. As a result, an adjudication of delinquency can carry the possibility of very significant and lifelong effects, including out-of-home placement, disqualification from military service, Megan's Law registration, and enhanced sentencing for adult crimes. Given these possible consequences, children must be afforded constitutionally required due process protections with all the formality and associated procedural rigidity they entail.

On the other hand, society thinks of juvenile courts as "problem-solving courts." As problem-solving courts, they should have the flexibility and creativity needed to address the unique problems of childhood behavior and to be places of shelter and protection.

In Pennsylvania, as well as the rest of the nation, there are two parallel systems of justice—one for adults who commit crimes, the other for children who commit acts that would be crimes if they were adults. Indeed, the truism that children are different from adults takes on added power in the justice system. Adolescents, beset by impulsiveness, immaturity, hormonal tides, and vulnerability to peer pressure, are not as blameworthy as adults when they violate laws. When you ask young wrongdoers what they were thinking, one probable answer is that they weren't.

The Annie E. Casey Foundation notes that there is an abundance of research proving that children are not merely smaller versions of adults: "New brain imaging research revealed that 'the brain systems that govern impulse control, planning, and thinking ahead are still developing well beyond age 18.' Behavioral studies confirmed that adolescents remain far less able to gauge risks and consequences, control impulses, handle stress, and resist peer pressure. Finally, research revealed that perhaps the most important difference between adolescent and adult lawbreakers is that most youthful offenders will cease lawbreaking as part of the normal maturation process."

The issue of young people's culpability has been studied by the MacArthur Foundation Research Network on Adolescent Development and Juvenile Justice, and it concludes that punishment or other legal sanctions for young defendants should not be based solely on the harm they have caused but also on blameworthiness:

Many studies have shown that by the age of sixteen, adolescents' cognitive abilities—loosely, their intelligence or ability to reason—loosely mirrors that of adults. But how people reason is only one influence on how they make decisions. In the real world, especially in high-pressure crime situations, judgments are made in the heat of the moment, often in the company of peers. In these situations, adolescents' other common traits—their short-sightedness, their impulsivity, their susceptibility to peer influence—can quickly undermine their decision-making capacity.

However, the maturing process follows a similar pattern across virtually all teenagers. Therefore it is both logical and efficient to treat adolescents as a special legal category—and to refer the vast majority of offenders under the age of 18 to juvenile court, where they will be treated as responsible but less blameworthy, and where they will receive less punishment and more rehabilitation and treatment than typical adult offenders. The juvenile system does not excuse youths of their crimes; rather, it acknowledges the development stage and its role in the crimes committed, and punishes appropriately.

Such distinction and nuance seem to be absent among large numbers of people, not just in northeastern Pennsylvania, but throughout the United States. We are a nation that sees imprisonment as the best means of controlling crime. And why should kids be any different? What candidate for judge, or any other political office, ever got votes by promising to work toward rehabilitating criminals? Retribution trumps rehabilitation every Election Day. Thus it is that America, with only 5 percent of the world's population, is home to 25 percent of its prisoners.

This pervasive belief that more people need to be locked up was the rich breeding ground for the Luzerne County disaster. Like the coal mine operators a century earlier, Ciavarella (and, less directly, his co-conspirator Conahan) preyed on people too weak to fight back. They were easy targets. No sons or daughters of wealthy businessmen or professionals were hauled off in shackles. Many of the victims came from disrupted, impoverished households. Ciavarella ordered his probation officers to lull them into a false sense of security, and then he suckerpunched them when they got to his courtroom. Children and parents left separately and bewildered. There was no justice, and this is the real crime. That the judges took money to further these ends only made it a worse crime.

Like all true stories, this one has no end.

INDEX

CELEBRATING 20 YEARS OF
INDEPENDENT PUBLISHING

Thank you for reading this book published by The New Press. The New Press is a nonprofit, public interest publisher celebrating its twentieth anniversary in 2012. New Press books and authors play a crucial role in sparking conversations about the key political and social issues of our day.

We hope you enjoyed this book and that you will stay in touch with The New Press. Here are a few ways to stay up to date with our books, events, and the issues we cover:

- Sign up at www.thenewpress.com/subscribe to receive updates on New Press authors and issues and to be notified about local events
- Like us on Facebook: www.facebook.com/newpressbooks
- Follow us on Twitter: www.twitter.com/thenewpress

Please consider buying New Press books for yourself; for friends and family; or to donate to schools, libraries, community centers, prison libraries, and other organizations involved with the issues our authors write about.

The New Press is a 501(c)(3) nonprofit organization. You can also support our work with a tax-deductible gift by visiting www.thenewpress.com/donate.